Intellectuals, Universities, AND THE State IN Western Modern Societies

Intellectuals, Universities, AND THE State IN Western Modern Societies

EDITED BY
Ron Eyerman,
Lennart G. Svensson,
AND Thomas Söderqvist

UNIVERSITY OF CALIFORNIA PRESS
Berkeley / Los Angeles / London

UNIVERSITY OF CALIFORNIA PRESS
Berkeley and Los Angeles, California

UNIVERSITY OF CALIFORNIA PRESS, LTD.
London, England

Library of Congress Cataloging-in-Publication Data

Intellectuals, universities, and the state in Western
  modern societies.

  Greatly rev. versions of papers originally presented
at a conference held at Fiskebäckskil, near Gothenburg,
Sweden, in January 1984.
  Includes bibliographies.
  1. Intellectuals—Congresses. 2. Elite (Social
sciences)—Congresses. 3. Capitalism—Congresses.
4. Communism and intellectuals—Congresses.
I. Eyerman, Ron. II. Svennson, Lennart G.
III. Söderqvist, Thomas.
HM213.I548   1987   305.5'52   86-7035
ISBN 0-520-05701-5 (alk. paper)

PRINTED IN THE UNITED STATES OF AMERICA

1 2 3 4 5 6 7 8 9

Contents

Preface

Studies on intellectuals and their relationship to the state and the universities are of vital interest for all industrialized societies. Several theoretical approaches for such studies are confronted, evaluated, and elaborated in the articles of this book.

These articles are the greatly revised versions of papers originally presented at a conference, "Intellectuals, Universities, and the State," held at Fiskebäckskil, near Gothenburg, Sweden, in January 1984. Perhaps the cold weather helped heat up the debate and spark the collective interest in revising and reproducing these essays in book form. In any case, we are most grateful for the dedicated work of the contributors. We would also like to extend our thanks to the Swedish National Board of Universities and Colleges for the financial support they provided in making this conference possible. Special thanks go to Eskil Björklund, the director of the program Research on Higher Education.

R. E., L. G. S., T. S.

Lund, Gothenburg, and Roskilde
November 1985

1

Introduction

Ron Eyerman, Lennart G. Svensson, Thomas Söderqvist

I

The usual starting point for a discussion of the political impact of intellectuals in modern society is the Dreyfus affair. In his influential essay on the "new class," Daniel Bell follows a familiar pattern when he cites the petition placed by leading French men of letters in a newspaper as the origin of the politically loaded concept of the "intelligentsia."[1] However, one need only look a little further back into French history to discover that on the eve of the 1848 Revolution, French Prime Minister Guizot spoke out in the legislature against a proposed amendment to the voting-rights bill that would have given to intellectuals the right to participate in political life. For Guizot, such a formal recognition of the social worth of intellectuals would undermine the entire system of political rights based on property ownership which had been in place since the Revolution. Opening the door to intellectuals solely on the basis of their craft would be to reopen floodgates that had only recently been carefully closed.

This is certainly not meant to imply that contemporary French men of letters were politically radical enemies of the people, as Edward Shils has defined intellectuals in another influential essay.[2] On the contrary, the leading intellectuals of the period—men such as Stendahl and Baudelaire, as Cesar Grana so skillfully shows—were aristocratic in their views and entirely unconcerned with political rights and wrongs.[3] Besides revealing the eroding ground of property rights as the measure of political competence, what this does imply is that already in Orleanist France, with its restored "middle-class" monarchy, intellectuals could be readily identified by law as well as by common consciousness.

At a later period, in the 1920s, books such as Henri Barbusse's *Le Couteau entre les Dents*, Julien Benda's *La Trahison des Clercs*, and Pierre Naville's *La Revolution et les Intellectuels* summarized an entire epoch of critical discourse on intellectuals in France.[4] In Germany at the same time, intellectuals were becoming an important theme in academic debate. While the French considered intellectuals to be a proper political topic, the Germans were more concerned with sociological aspects. Typical though relatively unknown titles from this period are *Die Intellektuellen und die Gesellschaft*, *Soziale Probleme der Intellektuellen*, and *Zur Soziologie der Intelligenz*.[5] Better-known studies from the 1920s include Max Scheler's *Die Formen des Wissens und der Bildung* and Karl Mannheim's *Ideologie und Utopie*.[6] An exception to this Germanic sociological emphasis, and more in line with the French debate, was the work of the Austrian Marxist Max Adler, which is discussed in one of the contributions to this volume.

While these and earlier studies of intellectuals had little problem with identification of their objects, whether sociological or political, such easy identification is not possible today. In Western mass democracies, in any case, intellectuals receive no special formal recognition by the state. In common consciousness, whether because of the tremendous expansion and diffusion of education or because of the "degradation" of the cultural enterprise as such, the term *intellectual* has little substantive meaning. Contemporary Western society, it seems, has made all definitions of intellectuals ad hoc.

Recent studies have defined intellectuals more or less as they have seen fit—for example, as those with a university degree or those working in specified professions, such as writers, journalists, teachers, and so on. The work of Shils[7] and, more recently, of Regis Debray[8] are examples of definitions of intellectuals which concentrate on their alleged role or function in society. Another, equally ad hoc manner of defining intellectuals cites certain psychological or behavioral characteristics as typical of intellectuals. In an influential book, Lewis Coser defines intellectuals as "men who never seem satisfied with things as they are."[9] Generally, one can distinguish two broad alternative ways in which sociologists have defined intellectuals: a phenomenological approach, which takes as its point of departure the self-understanding and perceptions of the individual, as shown by his or her particular ways of thinking and acting; and a structural approach, which takes as its starting point an objective, observable position in the social structure. The contributions to this volume follow the second approach, relating intellectuals to class theory.

II

"From time to time the state, embarrassed by the increasing demand for positions in its service, is forced to open the sluices of its bureaucratic canals in order to admit thousands of new postulants and thus to transform these from dangerous adversaries into zealous defenders and partisans. There are two classes of intellectuals: those who have succeeded in securing a post at the manger of the state, whilst the others consist of those who . . . have assaulted the fortress without being able to force their way in." So wrote Robert Michels more than seventy years ago in his now classic *Political Parties*.[10] If these words ring familiar today, it is in a way that the author probably never intended. In writing about the German Social Democratic party of the time of imperial Germany, Michels never assumed that intellectuals might form a class in themselves, capable of generating their own interests and of using the state as a springboard to achieving them. Nor did this occur to the majority of writers at the time. Antonio Gramsci was typical in declaring intellectuals incapable of generating a set of common interests. They were forced to choose between aligning with either of the two main social classes: capital or labor.[11] This remains the most common view to-day, especially among Marxists. With this in mind, some elaboration of Gramsci's ideas on intellectuals can be of some use.

Gramsci distinguished between organic and traditional intellectuals. He saw the former as indigenous to a particular class and as the articulators of its specific, class-related interests, and the latter as a relatively autonomous, free-floating variety concerned with the more abstract problems of culture, something traditionally associated with a generic or normative view of intellectuals. In the conflict-ridden context of early twentieth-century Europe, and entirely in line with all strains of Marxist thought, Gramsci claimed that the subordinate working class was not in a position to create its own "organic" intelligentsia. With Lenin and Kautsky, he believed that parts of the traditional intelligentsia, déclassé, would join with the working-class movement to become, if not its leaders, at least the articulators of its class interests—that is, formulating its ideology. The bourgeoisie, however, as the dominant class controlling the social institutions vital to intellectual life, the institutions of culture and education, would have no difficulty in creating and reproducing its own organic intelligentsia. In both cases, Gramsci denied that intellectuals could themselves generate sufficient interest and a sufficient institutional basis to form a class by itself.

Even at that time there were exceptions to this line of thinking. Jan Waclaw Machajski, a harsh critic of Bolshevik intellectuals as a new cultural bourgeoisie, echoed Bakunin's thoughts of a half century earlier.[12] Machajski's writing, however, had no influence on the contemporary Western debate. In the 1940s, this suddenly began to change. Thus, the exiled German sociologist Theodore Geiger could write that "an entirely new social structure with new divisions begins—still vaguely—to stand out" and that the intelligentsia now had its "own particular platform in society."[13] The seminal work by James Burnham on the managerial revolution, which influenced early critical theory through the work of Horkheimer and Adorno as well as of later critics such as George Orwell and Alvin Toffler, imputed a special and independent role for that specific group of intellectuals concerned with planning and managing in the new bureaucratic societies.[14]

However important such thoughts may appear in retrospect today, these early contributions to the theory of the "new class" were generally discarded during their time. The views of intellectuals held by Michels, Mannheim, and Gramsci dominated the discourse until the 1970s. The situation has now dramatically changed. Perhaps due to shifts in social structure which are now more apparent, the possibility of the formation of a new intellectual class is on the sociological agenda today. The great expansion of the state and "public sector" in Western societies and the stabilization of state socialist regimes in the East have underpinned new attempts to conceptualize the relationship between intellectuals and political power. The "sluices" of the state may have opened wide enough and become extensive enough to provide the basis for a new type of ruling class in Eastern socialist and Western capitalist societies.[15]

Of course, just as there are many possible ad hoc ways to define intellectuals, there are many possible points of departure for a discussion of the rise of intellectuals to a position of dominance in modern society. Here also, a basic division seems to run between action and structural approaches. Alain Touraine's impressive work on postindustrial, or programmed, society is one example of an action approach to the study of intellectuals and power.[16] Emphasizing the cultural domain, as expressed in the concept of "historicity," Touraine gives the struggle over cultural orientations—and hence the role of intellectuals as the creators and manipulators of symbols—a central place in the "self-production of society."[17] As a consequence, his latest work has focused on the activities of social movements composed largely of "intellectuals."[18]

While Touraine's work lends itself to an action approach, others, such as Pierre Bourdieu and Alvin Gouldner, take a structuralist stance. Bourdieu's theory of cultural fields introduces a cleavage between dominant intellectual positions and dominated positions.[19]

Although this theory could easily be adopted to include a general theory of societal domination by intellectuals, Bourdieu has shown no inclination in this direction. Instead, Gouldner's *The Future of Intellectuals and the Rise of the New Class* stands out as the central work in this regard.[20] Gouldner defines his new class broadly enough to include Coser's more restrictive notion that intellectuals are those who "live for rather than off ideas"[21] and the technicians and engineers whom others have placed in a "new working class."[22] Gouldner's new class is made up of both humanist intellectuals and technical intelligentsia, whose common identity has been forged from a shared cultural background provided by the experience of higher education and a common relation to the means of production. The two groups have in common the possession of the technical languages of science and rational argumentative discourse and a common relation to the labor market: they live off their intellectual labor. Together, these factors form the ground for a collective identity and a set of common interests—that is, for a distinct social class.

Since Gouldner's book is so central to the debate contained in the essays collected here, a more thorough discussion seems necessary. Two theoretical foundations are necessary to the building of a general theory of a new class of intellectuals: a theory of its distinctive language behavior and a general theory of capital. Gouldner calls the distinctive language behavior the "culture of critical discourse" (CCD). Such language behavior is a key element in the "culture" acquired through higher education and refers to critical-reflective attitudes as well as to the technical languages and pragmatic orientations of science and scientists. It is this language behavior that provides the basis for a common identity of intellectuals trained in different fields of knowledge and for different occupations and professions. The effect is to place the university and other institutions of higher learning as the central institutional basis for the formation of the new class, for its common identity in the CCD, and for its claims to income and power. The new class deals in ideas and knowledge, and upon these its influence and its life-style depend.

The claims to income and power of intellectuals are grounded on knowledge as "cultural capital," which can be accumulated by its possessors and "cashed in" on economic and political markets. Gouldner defines capital as "a produced object whose public goal is increased economic productivity but whose latent function is to increase the incomes and social control of those possessing it."[23] In this sense, as Weber noted, education is as much capital in the modern economy as are factory buildings or machines. It is just this notion of capital and the relation between "cultural" and "human" capital which has been the center of a dispute between Gouldner and Ivan Szelényi, a dispute that is continued and perhaps resolved by the latter's contribution to this volume. Gouldner's intellectuals, then, are not those Chinese bureaucrats described by Weber in his comparative study of traditional and modern intellectuals, nor are they the nineteenth-century dandies described by Grana who consumed and displayed their superior knowledge and sensibility in forms of hedonistic narcissism in protest against the expanding "commodification" of relations.[24] Rather, these are intellectuals out to master the world. They are rational, instrumental modern actors seeking to better their "life chances" through individual and collective forms of action.

In his last work, the posthumously published *Against Fragmentation*, Gouldner complemented his theory of the new class by tracing one of its ideological roots to the origins of Marxism. His aim was to show that "theory," be it Marxism or any other intellectual paradigm, involves much more than a string of propositions making claims about the nature of reality. Theory in Gouldner's sense implies a form of life and, as such, a public practice that involves the strategic action of appropriating positions in organizations and commandeering resources for the purpose of influencing events in its name. Thus, it is fundamental to Gouldner's approach that intellectuals be considered strategic actors, not only in search of income and status but also—and, for him, more important—in the name of their culture of critical discourse.

Like economic capital, cultural capital serves as a basis for income and is legitimated through an alleged "contribution to the production of economic valuables or wealth." Central to such legitimating claims is the ideology of professionalism. The income claims as well as the power claims of the new class must be socially enforceable. Such claims must necessarily be broader than claims to increased productivity, with the latter given as a core value of industrial society. Productivity can be raised in many ways, not all of which necessarily entail the knowledge of educated experts.

The struggle of competing forms of expert knowledge as well as of competing social groups and the attempt to gain a monopoly over a particular field is a history now well recognized. Who knows best how to raise productivity is more than an economic struggle. In addition, traditional intellectual professions (here, one thinks of Gouldner's own) rarely base their right to exist as well as their right to income and to status on productivity claims. Sociologists, especially university teachers of the subject, are more likely to root income claims in the established nature of the discipline or in its usefulness in social control (in the case of research), or in an appeal to general cultural enlightenment, rather than in productivity in the narrow meaning. Be this as it may, in both productivity in an established and socially useful discipline the idea of professionalism is central to both the self-perception and the group awareness of intellectual actors.

If professionalism is a central power strategy of intellectuals, the CCD is a "historically evolved set of rules, a grammar of discourse . . . centered on a specific speech act: justification."[25] As such, and by its very nature as a culture of *critical* discourse, it must necessarily transcend whatever strategic or instrumental aims its bearers may have. For such a discourse, as it is learned and transmitted in institutions of higher learning, is committed to the depersonalized, situation-free language and the universalistic values of modern science. It claims that the only force should be "the force of better argument," and the presentation of evidence "forbids reliance on a speaker's person, authority, or status in society to justify claims."[26] It is this commitment to scientific discourse, power of words, and demonstration which tempers the strategic action of individuals (and of the "class") in the quest for status and power. In this sense Gouldner's intellectual class behaves in a manner similar to that prescribed by Foucault.[27] It is this inner tension that produces what Gouldner calls the "flawed" nature of the new class. The flaw in its nature, in its tragic and Hegelian meaning, results from the self-interest that almost necessarily accompanies even the most high-minded actions in modern, rationalized society. Yet, Gouldner claims, the internalized values and practices of the CCD provides intellectuals with the grounds and the motivation for transcending narrow self-interest, both as individuals and as a class. The CCD provides the basis for what Kant called "the enlarged mind," taking the wider perspective that underlies both scientific and political judgments.

At the same time, commitment to rational discourse in questions of science can lead, as Habermas has argued, to a commitment to rational public discourse on other issues as well.[28] Here it can be assumed that part of the universalistic values attributed to the new class by Gouldner would include a commitment to "the force of better argument" in a wide range, if not all, of the issues of public concern. Thus, underlying the universalistic values of the new class (in Gouldner's theory, at least) is a commitment to a form of social order in which legislation is attained through open, public discourse, a commitment to participatory democracy in some broad form. However, here again the "flawed" nature of self-interested modern actors might temper such commitment, leading at best to a form of society in which legislation is achieved through a combination of claims to expert knowledge and public argument.

Summing up, Gouldner claims that in both East and West the intelligentsia has become a "cultural bourgeoisie," a new class whose power rests on its ability to control the production and distribution of "cultural capital." Unlike the capital upon which rested the power of the original bourgeoisie, cultural capital is symbolic rather than material. Yet it is just as useful in commanding income, status, and power. And unlike material capital, symbolic captial directly involves social relations, the relations of domination and subordination in a society. The possessor of cultural capital is in a position to control and dominate other people. Modern, technically advanced society greatly enhances the symbolic value of cultural capital. In addition to possessing the technical information necessary for the functioning of modern society, intellectuals also control cultural institutions and are thus capable of "representing society's goals and meaning in logical, rational terminology."[29] In contemporary conditions, this traditional culture-creating role of intellectuals places them in key locations in educational institutions, mass media, and the arts and sciences. It thus affords them an unprecedentedly powerful voice in defining the social situation, equally capable of creating crises and of proposing solutions.

III

The subtitle from Gouldner's book formed the ground upon which the idea for the Fiskebäckskil conference formed: "A Frame of Reference, Theses, Conjectures, Arguments, and an Historical Perspective on the Role of Intellectuals and Intelligentsia in the International Class Contest of the Modern Era." From this general point of departure the intention was to explore the state of the art of the study of intellectuals and professionals, with special reference to Scandinavia. From the articles here, however, we hope the reader will agree that our intentions went beyond the narrow Scandinavian context into the more international and general debate.

Beyond the social and economic changes that directly concern the situation of intellectuals in modern society, there are other important conditions of concern in theoretical and empirical studies. One is the renewed discussion of the state–civil society relationship, that is, the relationship between the public and private sectors. Another condition (more particular, perhaps, to Sweden) involves the radical change in the structure of universities and professional colleges, which have recently been even more incorporated into one comprehensive, corporative, and centralized system. This has had the effect of changing the tripodal constellation—intellectuals, universities, and the state—into a qualitatively new phenomenon. With Gouldner's work as background and with these new conditions in mind, the articles included here attack the question of intellectuals in modern societies.

In their paper, *Bill Martin* and *Ivan Szelényi* directly confront Gouldner's views. In comparing Gouldner and Bourdieu on the notion of cultural capital and Gouldner and Erik Wright on the notion of human capital, they go to the core issue of the specificity of the power of intellectuals in modern society. They locate a weakness in Gouldner's theory by pointing out that unlike its economic counterpart, cultural capital is not easily transformed into economic ownership or political power. How is it possible, they ask, for the cultural dominance of intellectuals, which they readily grant, to become economic dominance? Next, in relation to the notion of social class and to the claim that intellectuals form a new class in both Eastern socialist and Western capitalist societies, they ask where the institutional means lie for this new class to subordinate the old bourgeoisie. After pointing out these lacunas in existing new-class theory (and including Wright and Roemer along with Gouldner), Martin and Szelényi go on to propose a solution in a new general theory of symbolic domination. By differentiating between knowledge as "practical mastery" and "symbolic mastery," they reformulate the theory of cultural and human capital into a theory of forms of domination.

In a spirited defense of Gouldner's ideas, *Cornelis Disco* takes up the debate on the notion of cultural capital. On one hand, he welcomes Martin's and Szelényi's contribution, especially their emphasis on the essentially postcapitalist character of new-class culture, a point that Gouldner's theory could not explain. On the other hand, Disco asserts that Martin and Szelényi themselves cannot account for the widespread anticapitalism of many intellectuals in capitalist societies. With them, he argues for a general theory of cultural capital, pointing to the notion of social closure as developed by Frank Parkin and Randall Collins as a possible means of uniting Gouldner with Martin and Szelényi.[30]

Sweden presents an interesting example of a society where a new class might emerge under "capitalist" conditions. Thus, it is no coincidence that the three Swedish papers that address theoretical aspects fo the new-class problem concentrate on organized-welfare capitalism as a precondition for the rising power of intellectuals. *Bengt Furåker* takes up the place of intellectuals in the division of labor. After discussing the importance of education in the reproduction of the privileged position intellectuals hold in modern society and the relative size of the public sector and its significance in the struggle between "old" and "new" segments of the bourgeoisie, Furåker predicts an expansion in the power of state and public employees and thus in the power of intellectuals. From his Marxist point of view, he maintains that the power of intellectuals rests on the declining power of capital. He also stresses the role of trade unions and political organizations, a topic usually neglected in discussions of the new class.

Also concerned with the place of intellectuals in the contemporary division of labor, *Edmund Dahlström* directly confronts the issue of professionalization and its role in the power strategies of intellectuals, linking an older, more established research area, the sociology of the professions, with the more recently established new-class approach used by the other contributors to this volume. Professionalization is also the topic of *Katrín Fridjónsdóttir's* contribution. In a programmatic essay, she addresses the interesting issue, blurred by Gouldner, of the relationship between traditional intellectuals and the scientific, technical intelligentsia.

In a paper that sums up and ties many of the loose ends from other contributions, *Adam Westoby* points out that the rise of the new "knowledge" class has its roots in production and in engineering and computing as much as in distribution and service. Like Martin and Szelényi, Westoby is concerned about the ambiguities contained in the notion of "capital" and offers a learned critique of those theories that depend upon it. In another context Westoby has structured the historical discussion of the new class along three lines: (1) the description of a new class in socialist and other industrialized societies; (2) descriptions departing from social structure or from political behavior; and (3) analytical or historical descriptions of the new class.[31] The contributions in this volume discussed so far have been dominated by analytical and conceptual issues, according to Westoby's schema, although Martin and Szelényi make use of the distinction between socialist and other industrial societies, and Furåker looks at the relationship between social structure and political behavior in Western democracies. Westoby himself elaborates on changes in the social structure which he sees as necessary preconditions for the growth of a new class.

Westoby's third area can be used to refer to the division in this volume between analytical and conceptual issues and historical and empirical ones. Two contributions in the second part of the volume analyze the political behavior of intellectuals in specific historical contexts, while another relates the action orientations of intellectuals to structural factors.

The two related case studies by *Carl Levy* and *Lennart Olausson* are concerned with the relation between intellectuals and working-class movements. Levy offers a wide range of historical material, covering Italy, England, and France in the period around the turn of the century. In line with the writing of Michels, cited earlier, the existence of a centralized and expanding bureaucratic state is of central importance in Levy's explanation of the relationship between intellectuals and socialist movements. Olausson, for his part, focuses on the attempts by Austrian intellectuals to win over their colleagues to the socialist cause.

The most elaborated empirical contribution is the longitudinal study of Finnish students from the 1960s presented by *Yrjö-Paavo Häyrynen*. His research reveals the fruitfulness of applying a definition of intellectuals which includes both structural and phenomenological aspects. The common denominator in his view of intellectuals is the performance of mental work. In line with Westoby's convincing argument about the notorious difficulties of separating manual from mental work, Häyrynen defines the latter in terms of anticipatory orientations or aspirations combined with such structural determinations as formal education and position in the division of labor. He then goes on to study the varying careers of students. In a sense, this study is an example of Bourdieu's thesis concerning the valorization or enrichment of cultural capital, a topic of concern in several other papers in this volume. Häyrynen concludes with a tentative and heuristic division of intellectuals into subgroups according to structural position, educational career, content of work, and central life orientation.

Finally, we have included a documentary account of part of the discussion from the conference as interpreted by the Swedish journalist *Anders Björnsson*. His commentary not only gives the reader a flavor of the lively debate that occurred but also gives expression to the importance of interdisciplinary exchange in discussions concerning the new class.

IV

The conference that preceded these essays brought together participants from a number of academic disciplines, including history, political science, the history of science, education, psychology, anthropology, and sociology. As the recorded discussion reveals, this interdisciplinary pluralism on the changing class structure of modern societies stimulated debate as well as the need to rethink an inbred narrowness, which resulted in the greatly revised papers printed here. While we do not believe that the conceptual difficulties involved in the notion of a new class have been finally resolved in this collection of essays, we are convinced that some essential progress toward that end has been achieved. The elaborated discussions on such central themes as capital, professional monopoly, institutional dependence/independence of mental labor, and so on have certainly qualified many of the elements in a theory about the changing class structure in a postindustrial context. Furthermore, the more empirically oriented studies presented demonstrate how conceptualizations drawn from new-class theory can enrich historical studies of the division of labor in society and can also have some consequences for political organization and practice. Some lacunas remain, to be sure—for example, in microstudies of how the degree of dependence in occupations involving mental labor relate to the growth of bureaucratic institutions, and in macrostudies of the effects of higher education on occupational structure and political behavior. We hope, however, that the reader will agree that the essays collected here make a significant contribution to the current debate about intellectuals, universities, and the state.

NOTES

1. D. Bell, *The Winding Passage* (Cambridge, Mass., 1980).

2. E. Shills, *The Intellectuals and the Powers and Other Essays* (Chicago, 1972).

3. C. Grana, *Bohemian versus Bourgeois* (New York, 1964).

4. H. Barbusse, *Le Couteau entre les Dents* (Paris, 1921); J. Benda, *La Trahison des Clercs* (Paris, 1927); P. Naville, *La Revolution et les Intellectuels* (Paris, 1928).

5. H. Kurella, *Die Intellektuellen und die Gesellschaft* (Wiesbaden, 1913); R. Kassel, *Soziale Probleme der Intellektuellen* (Wien, 1920); C. Brinckmann, *Zur Soziologie der Intelligenz* (Berlin, 1921).

6. M. Scheler, *Die Formen des Wissens und der Bildung* (Bonn, 1925); K. Mannheim, *Ideologie und Utopie* (Bonn, 1929).

7. E. Shils, *The Intellectual between Tradition and Modernity: the Indian Situation* (The Hague, 1961).

8. R. Debray, *Le Pouvoir intellectuel en France* (Paris, 1979).

9. L. Coser, *Men of Ideas* (New York, 1965), p. viii.

10. R. Michels, *Political Parties* (New York, 1915).

11. A. Gramsci, *Selection from the Prison Notebooks* (London, 1971).

12. J. W. Machajski, *Le Socialisme des Intellectuelles* (Paris, 1979).

13. T. Geiger, *Aufgaben und Stellung der Intelligenz in der Gesellschaft* (Stuttgart, 1949). Geiger also published an extensive empirical study of the changing recruitment of the Danish intelligentsia based on biographical lexical information.

14. J. Burnham, *The Managerial Revolution* (New York, 1941).

15. See, e.g., G. Konrád and I. Szelényi, *The Intellectuals on the Road to Class Power* (Brighton, 1979); B. Bruce-Briggs, ed., *The New Class?* (New Brunswick, 1979); J. Cohen, *Class and Civil Society* (Oxford, 1982).

16. A. Touraine, *La Sociéte Post-Industrielle* (Paris, 1969).

17. A. Touraine, *Production de la Société* (Paris, 1973).

18. A. Touraine, *The Voice and the Eye* (Cambridge, 1980).

19. P. Bourdieu and J.-C. Passeron, *Reproduction in Education, Society, and Culture* (London and Beverly Hills, 1977).

20. A. Gouldner, *The Future of Intellectuals and the Rise of the New Class* (New York, 1979).

21. Coser, *Men of Ideas* (n. 9), p. viii.

22. A. Gorz, *Strategy for Labor* (Boston, 1967).

23. Gouldner, *Future of Intellectuals* (n. 20), p. 21.

24. M. Weber, *Economy and Society*, vol. 1 (Berkeley, 1978); Grana, *Bohemian versus Bourgeois* (n. 3).

25. Gouldner, *Future of Intellectuals* (n. 20), p. 28.

26. Ibid.

27. M. Foucault, *Discipline and Punish* (London, 1977).

28. J. Habermas, *Toward a Rational Society* (Boston, 1970).

29. Gouldner, *Future of Intellectuals* (n. 20).

30. F. Parkin, *Marxism and Class Theory: A Bourgeois Critique* (London, 1979); R. Collins, *The Credential Society* (London, 1979).

31. A. Westoby, "På jakt efter den nya klassen" [Pursuing the new class], *Clarté* (Stockholm), no. 1, 1984.

2

Beyond Cultural Capital: Toward a Theory of Symbolic Domination

Bill Martin and Ivan Szelényi

INTRODUCTION

Recent theorists of cultural capital have been concerned with using the concept to explain the power of the highly educated in advanced capitalist and postcapitalist societies, but they often arrive
at contradictory conclusions about the level of autonomy enjoyed
by owners of cultural capital from other classes. The contrasting
theories of Pierre Bourdieu and Alvin Gouldner offer the most
striking and well-developed examples of this tendency. Bourdieu
claims that the "sphere of cultural production" is "relatively autonomous" from that of "material production" and that it is
therefore justified to regard those who have the ability to appropriate the mechanisms of cultural production as the *owners* of
cultural capital.[1] However, since cultural production is only relatively autonomous from material production, ownership of such
capital can only create substrata within the dominant capitalist
class. By contrast, Gouldner believes cultural capital to be
genuinely autonomous, and he uses the concept of capital literally rather than metaphorically.[2] In Gouldner's theory, ownership
of cultural capital is the basis for a new-class position, with the
humanistic intellectuals and the technical intelligentsia using
their cultural capital to unseat the "old class" of the moneyed
bourgeoisie.

In their new "general theory of exploitation," both John Roemer and Erik Wright offer compromise solutions to this debate. They replace the concept of cultural capital with the notion of "skill assets," and they claim that ownership of skill assets is an independent source of surplus expropriation and, hence, of exploitation.[3] Under capitalism, as long as private ownership of the means of production exists, ownership of skill assets can only offer a "contradictory class position." Under socialism, however, with the abolition of private ownership of the means of production, monopolistic owners of skill assets become the sole exploiters: they become a new dominant class. In this way Roemer and Wright put the Bourdieu-Gouldner debate into a historical perspective. They accept Bourdieu's view under capitalism and Gouldner's under socialism. We find this compromise persuasive, as far as it goes, but we feel that it fails to resolve one important contradiction between the position of Roemer and Wright and that of Gouldner.

Gouldner's work on the new class was so successful, in part, because it helped to explain the paradox of the "conservative working class" and the "radical middle class," the enthusiasm of intellectuals (and the relative indifference of the workers) for "progressive" causes—the anti–Vietnam war movement, feminism, the environmental movement, and so on—during the late 1960s and early 1970s. In Gouldner's neo-Weberian theory of history, the fate of social change is decided by the struggles between moneyed and cultural bourgeoisies, while the subordinated class does not have much to gain, since it does not have a chance to come to power anyway. On the basis of this theory one would anticipate intellectuals to be the most consistently anticapitalist group in capitalist societies.

Roemer and Wright offer a radically different hypothesis. According to them, the highly educated are "junior partners" in the system of exploitation. They will therefore be more procapitalist than the workers, though less so than the capitalists themselves. In Roemer and Wright's neo-Marxist theory of history, the driving force behind social change is still the struggle of the subordinated class.

Neither of these hypotheses can be dismissed out of hand. Examples such as the radical generation of the sixties or the

phenomenon of "adversary culture" theorized by neoconservatives from Schelsky to Podhoretz[4] give credence to Gouldner's
hypothesis, while the emergence of the New Right and its impact
on the highly educated seems to support the argument of Roemer
and Wright. This, then, is a central puzzle for new-class theorizing: which categories of the highly educated are more likely to
subvert existing class relations, to challenge rather than to
reproduce the status quo, and to come forward with their own
power aspirations, and under what circumstances are they likely
to do so? To solve this problem we may need a synthesis of the
cultural- and human-capital approaches. We hope that this paper
will contribute to such a synthesis.

Cultural-capital theories offer insights about the nature of
authority enjoyed by producers of culture which cannot be gained
from the human-capital/skill-exploitation perspective. Bourdieu
emphasizes that cultural-capital owners exercise "symbolic
mastery" of their areas of expertise, as distinct from the "practical mastery" of those who are deprived of cultural capital.[5] Similarly, Gouldner claims that it is their engagement in the "culture
of critical discourse" which enables cultural-capital owners to
exercise their own authority and to challenge all other authority,
including that of economic-capital owners.[6] Clearly, the difference
between those who exercise symbolic mastery and those who are
limited to practical mastery, between those who enter the culture
of critical discourse and those who only speak regular speech, is
not quantitative but *qualitative*. Symbolic capital does not require
more human capital (or skill) than practical mastery but instead
requires something *else*, a different type of knowledge or skill.

Furthermore, symbolic mastery, or the culture of critical discourse, offers authority without reference to any agency outside
the process of cultural production. Since, according to Gouldner,
cultural capital has to do with the norms that define the culturally accepted ways of doing things (rather than with the content
of what is done), the claim for authority or for material rewards
made by cultural-capital owners need not be understood by reference to narrowly defined economic efficiency or by contributions
to productivity gains. Instead, cultural-capital owners ground
their authority in the claim that they know about important mat-

ters in superior ways to ordinary people and that anyone who understands what they know can see that it conforms to rational rules for truthful discourse (the culture of critical discourse).

In other words, cultural-capital theories offer at least two insights that cannot be gained from human-capital (or skill-exploitation) perspectives: (1) They emphasize *discontinuity*, a qualitative break in the process of production or accumulation of knowledge, and (2) they propose that the claim to authority made by cultural-capital owners can be *self-grounded*. With these two insights, cultural-capital theory depicts features of the highly educated which may explain why they would and could come forward with autonomous power aspirations (i.e., by dividing the world into "knows" and "know-nots," with a self-righteous claim to authority by the "knows").[7] Although we think that Bourdieu and Gouldner were unable to come up with a consistent theory of cultural capital, and we are skeptical about the usefulness of the concept of "capital" in describing the phenomena they explore, we would still like to preserve these insights for a more comprehensive theory of symbolic domination.

In this paper, therefore, we entertain the idea that the knowledge of the highly educated may simultaneously have two different aspects or faces: one can be described as human capital, the other as cultural capital. It appears to be reasonable to regard the highly educated as human-capital owners, owners of scarce and economically useful skills, who, through the scarcity of such skills, gain privileges and (some) power and may therefore be conceived of as junior partners in exploitation. However, many of the highly educated not only use complex and sophisticated technical skills but at the same time also exercise symbolic mastery and produce theoretical knowledge and are thus involved in the culture of critical discourse. To this extent they are also cultural-capital owners, making a self-referential claim to authority which is not derived from the economic usefulness of their skills. Moreover, if the circumstances are favorable, they may use their cultural capital to undermine all other authority in society.

Using such a synthesis of human- and cultural-capital theories, we hope to offer the point of departure for a solution to the puz-

zle of new-class theory described above. Now we may hypothesize that—all other conditions being equal—the more cultural
capital the highly educated own, the more likely they will be to
challenge the status quo, to be anticapitalist, to have power aspirations of their own. By contrast, human-capital ownership mentality is the mentality of the junior partner in exploitation: it is
nonsubversive, and to the extent that the highly educated are
human-capital owners, they will fit quite smoothly into the existing class structure. Therefore, if we were able to measure the
human- and cultural-capital components of the knowledge of the
highly educated, we might be able to predict their political attitudes and behavior.

Of course, we have a long way to go before we are anywhere
near an empirical-research agenda. First of all, it is a rather complicated task to distinguish the human- and cultural-capital components of the knowledge of the highly educated. It would be
rather naïve to follow the example of Schelsky and identify the
critical-ideological, or humanistic, intellectuals as cultural-capital
owners.[8] Gouldner persuasively argues that humanistic intellectuals and the technical intelligentsia converge via the culture of
critical discourse. The division between human and cultural capital is not identical to a distinction between disciplines or professions. Instead, it typically crosscuts these boundaries, and it does
so in a historically variable manner. The claim about the emergence of a new class ought to be taken more seriously now than
it was twenty or fifty years ago, because cultural capital is becoming an integral component of the knowledge of wider and wider
circles of the highly educated and, more important, because symbolic mastery is gaining in importance in constituting the technical
intelligentsia, too. Yet the difficulties in elaboration of an
empirical-research agenda concerned with the new class are ex-
acerbated by the fact that most, if not all, of the highly educated
in our postindustrial societies have both human- and cultural-
capital components well represented in their knowledge. The
contradictions of human and cultural capital are internalized in
the personalities of modern intellectuals, and this is primarily
responsible for the social and political schizophrenia that is deeply
ingrained in our character. We are all tormented between the call

to subvert and the task of social reproduction, attracted to discipline and anarchy at the same time. Exploration of the prospects of the power aspirations of the highly educated—the intellectuals—will, therefore, require a research strategy that will skillfully fluctuate between the microlevel of ego formation and interpersonal relations and the macrolevel of political struggles and class formation. Factors operating both at the micro- and macrolevels will determine whether intellectuals will ever be able to make a successful bid for power.

The rest of this paper will be concerned with a detailed assessment of the concept of cultural capital in the works of Bourdieu and Gouldner. We will show that both authors use the concept in an inconsistent manner but that they still offer significant insights into the nature of the power of the highly educated in advanced societies. We will then assess how the recent work of Roemer and Wright on a "general theory of exploitation" could be interpreted as a synthesis of Bourdieu and Gouldner, and we will identify the unresolved aspects of this synthesis. Finally, we will briefly sum up our own proposal for a more comprehensive synthesis, a synthesis of the cultural- and human-capital approaches to the problem of the new class, a first step toward a general theory of symbolic domination.

CULTURAL CAPITAL AND THE INTERNAL DIFFERENTIATION OF THE BOURGEOISIE: BOURDIEU

We should note from the start some limitations on the usefulness to us of Bourdieu's work on cultural capital. These limitations are imposed by the way he uses the concept, since, after all, he is an economic reductionist.[9] From his theory of the "relative autonomy" of the sphere of cultural production, it follows that the basic class structure can be formed only in the economic sphere. At most, cultural-capital ownership will modify this basic class structure. Apparently caught up in the structuralist spirit of the late 1960s and early 1970s, when his theory of cultural capital was developed, Bourdieu "in the last instance" emphasizes that although cultural-capital reproduction is central to the reproduction of existing class relations, under no circumstances can it subvert those relations. In our view, this makes the application of the concept of cultural capital inflated and, ultimately, unnecessary. For Bourdieu, the term *capital* does not have the same status in economy and culture. Instead, he feels that capital can be linked to the notion of culture only in a metaphorical sense. Such a theoretical linkage is tenuous at best and may be extremely misleading. More significantly, Bourdieu's reductionism prevents him from accounting for his own theory, that is, from accounting for the existence of critical thought.

At the same time, there are important insights in Bourdieu's work. Unlike Gouldner, he does not flirt with the idea of "exploitation" based on cultural-capital ownership but accepts the centrality of the moment of domination in the concept of cultural capital. Methodologically we regard this as an important move away from economic reductionism and toward a *general theory of symbolic domination*. Finally, his distinction between symbolic and practical mastery impresses us as extremely useful for understanding the self-groundedness of any authority claim made by producers of meanings.

A theory of "relative autonomy" of the sphere of cultural production

Bourdieu defines economic and cultural capital respectively as "the means . . . of appropriating the mechanisms of the field of production and the field of cultural production."[10] The market of laissez-faire capitalism is necessary in order for economic capital to exist as a distinct means of appropriating purely economic mechanisms. Cultural capital, however, allows its possessor to appropriate the mechanisms of the dominant culture. This is a theory of "relative autonomy." The relativity of culture has two aspects. On the one hand, the "selection of meanings" that makes up the cultural system is *arbitrary* (in the sense that it cannot be deduced from universal nonsocial principles, i.e., it is not determined by the "natural world"). On the other hand, it is also "socio-logically *necessary*" insofar as it arises from a set of social conditions that also permit its intelligibility.[11] Here, "arbitrariness'' refers to the content of the cultural system, its selection of meanings, while ''necessity'' refers to the content of the social relations that are reproduced.

Like the theory of the relative autonomy of the state, this theory of the relative autonomy of cultural reproduction comes very close to a class-reductionist view. Though Bourdieu repeatedly emphasizes the variable nature of both arbitrariness and necessity,[12] the implications for class societies are spelled out in unambiguous terms. Different classes inculcate, within families, different sets of meanings which, presumably, are to be sociologically understood in terms of a more basic set of social conditions of the various classes (e.g., the relations of production). Furthermore, the processes of reproduction of these class cultures are determined by the reproduction process of the culture of the dominant class. Although Bourdieu carefully tries to avoid presupposing a mechanical connection between the dominant class and the culture and cultural modes it imposes, the explanation for *change* in meaning systems lies in the interests of that class. In pursuing these interests, which are defined not culturally but politically and economically, the dominant class instrumentally manipulates the modes of cultural reproduction. True, the owners of cultural capital do have a particularistic interest in the maintenance and extension of these very processes, since the relations between the dominant and dominated classes are ongoingly reproduced in the process of cultural reproduction. Still, this is not enough to constitute the owners of cultural capital as an autonomous cultural bourgeoisie, since they remain integrated within the dominant class. At best they can be understood as a relatively autonomous segment of the dominant class.

Consequences for class theory

On the basis of such a definition of cultural capital, the class structure of advanced capitalist societies could be presented in the schematic way shown in table 1. This scheme is a rather free interpretation of Bourdieu, and even our cautious distinction between moneyed and cultural bourgeoisies as fragments within the

TABLE 1

	Dominant class		Middle class	Proletariat
	Moneyed Bourgeoisie	Cultural Bourgeoisie		
Money capital	+ +	+	–	–
Cultural capital	+	+ +	+ +	–

same dominant class could not be substantiated textually from his work. The middle-class position in the above scheme also refers more to a semiautonomous stratum than to a class proper. For example, the teaching profession might occupy such a position, since its members would have cultural capital without having money capital. Such a middle class has a primary interest in the maintenance and extension of the cultural reproduction process itself. Because of the class-determined nature of the dominant culture, this still does not allow for any fundamental conflict of interest between the dominant class and the middle class: under no circumstances can this middle class be regarded as an ascending class. After all, Bourdieu's main interest is to demonstrate how the existing class structure is reproduced through the process of cultural reproduction, not how it is subverted.[13]

Centrality of "domination": Cultural capital—a metaphor

In the Marxist theory of class, the term *capital* contains two twin moments: appropriation and domination. Though the relationship between appropriation and domination is "dialectical," at least under the conditions of capitalist society, the moment of "appropriation" seems to precede the moment of "domination."[14] In Bourdieu's theory of cultural capital, the moment of domination is central. Although cultural capital allows its possessor to "appropriate" the mechanisms of the field of cultural production, *this is cultural domination rather than "exploitation" in the narrower sense of the term.* To put it simply, no attempt is made to derive economic exploitation from cultural-capital ownership.

Cultural-capital ownership assures cultural domination, while economic exploitation is explained by ownership of "money capital." In conceptualizing cultural capital, Bourdieu does not consider it as a source of income (which is the key to Gouldner's definition of cultural capital); he does not reflect on the relationship between income from cultural-capital ownership and contribution to productivity gains; and he does not reflect on whether income from cultural capital is rentlike or wagelike income (these issues are central for Gouldner and for Roemer and Wright). On this basis we are inclined to conclude that there is little reason for Bourdieu to refer to his system of meanings as cultural capital. For him, the term *capital* is hardly more than a metaphor.

However, we do not criticize Bourdieu for his metaphorical usage of the concept of "cultural capital"—actually, this may be the strength of his conceptualization. To emphasize the centrality of the problem of domination rather than of appropriation or exploitation may be very appropriate to an understanding of the power and privilege of the highly educated.[15] We criticize Bourdieu for his structuralist class (and economic) reductionism and for his general reluctance to consider the *potential* autonomy of cultural domination from economic exploitation.

To be more precise, in Bourdieu's analysis of premodern societies—particularly premodern African societies[16]—he concedes the autonomy of the symbolic system. In no way can he be accused of economic reductionism. But he certainly seems to think that with modern capitalism a kind of irreversible colonialization of the symbolic sphere by the economic sphere has occurred, and he does not seem to see the possibility of the reemergence of the autonomy of the former. This prevents him from accounting for himself, for critical theory, or, indeed, for the subversive potential of critical thought.

"Symbolic mastery": a domination without reference to outside agency

We must qualify this criticism somewhat, since it is possible to identify elements in Bourdieu's analysis which allow for the existence of cultural domination without reference to outside agency. In their analysis of the process of cultural reproduction, Bourdieu and Passeron discuss the social significance of the theorization of primary cultural practice (in the sense of everyday practice of systems of meaning). According to Bourdieu and Passeron, the process of cultural reproduction may subordinate practical mastery of practices (of all sorts) to symbolic mastery of those practices. Thus,

> the mere fact of using theoretic discourse to make explicit the principles of techniques of which working-class children have practical mastery is sufficient to cast the knacks and tricks of the trade into the illegitimacy of makeshift approximation, just as "general education" reduces thier language to jargon, slang, or gibberish. This is one of the most potent effects of the theoretic discourse which sets an unbridgeable gulf between the holder of the principles (e.g., the engineer) and the mere practitioner (e.g., the technician).[17]

This formulation demonstrates clearly that cultural practice itself can set up a categorical relationship between two groups: those who possess the cultural tools necessary to participate in theoretical construction of everyday techniques, and those who do not. Here, there is no outside agency or relation that underlies the domination of the "holder of principles" over the "mere practitioner." Instead, *the relation is purely within the system of cultural production.*

But even in this analysis Bourdieu reverts back to some extent to his "class reductionism": he emphasizes that the educational system reproduces the content of existing class relations. His research indicates that although universal educational systems offer symbolic mastery of the dominant culture to all students, only those whose families provide practical mastery of the dominant culture can achieve symbolic mastery. For example, schools always teach the grammar of a native language on the basis of an already achieved practical mastery of grammatical rules in everyday speech. Children from lower-class families rarely possess this orthodox practical mastery, so that "general education" indeed reduces their language to "jargon, slang, or gibberish." This process ensures that those who do not achieve symbolic mastery recognize as legitimate the right of those who do achieve such mastery to pronounce on the truly correct way to go about things. Thus, the educational system does not merely legitimate an abstract dominance of a dominant culture but also practically ensures that those who possess that culture are dominant over those who do not.

The distinction between practical mastery and symbolic mastery, the recognition that an unbridgeable gulf exists not only between the dominant and dominated classes but also between the "holders of principles" (engineers, psychiatrists, priests, etc.) and everyone else, is of major significance for conceptualizing the nature of the power of intellectuals. Of course, in a capitalist society children of the bourgeoisie are more likely to achieve symbolic mastery, but this is beside the point. The main point is that by symbolic mastery the "mere practitioner" is subjected to *a new type of domination*. In order to construct a theory of the power of intellectuals we must comprehend the anatomy of this symbolic mastery, just as Marxists had to develop a theory of the political economy of the capitalist mode of production in order to grasp power under capitalism. It may be better, therefore, to define cultural capital not as an asset that simply allows the appropriation of mechanisms of the dominant culture but as one that allows the appropriation of symbolic mastery (without prejudging the relationship between symbolic mastery and a culture that corresponds to the interests represented by reproduction of existing class relations). We are inclined to believe that one should accept the metaphorical nature of the term *capital* in the concept of cultural capital. But, unlike Bourdieu's acceptance of this, our acceptance does not lead us to conclude that since cultural capital is not capital proper, it is in the last instance always subordinated to the logic of money capital. Cultural capital is a metaphor for us because with this notion theorists such as Bourdieu and Gouldner first began to explore a new type of domination, one that has certain analogies to domination by money capital but that may be structured differently and may follow a different logic.

CULTURAL CAPITAL AND THE NEW CLASS: GOULDNER

Gouldner does not simply borrow the term *cultural capital* from Bourdieu. Rather, he reconstructs the concept and radicalizes the theory. In one sense Gouldner uncompromisingly transcends the economic reductionism of Bourdieu. The term *capital* gains the same status in the concept of cultural capital as it has in economic or money capital—if economic capital is one source of class power, then cultural capital is another. The concept of the culture of critical discourse is a very important step toward the comprehension of the self-groundedness of the authority of intellectuals. In another sense Gouldner's horizons remain limited, particularly methodologically, by economism.[18] In the end he takes cultural capital too seriously and pushes the parallel with economic capital too far.

This causes several problems. First, by insisting that cultural capital is not a metaphor, Gouldner creates an internally inconsistent account of the new class. Thus, for instance, his failure to show that cultural capital is as much a necessary precondition for production as economic capital creates difficulties in explaining the emergence of a "cultural bourgeoisie" at all, difficulties that are not solved by reverting to the argument that connections between capital and productivity are only "imputed." Second, and more important, Gouldner's undifferentiated labeling of all knowledge of the highly educated as cultural capital conforming to the culture of critical discourse, his inability to distinguish situations in which practical mastery matters more than symbolic mastery, leads him to overemphasize the integration of different categories of the highly educated. In this way he arrives at wrong empirical predictions of the political behavior and attitudes of the highly educated. He attributes too much anticapitalism to them and cannot explain middle-class conservatism.

A generic concept of capital

Gouldner leaves no doubt that he intends the notion of cultural capital to be taken seriously: for him the notion of cultural capital is not merely a metaphor; cultural capital is not merely *like* economic capital, it *is* a form of capital. To ground the idea that cultural capital is capital in just the same sense as economic capital, Gouldner produces a generic concept of capital:

> Capital . . . is: any produced object used to make saleable utilities, thus providing its possessor with incomes, or claims to incomes defined as legitimate because of their imputed contribution to economic productivity: these claims to income are enforced normally by withholding, or threatening to withhold the capital-object.[19]

Given this general notion of capital, what, then, is the specific nature of cultural capital? Remarkably, Gouldner spends little time on this question, preferring to elaborate the distinctiveness of the cultural capital possessed by the new class. He does indicate that cultural capital is possessed to some degree by all classes—but what is it? Maintaining a focus on the system of economic production and the social determination of the technical basis of production, he emphasizes that labor is carried out in "conformity to some cultural requirement or standard, a norm."[20] It is this necessary cultural investment that should be considered as cultural capital.

Gouldner's point seems to be that all "technical" skills are embedded in norms about how things are done, and that it is not a straightforward matter to distinguish those components of skills which are technical from those which are "normative." His argument against human-capital theorists is that they fail to see that a significant part of the claim to high incomes made by some people (such as professionals) is that they do their jobs in conformity to certain norms, and that those who produce the same end result without conforming to such norms would not have the same claims on high incomes. Thus, it is the capacity to perform tasks in culturally acceptable ways that Gouldner calls "cultural capital." As we have already noted, this definition of cultural capital prevents Gouldner from declaring cultural-capital ownership to be the defining characteristic of the new class, since all labor is performed in conformity to norms.

Gouldner is undoubtedly correct to criticize human-capital theorists for their naïveté in assuming an inevitable correspondence between higher education and increased productivity as the basis for income stratification. Instead, he suggests, it is the *imputed* relation between productivity gains and education that results in high incomes for the highly educated. However, we believe that this one-sided emphasis on rejecting any close relation between productivity and income prevented Gouldner from achieving an interesting synthesis of the human-capital account and his own insight.

Such a synthesis would have suggested that human-capital theorists are right with respect to some labor-market positions, in the sense that the normative aspects of the labor performed in these positions is subordinated to the technical ones: what matters is getting the job done, not how it is done. Gouldner is correct in pointing out that even in those jobs the technical aspects of the job remain embedded in a cultural medium, but he fails to see that the cultural medium has no stability, no capacity to resist the technical demands of the labor being performed. For people occupying these positions, the "real" and "imputed" relation between the skills they hold and productivity is very close, and hence their income really is closely related to their productivity. Hence the Gouldnerian notion of cultural capital tells us little about the claim on income enjoyed by occupants of these positions. By contrast, there are other jobs where Gouldner's notion of cultural capital and an "imputed" connection between productivity and skills tell us far more about income and other aspects of position in the occupational structure than do the notions of the human-capital theorists. People in these positions are able to control the normative aspects of their work (i.e., the "imputed" relation of cultural possessions to productivity) and to subordinate the technical aspects (i.e., the "real" relation of cultural possessions to productivity) to those normative aspects.

By Gouldner's definition both groups would still be defined as cultural-capital owners. But it may be more useful to suggest that only the latter should be so defined, with the former group (those for whom technical skills are dominant over cultural norms) viewed as human-capital owners with no cultural capital. This synthesis would then suggest an empirically testable hypothesis: those who are cultural-capital owners are more likely to collect "rent" on their investment in education—that is, they are more likely to gain a surplus from possessing cultural capital. Those who do not possess such cultural capital, who possess skills where technical aspects are dominant (human-capital owners), would merely expect a return of their educational investment over their lifetime earnings, with no rent. It would certainly be an interesting research project to find those skills where people collect rent on their educational investments and to try to link their ability to collect rent to the socially defined character of the skills they possess. Besides producing an empirically testable hypothesis, this synthesis would also have forced Gouldner to scrutinize the notion of "imputedness" to try to find an explanation for why cultural-capital owners collect rents while human-capital owners do not. Where does this rent come from? As we will see, Roemer and Wright confront some of these problems in their theory. They explicitly define exploitation by rent (e.g., that collected by owners of certain skills). But, like Gouldner, they are also silent concerning the source of this rent.

Before moving on we should note the sharp contrast between the directions of Gouldner's and Bourdieu's analyses. While for Bourdieu the essence of cultural capital is the gaining of access to the "mechanisms" of cultural domination, for Gouldner the key point in the definition of capital in general and cultural capital in particular is access to income and the emphasis on the "imputedness" of the contributions of cultural capital to productivity gains. While for Bourdieu the moment of "domination" is central (if not exclusive) for the concept of cultural capital, Gouldner emphasizes the nonmetaphoricality of the concept of capital in cultural capital and thus brings back to a central place the moment of appropriation. We will return to the issue of the correct place of domination and appropriation in the theory of the new class.

The Culture of Critical Discourse

Having established the notion of cultural capital, Gouldner is next concerned with specifying the distinctiveness of the type of cultural capital possessed by members of the new class. It is not merely that they possess more of such capital than any other group (although this, too, is the case) but also that they ensure that their knowledge conforms to a special set of rules: the culture of critical discourse (CCD). The basis of CCD is that assertions are justified purely on the basis of argument; there can be no invocation of authority which cannot itself be legitimately questioned. Possession of cultural capital (in Gouldner's sense of the term) per se offers only privileges, but those who enter CCD form a new class: if cultural capital takes the form of CCD, then it begins to undermine all authority, including the authority of the old moneyed class. The new class is composed of both the humanistic intellectuals and the technical intelligentsia, that is, by all those who share CCD. Gouldner characterizes those who enter CCD, the new class, as a speech community, thus emphasizing his indebtedness to the sociolinguistics of Basil Bernstein.[21] Building on Bernstein's notion that some groups use more "situation-free" forms of speech than others, Gouldner suggests that CCD is characterized by its high level of "context independence." In order to avoid reference to authority as the ultimate justification of assertion, CCD also requires the capacity to make explicit the rules of "good speech." This capacity is referred to as the "theoreticity" of CCD (note the similarity with Bourdieu's notion of "symbolic mastery").

Perhaps the most important implication of this characterization of CCD is that it allows Gouldner to specify the element common to the professionals, intellectuals, and technical intelligentsia who, he argues, make up the new class. It is precisely the fact that CCD is a set of norms about what constitutes "good speech" in any context that makes it the unifying characteristic of the new class. CCD crosses all disciplinary boundaries, providing a common standard for all disciplines. The form of cultural capital possessed by the new class is thus precisely the capacity to engage in speech governed by the rules dictated by CCD.

The scheme of class structure which corresponds to this concept of cultural capital and CCD is shown in table 2. Gouldner solves the central contradiction of the theory of Bourdieu, that is, that "cultural production" is irreducible to "material production"

TABLE 2

	Descending Old Dominant Class:	Ascending New Dominant Class:	Proletariat
	The Moneyed Bourgeoisie	The Cultural Bourgeoisie	
Money Capital	+	−	−
Cultural Capital (in the form of CCD)	−	+	−

but that the basic class structure can only be formed within material production. The most important empirical contribution of Gouldner is that he can now account for the "anticapitalism" of the intellectuals, the feature Bourdieu was unable to account for. On the basis of his theory Gouldner can now coherently argue that the major structural conflict of advanced capitalist societies is between the old, moneyed bourgeoisie and the new, cultural bourgeoisie.

Internal inconsistencies of Gouldner's concept of capital

Gouldner takes the concept of cultural capital too seriously. He pushes Bourdieu's idea to its logical conclusion, but in the process he shows us the impossibility of the project. By insisting that cultural capital is not a metaphor, Gouldner forces the logic of Marxist class analysis, based on the notion of economic capital, onto the analysis of the nature of the power of intellectuals. This methodological economism creates internal inconsistencies in the way his concept of cultural capital is constructed and in the way it is used to define a new class. At the same time it is also at least partially responsible for Gouldner's inability to account for the internal diversification of the educated elite.

The problem related to the inconsistencies in Gouldner's conceptualization of cultural capital and the new class tend to fall into two categories: those associated with the parallel between the accepted notion of material capital and that of cultural capital, and those associated with the way in which Gouldner conceives of capital in general.

In the first set of problems, cultural capital cannot be detached from the individual who owns it. Whereas a capitalist (in the old sense) can lose his capital through bad business or simple bad luck, the professional, for example, cannot in the same sense lose cultural capital; not even the state can take it away (although it can make its use illegal). This also means that the owner of cultural capital must put it into action himself if it is to be used in the process of production (irrespective of whether or not it contributes to increasing productivity). To revert to metaphor, it is not clear how the cultural capital of one person can be used as the ''means of production'' by another, especially without the first person's doing some of the productive labor. At least at first sight, there appears to be no room for ''surplus-value'' creation by the owners of cultural capital.

This brings us to the second point, which is that cultural capital is not consumed in production in the way in which economic capital appears to be. The capacity of a person to engage in CCD is not ''worn away'' in production in the sense that the means of production are. If anything, cultural capital is likely to be enhanced by its use (the value of experience, etc.). Among the theorists of technocracy this feature of the dominant productive force (''science,'' in Daniel Bell's view)[22] has already been extensively commented on. Essentially, their view is that the revolutionary effect of science on production is largely due to the fact that, unlike the old productive forces of industrial society, the new means of production—that is, knowledge—is not diminished in any way by production.

However, these issues do not seem to be decisive for the theory of cultural capital. The first problem may be overcome by reverting to the argument that capital is a relation, not a thing. Hence, what most capital owners use their capital for in production is to establish a relation between themselves and workers. Similarly, cultural-capital owners may be able to direct others by virtue of their ''ownership'' of cultural capital. Second, the problem of the ''wearing away'' of economic capital is wrongly posed. The means of production are not coterminous with capital in the process of production, since the portion of the means of production that is worn away in production is not capital lost as much as it is capital transferred to the finished product. Cultural capital simply does not foster this confusion, for it is clear from the outset that production (whether cultural or economic) will not diminish it.

The second set of problems is associated more with the way in which Gouldner chooses to define capital. As noted above, there is a problem in Gouldner's attempt to claim that there is no necessary relation between the activation of capital and levels of productivity. The basis for the existence of economic capital in capitalist societies is the separation of the worker from the means of production and from the embodiment of capital in these means of production. Gouldner had much to gain by his generic definition of capital. By defining capital in terms of its imputed contribution to economic productivity, he sought to imply that cultural-capital owners could dominate the processes of material production, just as owners of economic capital had. The danger, however, is that if Marxists can show that economic capital necessarily affects productivity whereas (as Gouldner is the first to admit) cultural capital need not, then the theoretical support for the notion of a dominant class of cultural-capital owners is undermined. For, in this case, owners of economic capital seem to have a more fundamental claim on control of economic production than a cultural bourgeoisie could ever achieve.

Gouldner's definition of capital is problematic in another very important way. One of the most significant characteristics of money capital is its convertibility. If it were not possible to convert all economic capital into money or its equivalent, then such basic processes as accumulation would not be possible. For instance, a capitalist does not merely accumulate machines for making shoes. Rather, he or she accumulates abstract capital that may at any moment be converted into machines for making shirts. Economic capital is defined precisely where there is an institutionalized market that allows the valuation and convertibility of all capital goods. In leaving out this aspect of capital, Gouldner sidesteps a major problem of the notion of cultural capital. Such capital is, at least in his definition, unavoidably differentiated. For example, the possessor of an engineering degree is employed precisely because his degree is in engineering, not merely because he possesses a degree. His qualifications are not convertible to those required for a lecturing position in sociology. The notion of CCD does not solve this problem. Although CCD may be a mode of speech common to all intellectuals, in Gouldner's definition it alone does not constitute cultural capital. For example, a civil engineer's cultural capital will consist of a store of knowledge about how to build bridges, roads, etc. While this knowledge will be carried in a form appropriate to the demands of CCD, it is clear that CCD does not constitute it. It is this technical knowledge base of which CCD can be applied which is not convertible to some other form of cultural capital by its owner. In short, it seems that many of the people whom Gouldner would regard as cultural-capital owners can use their cultural capital only to achieve very circumscribed power over others.

A final drawback of Gouldner's definition of cultural capital is its failure to imply that the cultural bourgeoisie is distinguished simply by possession of a form of capital which the rest of the population does not possess at all. If one wishes to define a new class on the basis of cultural capital, it would seem to be necessary to locate another nonowning class (which is subordinated). To put it crudely, the criterion of a class theory as opposed to a stratification theory is precisely that classes are defined by qualitative or categorical differences rather than by the quantitative variations that differentiate strata. Gouldner is obviously not unaware of this point, hence his emphasis on conformity (as opposed to nonconformity) to CCD as the distinctive mark of the new class. He is careful, however, not to equate cultural capital with CCD, and in fact he implies that all classes possess some cultural capital. The reason Gouldner is unwilling to define cultural capital as knowledge that is subject to the rules of CCD is, apparently, his insistence on defining capital as that which is imputed to contribute to *economic* productivity. It would be impossible for him to argue that only knowledge conforming to CCD has an imputed contribution to economic productivity.

These internal inconsistencies demonstrate that the nonmetaphorical usage of the term *capital* in the concept of cultural capital has created more problems than it has solved. The underlying methodological economism may also be at least partially responsible for the major substantive weaknesses of the Gould-nerian theory of the new class: Gouldner's inability to account for the procapitalism of certain professions and his overemphasis on the radicalism of intellectuals and of the immediacy of their rise to power. Thus, in 1979, Gouldner wrote:

> From the American side, détente was grounded in the split within the Republican Party. This split was made public at its 1976 convention, where the most politically backward and less educated section of the old class rallied to the standard of Ronald Reagan. His appeal was most especially to die-hard, anti-communist small businessmen, farmers, ranchers, who are most hostile to the "long hairs" and "theorists" of the New Class. Gerald Ford's victory against Reagan spelled the final defeat of Cold War Communism (sic) in the Republican Party by those sectors of the old class in large scale late-capitalism most allied with the New Class, as well as by many in the New Class itself.[23]

The money-capital/cultural-capital dichotomy (which follows from what we call "methodological economism"), the identification of all intellectuals as cultural-capital owners, the lack of differentiation between "symbolic" and "practical" mastery within the category of the highly educated, and an overempha-sis on the unity of humanistic and technical intellectuals may be partly responsible for this premature prophecy about the "final defeat" of the old class as represented by Ronald Reagan. The po-litical history of the United States since 1979 has once more un-derlined our need for a theory that can also explain the readiness of the "educated middle classes" (or at least of certain fractions of these classes) to ally with the old class and turn against their own, that is, against the "long hairs" and "theorists" of the new class. The disaster of the new-class project during the last five years, not only in the United States but also in several other ad-vanced or "late" capitalist societies, can only be understood if we break away from the economic-capital/cultural-capital dichotomy and understand the internal divisions within the highly educated strata.

THE CONCEPT OF "CONTRADICTORY
CLASS LOCATIONS"

In offering the first neo-Marxist theory of the new knowledge class, Roemer and Wright[24] to some extent achieve a synthesis of Bourdieu and Gouldner. Roemer and Wright basically accept Bourdieu's theory for capitalist conditions, that as long as private ownership of the means of production exists knowledge can only restratify existing class relations. For postcapitalist societies, Roemer and Wright side with Gouldner: if private ownership of the means of production has been eliminated, then access to scarce skills becomes the basis of a new-class domination.

Roemer and Wright achieve this synthesis by disposing of the concept of cultural capital and basically relying on a somewhat modified version of human-capital theory. By getting rid of the muddy concept of cultural capital they can present a more internally coherent account of the economic privileges and the resulting interests of the highly educated. However, they completely lose sight of the sources of intellectual radicalism under capitalism. They also offer a rather narrowly economistic interpretation of power under socialism. From their theory it appears that the major contradiction under socialism could be reduced to income inequalities. They miss the much crucial problem of political/cultural domination.

First, we should reconstruct how Roemer develops his general theory of exploitation and how Wright adapts it to his project for a general concept of class which could account for the emergence of a new knowledge class as well as it explains the existence of the bourgeoisie. In *A General Theory of Exploitation and Class*, Roemer argues that Marx only described a particular case of exploitation, one that is based on ownership of "capital assets." Roemer suggests that there are other productive assets besides capital and that a different system of exploitation can be based on control of each of them. For the purposes of the present analysis it is sufficient to mention one such asset, namely, "skill assets." Under capitalism, according to Roemer, there is a dual system of exploitation based on the ownership of capital assets and skill assets. With the elimination of private ownership of the means of

TABLE 3

	Unequal distribution of:	
	Capital assets	Skill assets
Capitalism. Here a dual system of exploitation exists. The dominant class owns capital assets and exploits everyone else. The intellectuals, owners of skill assets, are in a contradictory class location, but they themselves exploit the working class.	+	+
Socialism. Here intellectuals rise from their earlier contradictory class location and become the sole exploiters, the new dominant class.	−	+
Communism. Classless society; no productive assets are unequally distributed; no exploitation exists.	−	−

production, exploitation based on the ownership of skill assets remains (Roemer calls this "skill exploitation"). Socialism is, therefore, a new-class society in which skill exploiters replace capitalists as a dominant class. But why are those who own skill assets exploiters? Roemer offers a complex game-theoretic explanation. It is not necessary to present this analysis here; suffice it to say that owners of skill assets are exploiters to the extent that they earn more than they have invested in their education. Skill exploitation can be measured by the difference between returns on human-capital investment and actual incomes.

In a recent book,[25] Wright has used Roemer's general theory of exploitation to develop a general theory of class and to redefine his own earlier theory of contradictory class locations.[26] He analyzes the class structure of four social formations (feudalism, capitalism, bureaucratic socialism, and socialism) by describing the unequal access to one of four "productive assets" (labor power, means of production, organizational assets, and technical skills). We will limit our analysis here to the capitalism/socialism comparison. Using Roemer's idea of skill exploitation, Wright describes the nature of class relations and sources of exploitation under capitalism and under socialism as shown in table 3.

This conceptualization of the new class has several advantages when compared with the theories discussed above. Unlike Gouldner, Wright clearly defines the historic condition that is required for the ascendence of a "knowledge class" to power: the abolition of private ownership of the means of production. Furthermore, this is not simply achieved by the subversive effect of a culture of critical discourse but instead involves a historical struggle against exploitation based on ownership of capital assets. Wright also perceives the working class, who are the most exploited, to be the major force in this struggle (while in Gouldner's analysis the "masses" are invisible). Wright's theory offers us an account of the structural limits of the power aspirations of the highly educated and an explanation of how these structural limits can be removed—not through infighting within the elite but through the struggle of an exploited working class.

Wright's new version of the "contradictory class location" theory is also of great interest for our analysis. Unlike Bourdieu, who emphasizes the unity of the dominant bourgeois class, Wright captures the contradictoriness of the situation of the highly skilled under capitalism. A certain degree of anticapitalism is to be expected from the highly educated who do not own money capital. After all, they, too, are exploited.

By and large we regard this theory as a fairly successful synthesis. At the same time, we think that since it relies exclusively on human-capital theory it misses the important insights of the cultural-capital approach to the new class. It therefore cannot give a sufficiently sophisticated account of the internal divisions of the highly educated under capitalism and the nature of domination under postcapitalist societies. We will now elaborate in some detail what we see as the shortcomings of this theory which are attributable to its exclusive reliance on the human-capital approach.

First, while the "general theory of exploitation and class" is impressively coherent, we think we can detect a telling inconsistency in the notion of skill exploitation. As already mentioned, the idea of skill exploitation implies that owners of scarce skills collect rent on their human-capital investments. This is a reasonable argument, as it makes sense to draw a distinction between "salaries" received for highly skilled labor and "rent" collected on human-capital investment. At the same time, it is unclear where this rent comes from. Under perfect market conditions one would anticipate that no rent would be collected on human-capital investment. Here we can detect an interesting asymmetry between capital assets and skill assets as sources of exploitative practices. Ownership of capital assets will bring rent under perfect as well as imperfect market conditions, but ownership of skill assets will not. Human-capital investments are sources of rent only if skills are "scarce." Most important for the conceptualization of the nature of intellectuals' power, a "scarcity" of skills can only be explained by extramarket—and extraeconomic—factors. So, for instance, probably the most important source of such rent under capitalism is the existence of professional associations, insofar as they achieve effective market control over the supply of skills and services offered by the profession. Medical associations around the world have often been successful in guaranteeing such rent for their members by limiting the enrollments of medical schools. But how can one explain the power of medical associations to achieve effective market control? One can hardly explain this from the market or the economy. One would instead have to make reference to the *type* of knowledge possessed by doctors. In other words, the existence/nonexistence of rent collected from human-capital investments may have very little, or nothing, to do with the actual contribution of such investments to productivity or with the amount of human capital accumulated. The existence of such rent may indicate the presence of what Bourdieu and Gouldner called cultural capital, the self-grounded authority of the knowledge possessor.

Another typical example of the source of rent in human-capital investment may be the bureaucratic regulation of income levels in internal-labor markets. The extreme example would be the income of the Soviet bureaucrat, which is set by himself or herself: one should not search for the source of this income in the economy, since it is instead in the cultural/political system. In other words, unlike the case of owners of capital assets, in the case of owners of human capital or skill assets, it is not their income that is the source of their authority. On the contrary, it is their authority that is the source of their income, particularly their "unearned," rentlike income.

All of this suggests a reservation about one of the main assumptions of human-capital theory which seems to be accepted by Roemer and Wright, and that is the assumption of the "continuous" distribution of skill assets. As we noted in our analysis of the cultural-capital theory of Gouldner (which is also based on the assumption of "continuous" rather than "categorical" distribution), it is problematic to base a class dichotomy between "exploiters" and "exploited" on the distribution of an asset whose ownership is spread across the whole of the social hierarchy (the difference between the worker and the capitalist, after all, is not that the worker owns *less* capital . . .). Indeed, if everybody has some skill, where can we draw the dividing line between the exploiters and the exploited? Don't we need a more specific theory about the nature of these skills in order to perform this operation? The answer to this question is almost inevitably yes. But there is absolutely nothing in human-capital theory or in the "general theory of exploitation" which would enable us to make such a judgment. What we need are insights that can only be gained from the cultural-capital approach.

But let us be more specific and empirical. From the point of view of empirical research, the major weakness of Wright's theory is that he assumes that a simple gradation of anticapitalism in political attitudes runs from the working class to the professionals and that this scale somehow reflects the quantity of human capital invested. This hypothesis is, of course, empirically untenable. First, some of the most radical and anticapitalist groups are not workers but people with high investments in education. The theory is unable to predict why they behave the way they do. In other words, what can the theory do with the elementary observation that some intellectuals are far more radical than most workers? Furthermore, there is no empirical evidence whatsoever that there is any correlation within the group of the highly educated between the level of education and anticapitalist radicalism. It would be more plausible to assume that a qualitative break

in pro–status quo attitudes is to be found as human-capital investment increases rather than that a simple quantitative change in
such attitudes occurs with a change in the level of human-capital
investment. But if this is the case, then one needs the insights of
the cultural-capital approach.

CONCLUSION: TOWARD A GENERAL THEORY OF SYMBOLIC DOMINATION

We have to be rather sketchy at this point, since this paper is
of an exploratory character and does not pretend to have the final
solution to the questions raised by human-capital and cultural-
capital theories. We are very uneasy about using the term *capital*
(human or cultural) in analyzing power aspirations and claims for
rewards or privileges by the highly educated. We are quite certain that it can only be done metaphorically, and we are not convinced that such usage is justified at all. We are also very uneasy
about calling the relationship between the "knows" and the
"know-nots" (to use the picturesque language of Nomad) "exploitation." We are aware that terminological precision is not in-
significant. Metaphors can easily mislead us: by using the
language of "capital," "exploitation," and "class" we can easily drift along the conventional routes of class analysis which were
designed to comprehend the nature of capital owners' power and
which may, therefore, be highly inappropriate to the analysis of
the nature of the power of the highly educated. Still, at this stage
we do not want to get bogged down in a terminological exercise.
Instead, we would like to confront the substantive issues brought
up by the theorists discussed in this paper.

We will now return to the puzzle of new-class theory posed at
the beginning of this paper (i.e., the unpredictability of the political attitudes of the highly educated). Our analysis has suggested
that this can be understood as a reflection of the two facets of the
knowledge possessed by the highly educated.

On one hand, the human-capital aspect is the technically useful aspect of their knowledge. It is the capacity to achieve the ends

set by others, particularly by employers or clients, and it is the practical mastery of which Bourdieu speaks. We would expect all participants in labor markets to have this kind of knowledge to some extent. Moreover, all other things being equal, incomes will reflect the economic investments made by people with this kind of knowledge.

On the other hand, the cultural-capital aspect of the knowledge of the highly educated is the capacity to describe the principles by which those with merely technical knowledge manipulate their worlds. It is the capacity to gain symbolic mastery of practices. This knowledge conforms to Gouldner's culture of critical discourse in that its legitimacy is self-referential. Moreover, it is dichotomously distributed and affords those who have it the capacity to exercise domination over those who do not. It divides the world into the "knows" and the "know-nots." This aspect of the knowledge of the highly educated does not conform to any laws but its own—even in the final instance, its character, objects, development, and political implications cannot be deduced from the demands or interests of other groups, such as capitalists or workers. Finally, we can hypothesize that the relationship between this facet of knowledge and income is not dependent on the economic investment in education necessary for its acquisition. In other words, it is the "imputed," not the "real," relation to productivity that matters in income determination for this aspect of the knowledge of the highly educated.

Our synthesis of human-capital and cultural-capital approaches suggests that crucial aspects of both the class position and the political attitudes of different categories of the highly educated can be understood by the relation of the two facets of the knowledge they possess. In conformity with our belief that the notion of cultural (or human) *capital* is becoming a hindrance to theorizing the new class, and in deference to the importance of Bourdieu's notion of symbolic domination, we would like to refer to these two aspects of knowledge as practical mastery and symbolic mastery. We believe that whichever of these aspects is dominant over the other (as well as the extent to which it is dominant) in the knowledge of a particular category of the highly educated significantly influences the structural position and political attitudes of that category. By "dominance" in this context we mean the capacity for the logic of development of one aspect of knowledge to dictate the progress of the other. Dominance of practical mastery over symbolic mastery means that productivity demands generated by the (capitalist) economy dictate the development of knowledge. In this case the positions, interests, and political attitudes of the highly educated group concerned conform to those of the basically capitalist society in which they exist.

If, however, symbolic mastery becomes dominant in the knowledge of a segment of the highly educated, the logic of knowledge production conforms to the laws of CCD and the interests of the knowledge producers, not to the demands of a capitalist economy. Most significantly, this situation offers the capacity for "symbolic domination," as Bourdieu termed it, to the highly educated. In this case there is no allegiance to the interests of capitalists, and anticapitalist political attitudes are likely to emerge where the logic of symbolic domination contradicts that of capitalist appropriation. Of course, we regard these two extremes as ideal types: the relation between symbolic and practical mastery in the knowledge of empirical categories of the highly educated is variable and so, therefore, is the strength of procapitalist or anticapitalist attitudes. Moreover, the stability of such attitudes will also depend on the stability of the domination of one aspect of knowledge over the other.

In agreement with Roemer and Wright's analysis, we suggest that there is a broad historical movement toward the appearance of a class based on domination through symbolic mastery, although we believe that this trend is more historically contingent and subject to reversals than Roemer and Wright seem to admit. Nevertheless, it is clear to us that as long as ownership of money capital remains a major source of social power and privilege, symbolic mastery will be only a limited source of such power and privilege. Yet, there are clearly categories of the highly educated in advanced capitalist societies which represent the seed of a potential new class—truly, to steal a phrase, the seeds of the new form of domination appear in the womb of the old society.

This broad synthesis may be represented in the setup shown in table 4, which draws heavily on a similar schema of Wright's but adds the implications of Gouldner's and Bourdieu's analyses.

We hope that our consideration of the human-capital and cultural-capital approaches to the knowledge of intellectuals and other highly educated groups could achieve at least two things. First, we hope that it has pinpointed the new quality of power held by knowledge monopolists in a postcapitalist society. In earlier work, one of us emphasized the differences between the "technocrats" of market economies and the "teleocrats" of post-capitalist societies (also noting that, paradoxically, in Soviet-type societies it is the technocratic component of intellectual thought which is more subversive and around which dissent is organized, while the opposite is, of course, true for Western societies, where

TABLE 4

Money capital	Practical mastery	Symbolic mastery	Nature of the position
Sources of power/privilege under capitalism			
+ +	+	−	Entrepreneurs/owners: dominant class
+	+ +	+ or −	Technocratic intelligentsia: privileged stratum of bourgeois character
− or +	+	+ +	Countercultural intelligentsia: in "contradictory class location"
Sources of power/privilege in postcapitalist societies			
−	+	+ +	"Teleocratic intelligentsia" (like teleocratic planners): a new dominant "class"
−	+ +	+	Technocrats, dissenting intellectuals: in "contradictory class locations"

the antitechnocratic, countercultural intelligentsia is the focus of social and political dissent).[27] Second, we hope that the distinction between symbolic and practical mastery as we have developed it will enable us to begin exploring the internal differentiation of the highly educated in capitalist societies and will help us to comprehend the basic procapitalism of technological thinking.

Finally, this macrolevel conceptualization will need to be complemented by a microlevel analysis. It is reasonable to try to explore the problems of integration of these two facets of the knowledge of the highly educated at the level of personality and to begin to explore the nature of domination by the "knows" over the "know-nots" at the level of interpersonal interaction. Studies of the relationships between the psychoanalyst and the patient, the priest and the believer, and so on could be used almost as laboratory experiments to comprehend the dynamics of the power of knowledge monopolists.[28] Such analysis would perform the same function for new-class theory that the study of the labor process does for Marxist class theory. Of course, the exploration of such research strategies, and in particular the integration of macro- and microlevels of analysis, is beyond the scope of our paper. This paper is a call to move beyond cultural-capital theories and to begin to develop a more comprehensive theory of symbolic domination. Such a theory will only be achieved when the integration of macrolevel and microlevel analyses has been accomplished.

NOTES

1. P. Bourdieu, *Towards a Theory of Practice* (Cambridge: Cambridge University Press, 1977), p. 184.

2. A. Gouldner, *The Future of Intellectuals and the Rise of the New Class* (New York: Macmillan Co., 1979), pp. 18 ff.

3. See J. Roemer, *A General Theory of Exploitation and Class* (Cambridge, Mass.: Harvard University Press, 1982); and E. O. Wright, *Classes* (London: Verso, 1985).

4. See, for example, N. Podhoretz, "The Adversary Culture and the New Class" in B. Bruce-Briggs, ed., *The New Class?* (New Brunswick: Transaction Books, 1979); and H. Schelsky, *Die Arbeit tun die Andren,* (Opladen: Westdeutscher Verlag, 1975).

5. P. Bourdieu and J.-C. Passeron, *Reproduction in Education, Society, and Culture* (London and Beverly Hills: Sage, 1977), pp. 47–50.

6. Gouldner, *Future of Intellectuals*, pp. 28–31.

7. Here we use the picturesque language of Max Nomad. See M. Nomad, "Masters Old and New," in V. F. Calverton, ed., *The Making of Society* (New York: Modern Library, 1937).

8. Schelsky, *Die Arbeit.*

9. This is most clear in the first part of Bourdieu and Passeron, *Reproduction in Education.*

10. Bourdieu, *Towards a Theory of Practice*, pp. 183–184.

11. Bourdieu and Passeron, *Reproduction in Education*, p. 8.

12. Bourdieu and Passeron, *Reproduction in Education.*

13. Cf. B. Ehrenreich and J. Ehrenreich, "The Professional/Managerial Class," in Pat Walker, ed., *Between Labor and Capital* (Boston: South End Press, 1979). In this piece the Ehrenreichs present a Marxist-influenced theory of how the group charged with the culturally based functions of reproduction of the relations of production in a capitalist society (the so-called managerial/professional class) can be defined as a distinct class. In other words, they use the same theoretical strategy as Bourdieu, trying to understand processes of reproduction, but they are open to the possibility that the agents who carry out these processes could have interests divergent from those of both major classes in capitalism.

14. In the sense that most Marxists would regard the exploitative practices of the dominant class as the "material base" of its cultural and political domination.

15. By contrast, Gouldner may do more damage than good to the theory of the new class by emphasizing the nonmetaphoricality of the concept of cultural capital. This turns out to be even more so in the "general theory of exploitation" of Roemer and Wright, where the moment of "domination" almost completely disappears.

16. Bourdieu, *Towards a Theory of Practice.*

17. Bourdieu and Passeron, *Reproduction in Education*, p. 50.

18. By methodological economism we mean that his theory assumes that knowledge monopolists' power is structured in the same way as that of owners of economic capital. In analyzing the power of the new class he effects a methodological *imitation* of Marxist class analysis rather than

realizing that he needs a new method to describe the new type of domination.

19. Gouldner, *Future of Intellectuals*, p. 21.

20. Gouldner, *Future of Intellectuals*, p. 27.

21. See, for example, B. Bernstein, *Class, Codes and Control*, vols. 1–3 (London: Routledge & Kegan Paul, 1971, 1973, 1975).

22. D. Bell, *The Coming of Post-Industrial Society* (New York: Basic Books, 1973).

23. Gouldner, *Future of Intellectuals*, p. 92.

24. See Roemer, *A General Theory of Exploitation*, and Wright.

25. Wright, *Classes*.

26. See E. O. Wright, *Class, Crisis and the State* (London: New Left Books, 1978).

27. See G. Konrád and I. Szelényi, *The Intellectuals on the Road to Class Power* (New York: Harcourt, Brace, Jovanovich, 1979).

28. For this point, we are indebted to T. Söderqvist, "The Microfoundation of the Intelligentsia Concept" (paper presented at the conference "Intellectuals, Universities, and the State," Fiskebäckskil, Sweden, January 12–15, 1984).

3

Intellectuals in Advanced Capitalism: Capital, Closure, and the New-Class Thesis

Cornelis Disco

> These metaphysics of magicians (opens another
>   book raptly)
> And necromantic books are heavenly;
> Lines, circles, letters, characters—
> Ay, these are those that Faustus most desires!
> O, what a world of profit and delight,
> Of power, of honor, and omnipotence
> Is promis'd to the studious artisan!
> All things that move between the quiet poles
> Shall be at my command. Emperors and kings
> Are but obey'd in their several provinces
> But his dominion that exceeds in this
> Stretcheth as far as doth the mind of man—
> A sound magician is a demi-God![1]

INTELLECTUALS AND THE TRANSFORMATION OF CAPITALISM

Manifestly as Bengt Furåker shows in his contribution to this volume, even those capitalist societies that have not succumbed to socialist revolution in the twentieth century have undergone a number of fundamental transformations. Recalling several of these will suffice to underscore the key role of the so-called educated strata in the making of contemporary capitalism:

1. *The pervasive mediation of modern lives by technical artifacts, from work to leisure, from war to love, from public space to private intimacy.* Contemporary life in the West is mediated (and also simultaneously enhanced, contained, and jeopardized) by personal and collective dominion over increasingly potent, clever, and even intelligent devices and technical systems. In numerous ways these made advanced capitalist "mass society" and its characteristic patterns of production/consumption, political organization, demography, and culture possible.

2. *The rationalization of the exercise of power.* Such rationalization is manifest in the emergence of the "smart" bureaucracy, which not only pursues the formalized and rule-bound deployment of centralized authority in the tradition of its Weberian ancestors but also senses, theoretically comprehends, plans, and selectively reconstructs its particular environment. While so doing it pays particular attention to the effects of its own interventions, utilizing each instance as a learning experience in which to sharpen and streamline future policy. Undoubtedly the most impressive examples of such "smart" bureaucracies exist within the "teleological states" of present-day socialisms, but the agencies of advanced capitalist "welfare states" are not far behind.

3. *The "information explosion."* The historical conjunction of increased leisure time, the exponential development of electronic media, and the vastly expanded requirements of "smart" bureaucracies for information with which to interpret and control their "fields" have resulted on one hand in the invasion of formerly private and intimate space by the mass-entertainment industry and on the other hand in the creation of an extensive and expanding data-processing and data-transmitting sector.

4. *The rise of the "caring estate."* On the basis of such developments as increased urbanization, the rise in living standards,

and the gradual construction of a welfare state, entire professions have emerged which are devoted to the physical, mental, and social care of populations. These professions have
arrogated to themselves the prerogatives of defining nor-
malcy, of diagnosing ill-being, and of prescribing remedies.
In a Laschian vein, the "caring estate" has thereby substituted cool professional expertise for the dense and sup-
portive traditional relations of caring and has thus
contributed to increasing dependency and powerlessness
among large sectors of the populations of advanced capitalist
societies.

The simple fact of developments such as these does not, of
course, compel us to speak of them as manifestations of the rising power of a new class of intellectuals.[2] Such a discourse is a
matter of theoretical and practical *choice*, as, indeed, is the discourse of "class" in general. However, as a theoretical strategy,
class theory—particularly of the Marxist variety—is a seductive
option because of its capacity for integrating the study of personal
biography, social stratification, and historical change. Class
theory, in this sense a paragon of Occamite virtue, promises to
reduce theoretical complexity by limiting the proliferation of concepts and hypotheses. It does this, as Frank Parkin argues, by
focalizing the basic "cleavages" in social order between haves
and have-nots, producers and profiteers, the knowledgeable and
the ignorant, the meek and the mighty.[3] Class theory thus
premises that structured social inequalities and the exploitative relations these entail are the primary facts of social existence and,
hence, the key to understanding society and history.
    Theories of intellectuals as a new class emerging from this tra-
dition are, in the first place, proposals for revising the Marxist
historical scenario.[4] Such theories will tend to reinterpret actually
existing socialisms as the dictatorship of the new class of intellectuals rather than that of the proletariat.[5] They will tend to redefine the crucial class contest in capitalist societies as a contest
between the capitalist class and the new class rather than between
the capitalist class and the proletariat.[6] *Marxist* theories of the new
class, in other words, do not merely insert a new class into the

orthodox Marxist class scenario but postulate a new "universal" class that will take the place of the proletariat in a radically demystified Marxist scenario.[7]

Whatever one's judgment about the desirability of such a theory, however, orthodox Marxist class theory constrains its development, both because it is an exemplary model and exclusionary class theory of society and history. Much of Marxism's strength in both of these respects appears to derive from the complex and tightly interwoven set of assertions around the concept of "capital." In particular, the ability of capital to assume both a physical form (as a means of production) and a purely quantitative money form (as a medium of exchange, as wages, and as profits) allowed Marx to integrate ownership rights, technologies of production, competition, and exploitation into a unified theory of capitalist development and class struggle. A central problem for a neo-Marxist new-class theory seeking to compete with orthodox Marxism on its own terms has thus been to develop a concept of "cultural capital" analogous to that of "material capital" in the Marxist theory of class.[8]

MATERIAL CAPITAL, CULTURAL CAPITAL, HUMAN CAPITAL

Both Gouldner and Szelényi have attempted, albeit in different ways, to define a version of cultural capital as a conceptual primitive equivalent to material capital and thus as a basis for the structuralization of a new class.[9] Gouldner's basically economistic approach proceeds from an attack on the conventional view that the incomes accruing to a capital depend on its contribution to productivity. In his view, the incomes accruing to any capital are in large part the result of a process of social negotiation in which the threat of withholding the capital and *claims* about its productivity play an important role. Gouldner thus explicitly defines capital as "any produced object used to make saleable utilities, thus providing its possessor with *incomes*, or claims to incomes defined as legitimate because of their imputed contribution to economic productivity."[10] Although Gouldner remains flexible about the *form* in which incomes accrue to holders of cultural capital (e.g., as wages, as copyright claims, and as the "preemption of certain offices"), it is clear that the ultimate measure of capitalization is the equivalent of these mediate forms in ready money (e.g., as lifetime earning).

Clearly, as Szelényi has argued in his recent critiques of Gouldner, this comes down to a merely distributive, neo-Weberian theory of class.[11] If the *only* concern of a new class is with its incomes, it is indeed hard to see how intellectuals in a capitalist society could be interested in anticapitalist politics or economic arrangements—certainly, a prerequisite for a class that is held to be a serious challenger to capitalist hegemony. The horizon of such a new class would have to remain restricted to professionalization projects aimed at cornering markets in expertise and could not be expected to include opposition to capitalism as such. Especially damaging is the difficulty of aligning this rather cynical thesis on the new class as a cultural bourgeoisie with the basically Hegelian and romantic thesis on the new class as a speech community. While the former depicts the new class as adaptive, strategic, and dedicated to the control of markets in knowledge, the latter depicts it as revolutionary, ideological, and essentially dedicated to the overthrow of all authority not founded on the "good argument." Although this is admittedly a charged rendition of Gouldner's position, and in spite of his repeated assertions that the new class is "morally ambiguous," a considerable theoretical problem obviously exists here. This problem is rooted in Gouldner's own ambiguous relationship to Marxism as well as in Marxism's own ambiguous relationship to bourgeois political economy.

Classical political economy introduced a conception of capital which may be characterized as "naïve realist." In this conception, capital was viewed simply as the material requisites of industrial production (e.g., building, machines, raw materials) and their equivalents in money. There seemed little reason to question either the evident productivity of such material requisites or the justice of the incomes accruing to those who financed their development and production and organized their interfacing with human labor. Classical political economy was, in effect, an attempt to describe and legitimate the emerging economic dominance of an increasingly potent manufacturing fraction of the bourgeoisie. Its eternalization of primitive bourgeois categories, such as the deeply embedded postulate of "possessive individualism," served both as a mystification of the bourgeoisie's less-than-glamorous historical origins and as a legitimation of its impending domination of "free" labor.[12] In essence, political economy tacitly redefined human beings as *bourgeois* human beings and civil society as *bourgeois* civil society.

Marx's critique of political economy shattered this glossy realist surface, not by challenging the productivity of capital as a means of production but by challenging the productivity of the labor of its owners. While Marx shared the common view that material capital conjoined with human labor produced use-values, he exerted himself in demonstrating that the labor of the capital owner himself produced nothing but his profits. Marx thus analyzed the labor of the capitalist as "unproductive labor," aimed solely at monitoring and organizing productive labor for the purpose of extracting the surplus value on which the capitalist's incomes depend. Envisaging a future mode of production in which the "direct producers" would themselves manage material capital as a means of production, Marx could dismiss the labor of capitalists as superfluous and, of course, their incomes as the wages of exploitation rather than of true labor. It is thus evident that Marx recognized a systematic discrepancy between the contribution of capitalists to productivity and their incomes.

The Marxist problem around which Gouldner develops his thesis on the "cultural bourgeoisie" is that of how, under conditions of formal political freedom, the capital owner succeeds in disciplining workers to such a degree that the extraction of surplus value becomes possible. Marx couched his answer in terms of the acute dependencies that the monopolization of capital ownership produced in the working class. The proletarian is literally dependent on the capitalist for his livelihood; access to the means of production as the only legitimate source of income is a matter of life or death for the worker, and where labor is relatively plentiful, unskilled, and consequently interchangeable, he simply has no choice but to accede to the capitalist's terms. Gouldner fixates his general theory of capital at precisely this point by arguing that capitalists *in general* succeed in commanding exploitative (i.e., "unearned," "exploitative") incomes on the basis of the threat to withhold their capital good, that is, on the basis of structured dependencies. Thus, economic monopolization produces market domination.

Given, however, that Marx never got around to a systematic theory of class, or even of the state, and that his critique of political economy therefore looms unnaturally large in his total oeuvre, it is questionable whether a "*general* theory of capital" taking its inspiration from Marx ought to have been pitched at this level. Marxism is not only a detailed analysis of the capitalist mode of production and a historical materialism but it is also more generally—as such post-Marxists as Lenin, Lukacs, Gramsci, and even Gouldner himself have reminded us—a class theory of historical transformation. In venturing a general theory of capital, therefore, we should be sensitive to the fact that capital—any capital—is not some kind of palpable object but is itself a historically produced structure of domination/dependence. One, but only one, aspect of this domination is the ability to extract exploitative incomes from dominated/dependent populations. Insofar as the social construction of a capital good can be said to underlie class formation, members of that class will also seek to reconstruct the world as one in which possessors of its capital good legitimately hold sway in all areas of life. One example of such reconstruction on an ideological plane is, of course, bourgeois political economy itself.

In an important sense, however, Marx was obviously correct in regarding capital owners as being in the game chiefly for the money. For the bourgeoisie, amassing money is not merely a route to status-enhancing consumption or increased leisure (though it may become this as well) but is also its royal road to economic, political, and cultural domination. As money becomes the universal medium of exchange and populations become increasingly dependent on purchase rather than on direct production, petty exchange, and barter for their livelihoods, the need for money becomes acute. Its successful concentration in the hands of a relatively small number of families—especially in the form of industrial capital, that is, as a means of production—produces intense dependencies. Consequently, it produces the need among ever larger and more diverse sectors of the population to be, as it were, bought. Moreover, the bourgeoisie's disposition over massed wealth enables it to buy out, buy up, buy off, or otherwise co-opt and control potential adversaries and possible allies—including, of course, those whom Gramsci described as the "organic intellectuals" of the bourgeoisie. In this way, the monopolization of access to the means of material survival (and, for a happy few, the means of distinction and the "good life") has hitherto enabled the money-capitalist class to dominate all sectors of social life in those sorts of societies which still bear its name.

Money incomes, however, do not play the same role in the life of the putative new class. For intellectuals, money incomes are primarily consumptive incomes and, at best, allow them merely to lead distinctive and relatively sumptuous lives. The capitalizable resource on the basis of which intellectuals may make a bid for class power consists of particular styles of discourse and derivative bodies of specialized knowledge and theory-based skills. Their ownership of wealth—at least in the form of personal possession of money capital—is not the pivotal determinant of their future as a new class. The possible structuralization and potential hegemony of the new class is, therefore, *pace* Gouldner, less a question of the political economy than of the politics of culture. Knowledge, in other words, is not the key to new class power by virtue of its ability to command extraordinary money incomes but by virtue of its ability, in the monopolistic form of "cultural capital," to exploit dependencies arising from the relative lack of crucial kinds of knowledge among other social groups. The key to the rise of a new class in capitalist societies, of course, is that the lack of knowledge increasingly threatens the process of the accumulation of money capital itself at corporate, national, and international levels. The point, however, is not that intellectuals thereby become the recipients of extraordinary salaries (although this may well serve as both a motivation and a means of control) but that they come to hold authoritative disposition over increasing masses of liquid and embodied money capital, both private and public. Whether this is, or can develop into, a substantial challenge to capitalist hegemony is a matter for closer analysis.

If Gouldner's strategy in arriving at a theory of cultural capital may be said to take its inspiration from that part of the Marxist legacy rooted in bourgeois political economy, it is fair to say that the contribution by Martin and Szelényi in this volume aims at a concept of cultural capital true to Marxism's Hegelian roots. For the latter, more or less content to leave Marx's materialist political economy for what it is, the specific capital of the new class is its capacity to institute a new regime of state domination. This regime is characterized by what Konrád and Szelényi, in their original analysis of the new class in state socialist societies, called "teleological redistribution"—that is, the politically coerced and ideologically steered central planning of economic systems.[13] This specific definition of the "capital" of the new class rules out the possibility of a new class within a capitalist mode of production, simply because the exigencies of private accumulation block teleological redistribution on any significant scale.

In the original formulation in *The Intellectuals on the Road to Class Power*, Gouldner did not view the new class as a new *capitalist* class but simply as the new hegemonic class of the postcapitalist state. Insofar as socialism was still held to represent the "universal" interest in the overthrow of capitalism, such a class could be depicted as the "new universal class." As critical sociologists writing in the tradition of Bakunin, Machajski, and Djilas, however, Konrád and Szelényi were primarily interested in discrediting old Marxist myths by showing that, far from being the promised classless societies, actually existing socialisms were generating a new class corresponding with new modes of domination and new social inequalities. It is for this reason that in Szelényi's earlier critiques of Gouldner he shows himself much taken by the latter's concept of the "*flawed* universal class."

"Flawedness," however, remains a metaphysical characterization in search of theoretical and empirical content. Both Gouldner's and Szelényi's intentions were to express the idea that, in spite of the "universal" challenge to capitalism which the new class represented, its members were in some sense "in it for themselves" and were thus interested in instituting new exploitative relationships. Gouldner theorized this self-centered "flawedness'' by describing his new class as in part a ''cultural bourgeoisie'' in pursuit of returns on its capital. Szelényi, rejecting both Gouldner's postulate of a new class under capitalism and consequently the ''general theory of capital'' which made such a postulate possible, had until recently devoted little attention to an equivalent systematic conceptualization.

The significance of the present contribution by Martin and Szelényi is its focus on a theory of symbolic capital as a medium for making both the ''universality'' and the ''flawedness'' of a new class, as they understand it, theoretically manageable. Though this does imply a rapprochement of sorts with Gouldner, the differences remain striking. Particularly obvious is the divergent usage of the concepts of ''cultural capital'' and ''human capital.'' Gouldner, it will be recalled, criticized the theory of human capital—in Theodore Schultz's sense—as an ideological pose seeking to legitimate extraordinary incomes for intellectual labor on the basis of its putative extraordinary productivity.[14] His conception of cultural capital, while equally economistic, dissociated incomes from productivity by inserting social processes of exclusion, coercion, and the generation of dependencies. Capital, avers Gouldner, always ''seeks something for nothing.'' Martin and Szelényi, while apparently sharing this view, nonetheless muddy the waters by using the very same terms to make quite another distinction: that between symbolic capital as a claim on special incomes and symbolic capital as the transcendent potential to institute a new mode of production/domination. For them, human capital describes the former sense of symbolic capital, and ''cultural capital'' describes the latter.

Although the terminological confusion could be cleared up in such a way as to retrieve Gouldner's critique of the well-established human-capital school, Martin and Szelényi obviously have a real point to make. It is this: a theory of cultural capital which could serve as the ''material basis'' of a new class cannot simply depict that class as deploying its culture to command incomes but must also depict that class's culture as inherently and essentially postcapitalist. Though they appreciate that Gouldner's idea of the culture of critical discourse (CCD) does fulfill this role, they see his theory of cultural capital as antagonistic to the former and as denying the possibility of a new *class* in favor of a theory of income stratification on the basis of symbolic skills. In their view, Gouldner has merely succeeded in describing the condition of intellectuals under capitalism, under "the primacy of material production," where they can only become a technocratic elite.

Martin and Szelényi's solution in essence splits "symbolic capital" into an economistic, "technocratic" component and a political, "teleological" component. Only the latter is cultural capital, that is, teleocratic capital proper to the "new class" on the basis of which its structuration proceeds. *Human* capital, in Martin and Szelényi's sense, is possessed not only by intellectuals but also by other groups who bring special and rare skills to the labor market. In this sense, symbolic capital as "human capital" is sufficient to underlie only a theory of *stratification*, not one of class formation.

This conceptual matrix is subsequently applied in a quasi-historical sense to the distinction between capitalist and post-capitalist societies. Human capital is viewed as the form of symbolic capital characteristic of the capitalist mode of production, thus explaining the procapitalism of technocratic professionals held to occupy a "contradictory class location." Cultural capital is the characteristic form under postcapitalist socialist societies, thus explaining the dominance of a hegemonic new class composed of teleocrats.

While Martin and Szelényi's criticisms of Gouldner's theory of cultural capital are well taken, their own solution does raise a number of knotty questions that may in the end prove more amenable to an approach such as Gouldner's.

First, there is the matter of the relationship among norms, technique, and theory. Human capital, in Martin and Szelényi's sense, is held to consist of "symbolic *skills*" that have a certain market value on the basis of their contribution to capitalist production. The intimate link of these professional "skills" to a theoretical mode of reasoning and to evolving bodies of theory is simply glossed over because of the requirement to reserve "theoreticity" for their concept of *cultural* capital. Gouldner focalizes this link by arguing that even professional technocratic cultures ultimately derive from the CCD. Glossing this connection, as Martin and Szelényi do, obviously eliminates all grounds for asserting the formation of a new class, rather than a mere skill stratum, *within* capitalism. Second, Martin and Szelényi's radical splitting of symbolic capital results in an ahistorical rendering of the structuralization of the new class. In their vision, the new class appears on the historical stage more or less as a deus ex machina only within postcapitalist society. While it is a tautology to argue that the new class can be the dominant class only in such societies, it does not follow that it cannot exist as a partly adaptive, partly oppositional "class-in-the-making" within capitalist society itself. After all, the capitalist class itself emerged "in the womb of the old order." Though Martin and Szelényi do in this connection recognize the existence of radical anticapitalist intellectuals in capitalist societies—and consequently of the cultural capital that makes such teleological opposition possible—they are unable to account for these phenomena on a theoretical level. Moreover, it remains a riddle how they conceive of the transformation of human capital into cultural capital with the advent of socialism. Vague Hegelian formulations about the primacy of symbolic over material production do not turn the trick. Lastly, the collapsing of Gouldner's human-capital/cultural-capital distinction—with its radical implications for the idea of capital as at once a productive *and* an income-generating social project—obscure the continuing pursuit by teleocrats in postcapitalist societies of exploitative incomes on the basis of their special cultural capital. In other words, some general equivalent to Gouldner's cynical thesis on cultural capital must be formulated which transcends the capitalism-socialism distinction. A concept of human capital which is limited to capitalist society is obviously inadequate for this purpose.

For these reasons, it does not seem desirable to follow Martin and Szelényi's lead. Neither, however, can their critique of Gouldner be ignored. One might say roughly that, *as far as their respective theories of cultural capital are concerned*, Martin and Szelényi cannot account for the anticapitalism of certain strata of intellectuals within capitalist society, while Gouldner cannot account for the hegemony of a new class in postcapitalist society.

CAPITAL AS SOCIAL CLOSURE

The foregoing argues for a general theory of capital which regards the relative salience of the command of extraordinary money-incomes as contingent on the nature of the capital good in question and which conceives capital formation as itself a risky and uncertain historical project. Though the theory being formulated by Szelényi et al. clearly meets this criterion, I consider it unsatisfactory because of its inability to comprehend the formation of "cultural capital" as a new class project within capitalism. What is required, therefore, is a theory of "capital" and "class" which is both flexible and empirically contingent. This theory must be capable of expressing the idea of class conflict between contending capitalist classes, each of which has the ability to proletarianize populations along different dimensions—even if the populations in question are in large measure one and the same.

In such a general theory, "capital" must refer to a specific kind of *resource* that is husbanded in such a way as to make possible the domination of populations by the class of resource holders. In such a theory, "capital" must refer to a socially produced and enclosed resource, the lack of control over which produces critical dependencies in excluded populations. The social transformation of a resource into a capital *may* provide a basis for class formation, where class is understood as an internally competitive social aggregate whose members (a) both consciously and unconsciously devote part of their energy to defending the perimeter of their common capital-good from intrusion and erosion by "outsiders," and (b) control critical aspects of the productive and organizational apparatus of a society by virtue of the exclusive control of a particular resource exercised as a capital.

The Weberian theory of closure, as it has been elaborated by such authors as Parkin, Bourdieu, and Collins, in principle provides such an approach.[15] Though it is possible to speak of a "school" of closure theory, there is little explicit recognition of the fact among its members and, indeed, except for Parkin, only peripheral concern with the lineaments of an explicit theory of closure. While it would take me too far afield to analyze the diverse ways in which individual members of this "school" conjoin the concepts of "capital," "closure," and "class," suffice it to say that none of the three abovementioned authors has regarded the accumulation of cultural capital as the basis for the formation of an independent new class. Insofar as "class" is a serious explanatory concept among these authors (as it is, for example, in Parkin's and, to a lesser extent, in Bourdieu's work), the tendency is to incorporate holders of cultural capital into a conglomerate "ruling class," composed of holders of material, social, and cultural capital. Though this has the virtue of emphasizing the exploitative dimensions of credentialism and of other strategies for monopolizing legitimated knowledge, by stressing the complicity of the knowledgeable with the reproduction of money capital it tends to gloss the ways in which accumulated cultural capital also limits and transforms the consequent domination. Conceiving of closure strategies around cultural resources as the basis of a new-class formation retrieves this oppositional potential while retaining a clear view of its exploitative dimensions.

The following general definition of social closure is an adequate point of departure. The term *social closure* refers to the efforts of a self-conscious group, the membership of which is restricted to persons sharing special characteristics, to establish and maintain the exclusion of others within a defined social field from access to special privileges or resources. The critical parameters in any attempt at closure are, therefore: (1) the scope and content of the "social field" in question, (2) the criteria on the basis of which "insiders" are distinguished from "outsiders," and (3) the nature of the privileges and resources that are "enclosed." I will argue that capital formation is a special result of attempts at closure defined by certain "values" obtaining for the three parameters. And I will argue that within the universe of closure strategies capable of generating capitals, an even smaller subset points in the direction of class structuralization.

Social Fields

As far as its "social scope" is concerned, closure is pursued in a wide range of social fields, running from informal groups through organizations, neighborhoods, and municipalities and to national and supranational organizations, markets, and platforms. There appears, nonetheless, to be considerable alignment among fields with regard to exclusionary criteria, microlevel closure in particular repeating with noteworthy fidelity the demarcation criteria deployed at macrolevels.[16] While it is, of course, conceivable that deviant "local" closure can produce the kind of critical dependencies associated with capitalization, these will likely be unstable if they threaten the penetration of capitals being established at a "cosmopolitan" level. Establishing a stable capital will thus require closure projects at national and supranational levels, even though the consequent distinctions and dependencies continue to penetrate to microlevels.

Aside from "scope," social fields are also differentiable according to their content. Important macrofields in this sense are those concerned with production and distribution of material goods, ideology and legitimation, production and reproduction of knowledge and technology, reproduction of human life, and politics. In the poetics of fields, as Bourdieu has demonstrated in a series of insightful researches, each specific field must be regarded as having a characteristic organization and as enjoying a relative autonomy.[17] Closure projects within specific fields, such as cartelization in the economic field or the monopolization of university chairs by a particular school in the field of knowledge production, can be integral components of overall closure projects issuing in capital and class formation. Nonetheless, unless these field-specific projects can be carried over into other fields, the local domination achieved can only be contingent on the weakness or indifference of closure-elites in other fields. The establishment and maintenance of a capital with society-wide currency, therefore, will require persistent efforts to abridge the autonomy of "alien" fields in such a way that correspondingly induced dependencies become more salient for participants in an "alien" field than the dependencies they may generate among themselves.

Such fields become, in effect, "colonized" by the alien capital.

Such "colonization" utilizes the resources of a pacified "core" to dominate a "periphery." The core of a given class-in-the-making is centered in the field in which its specific resource is generated and accumulated and of which it has become the effective and legitimate master as the result of persuasive performances. Its periphery, which may include another class's core, consists of alien fields within which it must seek to effect closure projects aimed at producing new dependencies and thus at further capitalizing its original resource.

Capitals generated in part by core closure projects at the national and supranational level and which may be deployed to effectively colonize a number of crucial alien fields are the matrices within which social classes may be expected to crystallize. Because the social closure of a resource and its transformation into a legitimate capital necessarily entails continuing acts of violence against both resourceless populations and bearers of competing resources, a class perimeter is defined which functions increasingly to align the private interest of each capital holder *in part* with the collective interest in its common defense. To the extent that purely local measures become structurally ineffective (as, for example, in the face of a national strike by industrial workers or of national measures to cut university budgets), dense, complex, and shifting networks of alliances arise, seconded by coordinating and representative organizations at all levels, to close the breach. Over time, such networks and their attendant agencies become public foci for the "collective consciousness" of the class. One key problem for students of class formation in this connection is that of theorizing the contradiction between the "war of all against all" characterizing the pervasive competition *among* capital holders and the necessary investments each may be called on to make in defense of the "common weal." This might well proceed by way of identifying the person who claims to represent the class (and on what grounds this claim is made), who calls the shots in class-wide coordinating and representative organizations, and whose partial interest thus has the greatest chance of being advanced as the interest of the whole.

Demarcation Criteria

Any number of criteria can be used to distinguish "insiders" from "outsiders." Particularly crucial types of demarcation are as follows: (a) "chance" criteria, such as gender and other physical distinctions or special capacities; (b) "inheritance" criteria, such as race, ethnicity, nationality, wealth, culture, and family background; and (c) "performance" criteria, based on individual achievements. It will be noted, as Parkin has been at pains to argue, that in practice these criteria overlap and contradict one another.[18]

One consequence is that in concrete cases of class structuralization, class membership is "overdetermined" along multiple criteria. Nonetheless, given that the exercise of a specific resource *as a capital* presupposes certain competencies in the individual capital holder, class demarcation (as opposed to status-group demarcation) will in practice proceed primarily according to criteria of performance and inheritance. The latter is particularly important insofar as it is both a tacit promise of the necessary competence as well as the locus of the intergenerational transmission of resources.

One caveat: demarcation criteria are neither hard-and-fast nor uniform. In particular, all insiders are not created equal, and all outsiders are not equally threatening. This points to both the existence of hierarchies (of competence, of inheritance, of virtue) within closure groups and to differentiated dealings with outsiders. As far as class formation is concerned, this should alert us at least to the fact of competition for dominance within classes and to the possibilities for alliances with outsider groups by contending factions. A hypothesis that may be advanced in this connection would be that the dominant players within a class's internal stratification system are those who control its core. Through their control over the production of the specific class resource, such class-elites may also be expected to represent the class interest vis-à-vis other classes as well as dominating the reproduction of capital holders, that is, formulating and exercising criteria of exclusion and inclusion.

Enclosed Resources

Closure, as a practice of selective exclusion, presupposes the existence of some "resource," the control of access to which is its object. As a general conception of strategic action, closure theory does not prejudice the nature of such a resource; it may be no more than a sense of exalted personal identity contingent on "belonging," or, at the other extreme, the very means of physical or psychological survival. A "resource," in this sense, is simply that which is held to be necessary for life to go on at a certain level; it is something that somebody, in some specific time and location, *needs*.

Obviously, however, in a Maslowian vein, there are some needs the very expression of which presupposes the prior satisfaction of others and, indeed, some human needs whose satisfaction brooks only temporary postponement. Although arguing the case would require much more room than I have here, a quick and dirty taxonomy of such "objective" anthropological needs would include the following: the perennial material needs (e.g., food, shelter, and clothing); diverse relational needs surrounding reproduction, identity, motivation, and sanity; and cognitive needs connected with existential orientation and instrumental action. When a specific resource required for the satisfaction of one or more of these basic needs is made an object of closure, a possible route to capital formation—and, consequently, to class formation—has been opened.

Whether such closure projects do in fact lead to capitalization and class formation depends on a host of historically contingent factors about which little can be said at this very schematic level. Given what has been said above about demarcation criteria and fields, however, it will be evident that a specific enclosed resource cannot long function as a stable and legitimate capital unless (a) holders of similar and competing resources are either expropriated or drawn into the fold of insiders, and (b) the capacity of the resource to generate dependencies is extended geographically and across other fields.

INSIDE THE NEW CLASS

Both Gouldner and Szelényi and his associates have argued that the new class is an essentially *transcendent* class. Gouldner has formulated this by describing intellectuals as the bearers of a common culture (the "culture of critical discourse") which is historically formed around norms of "good" speech, which stipulates that assertions must be judged by the quality of arguments rather than by the quality of speakers. Martin and Szelényi, while not openly antagonistic to Gouldner on this point, have collapsed the transcendent linguistic identity of intellectuals into a unitary conception of their cultural capital: the capacity to institute and maintain a *postcapitalist* mode of production/domination which they call "teleological redistribution." Martin and Szelényi thereby historically limit the possibility for class formation on the basis of the capitalization of transcendent linguistic cultures to societies in which the expropriators have already been expropriated. Gouldner's radical splitting of linguistic culture as a resource from its specific and historically contingent capital forms in principle allows a much suppler and more historically nuanced theory of the new class. In particular, of course, it allows for its formation within "the womb of the old society."

In essence, this discussion concerns the relationship among norms, theory, and technique. For both Gouldner and Szelényi et al., the particular significance of the new class is its historically novel fusion of these resources into cultural capital. But whereas Szelényi tends to ignore the substantive linkage between new-class techniques (which he and Martin classify as "skills") and its normative and theoretical resources (which produce cultural capital), Gouldner fails to show adequately how the capitalized theory and techniques entailed in professionalization projects retain a linkage to the norms of critical discourse and hence to a "transcendent universalism." The distinction he draws between "cultural bourgeoisie" and "speech community" and the tacitly parallel distinction between "humanistic intellectuals" and "technical intelligentsia" has led critics to question the possibility of speaking of a new class in these terms, much less of a new class conceived as potentially *hegemonic*.[19] The aggravation is scarcely mitigated by the apparent complacency with which Gouldner describes the new class as being simply "morally ambiguous."

Nonetheless, Gouldner does provide a point of departure for a theory capable of recovering the transcendent import of the *novum organum* that the new class's cultural capital is. That starting point is based in his observation that the norm of criticism, as the generative medium of the special and capitalizable cultures of the new class, remains embedded and mobilizable even in rather mundane bodies of professional technique. He casts this in terms of Thomas Kuhn's concepts of "normal" and "revolutionary" science, arguing that when "normal" theory fails to account for anomalous phenomena, previously marginal groups mobilize repressed linguistic potentials to generate new theory and exemplars. And, Gouldner implies, if the norms of the culture of critical discourse remain as a latent "repair" resource, they may also remain as a potential to question and reconstruct theories about other matters entirely. Such matters include the power relations prevailing within the field, the structures of domination within the field, and the economic and power relations in which the field as a whole is embedded. Although questions remain about the precise relationship between the norm of criticism and theory formation (questions that might be resolved by viewing concrete theoretical traditions as collectively enforced selective censorships of the right to criticize), the primary question is whether and how Gouldner's linguistic argument can be integrated with the sociologies of science and the professions under the aegis of a general theory of closure to produce an integral *sociological* theory of a professionalized new class.

Making concrete the abstract discussion of the previous section requires first locating the core and periphery of the new-class-in-becoming. The core, which, following Bourdieu, we might call the "scholarly field," comprises such institutions as universities, libraries, scholarly journals, research institutes, and their intersections with political parties and the press.[20] The periphery, consisting of professional "intrusions" into diverse social fields, comprises the conventional labor markets for university graduates, including large state and corporate bureaucracies as well as diverse forms of small-scale entrepreneurship. Intellectuals working in the core are primarily engaged in the *production* of theoretical knowledge such as scientific theory, ideologies, and the cognitive bases of technologies. Intellectuals working in the periphery are primarily engaged in the *application* and *reproduction* of theoretical knowledge in the form of material and social technologies, political programs and legal codes, and "finalized" educational curricula.[21]

Since the rise of the great medieval universities, the core has been the embodiment of the successful closure of the production of abstract theoretical knowledge, originally as the theologically dominated trivium and quadrivium, later with the addition of medicine, law, and philosophy, and finally, in the modern epoch, with natural philosophy and science. It is true that universities continue to be what they were from their inception, namely, theaters of intellectual and political rivalry, scarred by bitter and often inelegant struggles around the distribution of material and human resources. However, as institutions they have survived and have maintained some degree of autonomy by virtue of their success in claiming a superior method of producing and reproducing knowledge. That claim is legitimated by public demonstration of the universities' adherence to the "norm of collegiality," which refers to the university's organization as a community of intellectuals equal in the respect of the right to criticize one another. The university, in other words, in contrast to its environment and the conditions chronically prevailing there, has putatively been an enclave of "free speech," a place where one could speak one's mind—more or less—and get away with it.

The tacit assumption underlying the cultivation of such a deviant culture of critical discourse has, of course, been the conviction that persistent and thorough criticism was at least a necessary condition for the growth of knowledge—or, more cynically, that the appearance of persistent and thorough criticism was a necessary condition for the acceptance of academic knowledge as superior. But even though the reality has as often as not diverged from the claim, such divergence has always skirted the abyss of delegitimation and disfranchisement. What has held in this respect for the universities also holds, *mutatis mutandis*, for the other institutions of the core.

Whereas the core is organized according to the norms of collegiality and criticism, the peripheries are *grosso modo* "arenas of conflict," to use Gouldner's expression, between the former norms and the "norm of hierarchy." The latter norm states simply that it is not so much what is said that counts, but who says it. Though the bureaucratic institutions of the periphery are thus not "ruled" by intellectuals (i.e., their assertions are not uncontested merely because they are credentialed experts), neither does the "norm of hierarchy" prevail completely in the sense that the directives of senior functionaries—merely because they are hierarchically authoritative—are obeyed unconditionally. Rather, though formally subordinate to executive hierarchies, professionals within bureaucracies are able to exploit dependencies arising from lack of knowledge and consequent uncertainty to achieve a measure of control over decision making. Though this influence is cast in the face-saving structure of "consultation," it nevertheless acts to limit the scope of the "norm of hierarchy." Successful challenges of this kind are of crucial importance, especially in the field of state power. Whether politicians and civil servants conceive of state power as the handmaiden of money capital or develop their own teleological logic (and much of the checkered career of social democracy can be understood as such teleological invasions at the cost of the old class) is of the greatest consequence for the future of the new class in capitalism.[22]

Moreover, a measure of new-class penetration of peripheral institutions is evident in the institution of the "dual labor-market" through which hierarchical authority is conflated with educational credentials. The strong correlation of level of education with degree of bureaucratic authority (and, of course, lifetime earnings) is well established for contemporary advanced capitalist societies. And within large bureaucracies, staff divisions are structurally insulated from hierarchical meddling by the presence of bosses who frequently are themselves trained specialists. Such staff divisions may also be represented at the highest executive levels by special directors with sterling academic credentials. Though of course this implies an element of hierarchical control of professional independence, it also implies an element of professional control of hierarchical policy.

A dense set of relationships connects the core with the periphery and so makes plausible the continuing resonance of professional practice with the transcendent norms of the culture of critical discourse. First, the training and part of the socialization of professionals take place in the core. Though systems of tertiary schooling will differ in the extent to which they may, for example, require future engineers to assimilate Marlowe's *Faustus*, university education cannot do without instilling an abstract respect for the value of well-founded criticism. This potential, even though sharply circumscribed by limited notions of the term *well-founded*, is thus structurally embedded in professional practice via the biographies of its agents.

Second, the core theoretically underwrites the general "collective representation of the world" that prevails within a given profession, defining salient phenomena and providing *theoretical models* with which to analyze and solve practical problems. It does this both through the initial socialization of professionals and through various forms of continuing education, such as postgraduate courses, guest lectures, scientific journals, and special consultations. Through chairs endowed by institutions in the periphery and individuals whose careers meander between core and periphery, those in the core can remain abreast of practical problems in the periphery and channel resources into their theoretical clarification.

Third, the organization of professions across the specific peripheral institutions in which their members work provides professionals with a source of identity competitive with their identities as employees. This identity, stressing their collective command of a body of theory and practice, orients professional associations at least in part toward the core. Public debates within the profession over technical or ethical matters have the character of reflexive interludes in which the "norm of criticism" resurfaces as the medium of innovation. Such discussions may react upon model building in the core, modifying it or drawing it into new areas of development.

Although it is far from complete, the above framework for a theory of intellectuals in advanced capitalist societies seems to hold promise for negating the antinomies of "science" and "profession" and for theoretically reintegrating the normative and "universal" aspects of intellectual speech culture with strategies for social domination based on the capitalization of specific bodies of theory. Whether such capitalization projects will be able to threaten the firmly entrenched positions of holders of money captial and thus corrode capitalism from within is, of course, not a theoretical question but a practical one. In this matter, empirical research clearly has the task of keeping a finger on the historical pulse, resisting the temptation to interpret short-term faltering as the onset of a terminal crisis.

NOTES

1. Christopher Marlowe, *Doctor Faustus* (1604).

2. All of the developments referred to above have, of course, been described and explained without recourse to class models of social change. The increasing mediation of life by technological artifacts and systems has been variously explained as "functional adaptation" to system disequilibrium in the face of demographic and geopolitical changes, as an expression of the "autonomous" dynamics of technological development, and as the natural outcome of capitalist competition for markets and technological edges. The rationalization of the exercise of power has also been functionally explained as a necessary adaptation by political and economic bureaucracies to increasing scale and complexity or, alternatively (as in J. K. Galbraith's thesis on the "technostructure") as a means for extending and intensifying their control over markets, polities, and populations. The "information explosion" has been treated primarily as a spin-off of the more or less spontaneous development of new information and communication technologies, although rather more cynical theories of mass society and mass management have also had their say. Lastly, the rise of the "caring estate" has fallen under the purview of both functionalist and critical Marxist theories of professionalization. Though hardly sanguine about the willingness or ability of professionalized intellectuals to develop comprehensive anticapitalist attitudes or practices, studies from the latter perspective—such as Magali Sarfatti-Larson's *The Rise of Professionalism* (Berkeley, Los Angeles, London: University of California Press, 1977)—are deeply concerned with the problematic class location of intellectuals. A theory of the new class, however, would view professionalism as one of a number of possible strategies aiming at class domination.

3. See chapters 1 and 2 of Parkin's *Marxism and Class Theory: A Bourgeois Critique* (New York: Columbia University Press, 1979).

4. By no means do all "theories" of the new class aim at such a revision of Marxism. In particular, the 1970s spate of American establishment and neoconservative theorizing about the new class by such notables as Daniel Moynihan, Norman Podhoretz, and Irving Kristol exhibited an ironic and strictly quarantined use of class theory. Taking their direct inspiration from Milovan Djilas's thesis of the usurpation of socialist revolutions by a self-serving new class of state bureaucrats, these authors sought to construct a parallel equation for the relation of "liberal" intellectuals and politicians to their constituencies. By defining American political liberalism (New Deal, New Left, New Politics) as the ideology of a new class, these authors sought to debunk etatist politics and "liberal" values as mere ideological reflexes of crass economic and exclusionary interests.

This flirtation with Marxist categories cannot, however, be taken very seriously. Although they were clearly aware of the threat that a powerful "liberal" state would pose to cherished capitalist norms and procedures, it is hardly likely that any of these authors seriously entertained a Marxist view of social change or, indeed, defined American society as a "class society." Only panic in the face of a possible McGovern victory can explain their jiujitsu-like resort to class analysis. With the advent of the Reagan era, such talk from the right has evaporated.

For the complex genealogy of the concept of the new class emphasizing the American discussion in the seventies, see Barry Bruce-Briggs, "An Introduction to the Idea of the New Class," and Daniel Bell, "The New Class: A Muddled Concept," both in B. Bruce-Briggs, ed., *The New Class?* (New Brunswick, NJ: Transaction Books, 1979). For a comparative assessment of new-class theories with respect to their adequacy in explaining opinion-research data on intellectual groups, see also Steven Brint, " 'New Class' and Cumulative-Trend Explanations of the Liberal Political Attitudes of Professionals," *American Journal of Sociology* 90 (1984): 30–71.

5. The "revisionist" Marxist critiques of socialism emerge with Mikhail Bakunin's and Jan Waclaw Machajski's early attacks on the role of intellectuals in the leadership of socialist movements and with their predictions of the postrevolutionary hegemony of a new class of intellectuals and state bureaucrats. Milovan Djilas, *The New Class; An Analysis of the Communist System* (Praeger, 1957); Rudolf Bahro, *Die Alternative: zur Kritik des real existierenden Sozialismus* (Eur. Verlagsanstalt, 1977); and George Konrád and Ivan Szelényi, *The Intellectuals on the Road to Class Power* (Harvester Press, 1979) have all broadened and elaborated on this original insight. In spite of the common attack on the orthodox Marxist

scenario of the triumph of socialism and the transition to communism, they remain rather generously committed to the Marxist theory of class as a formal historiographic model. Their common investigation of the class structure of post revolutionary societies shows that the dictatorship of the proletariat has turned out to be not by but for the proletariat. And beyond this it has lifted the lid from a certain Marxist nightmare: namely, that the idea of a future "classless society" might turn out to be as mythical as the present idea of "workers' parties."

6. The most original current theorist of the new-class contest within capitalist societies is, beyond question, Alvin Gouldner. For his dense and suggestive analysis of this question see *The Future of Intellectuals and the Rise of the New Class* (Macmillan, 1979). This aspect of Gouldner's new-class theory has a number of academic sociological roots, harking back to Saint-Simon's identification of "les industrielles" as the new dominant class in industrial societies. Although Gouldner clearly owes a debt to the postfunctionalist sociology of the professions as developed in the work of, among others, Eliot Freidson and Magali Sarfatti-Larson, it seems fair to say that his case for the rise of a new class under capitalist hegemony draws most sustenance from the neo-Marxist hypothesis of the "managerial revolution." The canonical works here are, of course, A. Berle, Jr., and Gardner C. Means, *The Modern Corporation and Private Property* (New York, 1932), and James Burnham, *The Managerial Revolution* (New York, 1941). It should, however, be noted that Gouldner's originality is precisely that he reduces the rise of the new class to neither a "managerial revolution" nor professionalization projects. For an extensive bibliography of his critical-Marxist appropriation of academic sociology in the matter of the new class, see his bibliographic note in *The Future of Intellectuals*.

Though hewing to the Weberian concept of *"Priesterherrschaft"* instead of the neo-Marxist one of "new class," one can hardly fail to cite Helmut Schelsky's magisterial and acerbic *Die Arbeit tun die Anderen* (Westdeutscher Verlag, 1975) as a serious analysis of intellectual hegemony in advanced capitalist societies. What distinguishes Schelsky from the American neoconservatives is not a different moral or political evaluation of the growing influence of the intellectual "caste" but a profound appreciation of its real power.

7. The most explicit example of orthodox Marxist patchwork in this regard is the "Professional-Managerial Class" thesis of Barbara and John Ehrenreich. See their article "The Professional-Managerial Class" in Pat Walker, ed., *Between Labor and Capital* (Boston: South End Press, 1979). The same book also contains a number of relevant critiques of their effort.

The PMC thesis attempts to have the Marxist cake and eat it too by providing a class account of the new professional and managerial strata which leaves the original Marxist class scenario intact. The PMC is regarded as a new class specific to the monopoly stage of capitalism, whose specific place in the division of labor (read: specific *function*) is the reproduction of capitalist culture and capitalist class relations. The PMC is thus the most recent incarnation of the mysterious and interstitial "petty bourgeoisie" destined to disappear from the historical stage whenever the essential class contradiction between global capital and global labor reasserts itself. One might place Erik Olin Wright's assignment of professional strata to "contradictory class locations" within this tradition as well. See E. O. Wright, "Class and Occupation," in *Theory and Society* IX (1980): 177–214.

8. Though Bourdieu has not advanced a theory of the new class, he must be credited with the currency of the concept of "cultural capital." In Bourdieu's view, such capital is metaphorically equivalent to material capital and plays an equivalent role with regard to the stratification of social rewards. Nonetheless, he views the holders of cultural and of money capital as merely distinct strata within a single ruling class.

9. Gouldner, *Future of Intellectuals*; cf. the contribution by Martin and Szelényi in this volume.

10. Gouldner, *The Future of Intellectuals*, p. 21.

11. See his review of *The Future of Intellectuals* in *Telos* (1980): 189–192. See also "Gouldner's Theory of Intellectuals As a Flawed Universal Class," *Theory and Society* XI (1982): 779–798.

12. C. B. MacPherson, *The Political Theory of Possessive Individualism* (Oxford University Press, 1962).

13. Konrád and Szelényi, *Intellectuals on the Road to Class Power*.

14. Theodore Schultz, "Investment in Human Capital," *American Economic Review* (1961).

15. For a coherent summary of the present state of closure theory see Raymond Murphy, "The Struggle for Scholarly Recognition," *Theory and Society* XII (1983): 631–658. See also, for example: Parkin, *Marxism and Class Theory*; Bourdieu and Passeron, *La Reproduction* (Éditions de Minuit, 1970), and *Questions de Sociologie* (Éditions de Minuit, 1980), pp. 53–60, 113–120; Randall Collins, *The Credential Society* (Academic Press, 1979).

16. Basil Bernstein's research on the ways in which class-based linguistic codes influence performances, and hence educational demarcations and individual futures, is just one (albeit a very important) example of this correspondence of levels. See especially his *Class, Codes, and Control*, vols. 1–3 (Routledge & Kegan Paul, 1972, 1973, 1975).

17. Bourdieu and Passeron, *La Reproduction*; P. Bourdieu and Monique de St. Martin, "Le Patronat," *Actes de la Recherche en Sciences Sociales* 20/21 (1978): 3–82; Bourdieu, *Homo Academicus* (Éditions de Minuit, 1984).

18. Parkin, *Marxism and Class Theory*.

19. Michael Walzer, "The New Masters," review of Gouldner, *Future of Intellectuals* and Konrád and Szelényi, *Intellectuals on the Road to Class Power*, *New York Review of Books*, March 20, 1980; Charles Lemert and Paul Piccone, "Gouldner's Theoretical Method and Reflexive Sociology," *Theory and Society* XI (1982): 733–757.

20. Bourdieu, *Homo Academicus*.

21. Using a modified Kuhnian model, the "Starnberg Group" has viewed technology-relevant science as embodied in "finalized" (i.e., stable, exhausted, and universally accepted) paradigms. See Gernot Boehme, Wolfgang Van den Daele, and Wolfgang Krohn, "Finalization in Science," *Social Science Information* XV (1976): 307–330.

22. The continuing existence of active social-democratic parties in Western Europe—and their absence in the United States—may account for the rather different resonances that theories of the new class generate in those different national contexts. Certainly, social democracy, with its mandarin intellectual heritage, even now continues to provide Europeans with demonstrations of the political potency of teleological social theory. In the United States, where state power tends to be monopolized to a far greater degree by the old class, mobilizations of teleological theory have been strictly limited to the Keynesian management of severe crises, and even then such theoretical politics has been suspect as essentially un-American. For this reason, the role of intellectuals in American government has been limited largely to advisory and professional-technical roles, a situation hardly likely to impress superficial observers with the growing political power of a "new class."

4

The Future of the Intelligentsia Under Capitalism*

Bengt Furåker

INTRODUCTION

In modern capitalist societies there exist a great number of managers, engineers, bureaucrats, lawyers, doctors, intellectuals, and so on. These categories of persons are mainly sellers of "labor-power," although some of them (for example, some lawyers and doctors) exist in what can be described as a petty-bourgeois position. They sell their labor-power to private corporations, public agencies, and various other buyers from whom they receive salaries. Their work can be characterized as mental or intellectual labor. All work is, of course, mental to some degree, but theirs is essentially so, and most of them have gone through a long formal education. Although I am not convinced that it is the best one, I employ the term *intelligentsia* to signify these occupational groups.

---

* This paper was first presented at the Convention of the Austrian Sociological Association in December 1983.

The question of terminology is important because it is connected to separate ways of conceiving social structure in contemporary capitalism. The categories referred to have been called by very different names—"the new class of intellectuals and intelligentsia," "the professional-managerial class," "the new petty bourgeoisie," "the middle strata," "the new working class," and "contradictory class locations," to mention just a few examples from the sociological literature.[1] These terms express the lack of theoretical unity found among analysts of class structure and class relations in advanced capitalist society. Behind such theoretical divergencies are different ways of judging the present and future role of the intelligentsia. In this context distinctions can be made among at least three alternative views. The intelligentsia groups can be seen as (1) a segment of one or of several other classes (the bourgeoisie, the proletariat, and the petty bourgeoisie); (2) an essentially unsettled layer between the main social forces in society, perhaps leaning more toward one or the other; or (3) a relatively independent social force with clearly separate economic, political, and social aims.

It is not my ambition here to decide which one of these alternatives is correct. My purpose is, rather, to point out some aspects that must be further analyzed if more definite conclusions are to be drawn about the intelligentsia's future under capitalism. In order to do this I find it relevant to discuss the following issues: the social division of labor, the system of higher education, the public sector and the state, the ownership and control of the means of production, and the role of unions and political organizations. I will make some comments on each of these issues concerning their significance for the future of the intelligentsia.

THE SOCIAL DIVISION OF LABOR

In Western capitalist societies there has been a substantial growth of the intelligentsia over the last hundred years. With the scientific and technological revolution, the development of large corporations with advanced technology, and the expansion of education, culture and media, medical care, and other service sectors, the number of jobs with a considerable intellectual content has increased. At the same time the internal structure of white-collar work has undergone important changes. There are continuous processes of differentiation and homogenization within the intelligentsia; some positions are upgraded, others are degraded, and still others remain about the same.

The consequences of such changes must be analyzed carefully. They are important because they involve the heterogeneity and the degree of polarization within the intelligentsia and the relations between the intelligentsia and other social classes and strata. One may ask whether the intelligentsia is homogeneous enough to justify its being called a social class. In discussing this problem it may be relevant to consider differentiation among capitalists. Some capitalists are owners of huge industrial empires with production units in several countries and continents and with employees counted in tens of thousands. Others control small factories with, let us say, fifty or one hundred individuals on the payroll, and they may be living under a constant threat from their giant competitors. Still, they are all regarded as belonging to the same class. If we go over to the working class or the petty bourgeoisie, we find other divisions and rivalries. No social class is homogeneous, but the presence of internal differences, tensions, and conflicts cannot be taken as a reason for not using the concept of class.

To put the question in positive terms, however, are there any good reasons for bringing together the various intelligentsia occupations under the class concept? Alvin Gouldner tried to develop some arguments for an affirmative answer to this question.[2] According to Gouldner, the intelligentsia disposes of a cultural capital, something like a body of expert knowledge and skills, which is to a large extent acquired through education. All social groups possess cultural capital, but intellectuals and the intelligentsia have more of it than others, thereby occupying a specific position in relation to the means of production. This is the basis for their distinct class status. For Gouldner, "class" refers to "those who have the same relationship to the means of production."[3] This definition is his interpretation of what Marx would have said had he ever spelled out his conception clearly.

Gouldner's undogmatic interpretation of Marx offers a good starting point, but this general concept of class is still too vague and cannot be used for empirical analysis without being further qualified. The conceptual elaboration undertaken by the author still leaves many questions unanswered. Its very foundations are certainly debatable. Gouldner derives the two categories of cultural capital and economic capital for the same general concept of capital, that is, a humanly created object that can be legitimately used to provide its owner with income and power. One immediate objection is that cultural capital must be seen as a part of an individual's labor-power, while economic capital is something separate from a person's capacities for carrying out work. If we are to keep the distinction between labor-power and means of production, as I think we should, then neither Gouldner's general concept of capital nor his specific concept of cultural capital is well advised. They blur the division between sellers of labor-power (Gouldner has not even listed the term *labor-power* in his index of subjects) and owners of the means of production.

Cultural capital refers to professional knowledge and skills as capacities for performing certain kinds of work tasks. The members of the intelligentsia are to a large extent sellers of labor-power, but what they offer for sale is different from what manual workers bring to the labor market. Their specific capabilities are required for some positions in the social division of labor, and, by monopolizing expert knowledge and skills, they are able to claim a relatively large proportion of incomes, power, and prestige. Still, one may argue that there is a difference in degree rather than kind between the various groups of labor-power sellers, and, consequently, it is better not to conceptualize the intelligentsia as a class.

The intelligentsia not only occupies a privileged position compared to that of the proletariat but also fulfills particular functions in the division of labor. This fact is expressed in the social distance and the rather deep-rooted distrust between the two.[4] There are no doubt good reasons to accept Erik Wright's concept of "contradictory class locations'' in analyzing the role of, for example, some of the professional-managerial groups in private business.[5] Many of these groups are certainly in a contradictory position between the bourgeoisie and the proletariat, being subordinate to capitalists but having a superior and often supervisory role vis-à-vis workers. I am not sure, however, that Wright's formula as a whole can be applied in the way he suggests with regard to the publicly employed intelligentsia. Following is a brief quotation from his work:

> In terms of the educational system, for example, the bourgeois position would be held by top education officials (boards of regents, chancellors, superintendents of schools); the contradictory locations would be typically held by teachers; and the working-class location would be held by secretaries, janitors, school cafeteria workers, etc.[6]

In this passage many aspects could be debated, but here I will comment on only the first category mentioned. To assert that top education officials hold a bourgeois position is completely misleading, unless the analysis is restricted to private educational institutions (and this is not the case in Wright's essay). Top officials in the public system of education, like top officials in other state apparatuses, are not at all in the same position as the bourgeoisie, even though similarities as well as structural, political, and personal links exist between the two groups. Top-level state officials are part of a bureaucracy that is connected to a capitalist economic system but that nevertheless has an appreciable autonomy. They may instead be said to form a bureaucratic class or separate stratum all their own.

To sum up so far: in the social division of labor, the intelligentsia is located between the bourgeoisie and the proletariat in capitalist enterprises, in petty bourgeois positions, and in the various state agencies, where it performs administrative and/or intellectual tasks. Most of its members are sellers of labor-power, powerful enough to acquire a comparatively significant amount of power and privilege. This group has been increasing in number for a long period of time. Furthermore, the intelligentsia is internally heterogeneous, divided both horizontally and vertically, as a result of the current organization of economic and social life. Differences in economic conditions and power exist, and some members of the intelligentsia exercise power over other members of the same group. This can be seen, for example, in university hierarchies. In spite of all these grounds for competition and conflict, one has to admit that the intelligentsia is far from being completely atomized. There are many ties that keep the various groups together, and the question of whether the intelligentsia is now a class or has that potential remains unsolved. A lot of theoretical and empirical clarification is needed before this problem can receive satisfactory treatment.

Some of the ties within the intelligentsia stem from a common or at least similar educational background. The school system plays a key role in the analysis of the intelligentsia. Therefore, let me offer a few comments about the importance of education, especially higher education.

THE SYSTEM OF HIGHER EDUCATION

Members of the intelligentsia have usually spent many years in various educational institutions, since an academic degree or diploma is often required for the jobs they seek. Thus, most of them share the specific experience of student life during a period when human beings are mature yet still very malleable.

Although institutions of higher education differ, students are socialized into at least some common conceptions, values, and norms. Perhaps the most important function of higher education is to imbue students with an ideology of "professionalism,"[7] which stresses the need for autonomy in intellectual and professional occupations. Incumbents of intelligentsia positions are thus supposed to be independent of outside group or class interest. They are expected not to pay regard to anything but the internal requirements of the tasks to be performed. The basis for this autonomy, which is not merely illusionary but which can never be more than relative, is their disposal of a body of specialized knowledge.

Gouldner has put forward the idea that the new class of intellectuals and intelligentsia has acquired a specific language, which he calls the "culture of critical discourse."[8] Characteristic of this language is its mode of justification. Statements have to be justified in terms of reasonable arguments and not with reference to the speaker's social position or authority. The speech of the new class is thus relatively situation-free; it is "pattern-and-principle-oriented." The values and norms of "professionalism" are directly related to this form of speech. The culture of critical discourse according to Gouldner is, then, the general and common ideology of the intelligentsia, making it a speech community.

This analysis can hardly be reconciled with the view that the educational system only serves as a "transmission belt" for the dominant ideology in society. Gouldner argues that modern universities have a double function: they are at the same time reproductive and subversive. I believe he is right. The dominant values in society, which under capitalism are normally "bourgeois," are of course transmitted through the universities, but they are certainly also questioned through the antiauthoritarian ambitions of the culture of critical discourse. One can also say, using the terminology of Göran Therborn, that socialization always involves a process of both subjection and qualification.[9]

The formation of human beings means being subjected to a given order at the same time that it means being qualified to fill various roles in this order. There always exists the possibility that a contradiction will develop between these two elements of the process. When new types of qualification are required, conflicts may arise in relation to traditional mechanisms of subjugation, and such conflicts may lead to opposition and revolt. I think that the student rebellion of the sixties can in part be understood in these terms.

In my opinion, it is a matter of empirical investigation to determine the strength of the reproductive and subversive capacity of the universities in modern capitalism. In order to do this, one must study both the mechanisms of dependence between the system of higher education and the society at large and the internal power relations in the universities. Of course, no pure culture of critical discourse can exist, but there is a potential for critical examination of all aspects of human life to be found in intellectual and scientific endeavors. The ideals of the culture of critical discourse can also be seen as principles with important social effects. They give their adherents a common language, thus making them part of a speech community while simultaneously drawing a demarcation line in relation to outsiders. The ideological force unifying these processes must not be overlooked. There are no doubt many disputes, often hostile, within the intelligentsia over theoretical issues, but the fact that there are such disputes implies communication, and communication cannot take place without a common language. If the advocates of contradictory paradigms are to discuss their differences, they must find a metalanguage—and this is something that the culture of critical discourse may provide. In short, the culture of critical discourse fulfills a unifying function for the intelligentsia, but disputes are part of its core and will thus never cease to exist.

Another important aspect of the educational system is its role in establishing patterns of social mobility. In the advanced capitalist nations, formal education has expanded widely during the twentieth century. The average level of schooling has increased for all social classes, but the gaps between the classes seem to be more persistent. It has repeatedly been shown in various studies that educational success is related to social background.[10] Students whose parents are academics have a specific advantage with regard to the chance of entering a university. The educational system plays a role for the intelligentsia which is similar to that played by the hereditary estate for the classical bourgeoisie. This is very important, since if we are to call the intelligentsia a class we must find a mechanism for its reproduction over generations.

The educational system serves this function. In contemporary society the social division of labor is largely a division between manual and intellectual labor. More or less successfully, the educational system produces the qualifications demanded on the labor market. In doing this it also works as a mechanism for the selection and distribution of people to fill the available positions.

The stress put on formal education for the recruitment of individuals to jobs is of great importance for career patterns. With regard to the opportunities for acquiring educational credit, the offspring of the intelligentsia are favored because the family's cultural capital gives them a head start. The system of education is thus a key institution in the reproduction of the intelligentsia's position in the current class structure.

THE PUBLIC SECTOR AND THE STATE

A large segment of the intelligentsia is employed within the public sector (by the state or the municipality). Public employment has increased in the major capitalist countries since World War II, but its share of total employment varies from one country to another depending upon, among other things, the size of the privately organized service sector.

Those who are employed in the public sector work under very different conditions from those employed in private industry and other capitalistically organized areas. First, the latter are directly subordinated to the market and profit mechanisms of the capitalist mode of production, while public employees are usually freed from concern with what is salable and profitable. This is essentially a difference between the production of exchange values and use values.

Second, the state is not merely a separate sphere for the production of various kinds of services but is also an authority that can intervene in capitalist spheres of production and distribution. State intervention means legislation and economic measures of different types, handled by politicians and public officials. Although many of the measures taken by the state are well adjusted to the ways of the capitalist system (and many of them are initiated by capitalists themselves), there is always the possibility of conflict. This possibility is, of course, especially great when state action occurs in response to working-class demands.

Third, one central form of state intervention is taxation. Since public services are often free of charge or subsidized, they have to be financed through the taxation of individuals and enterprises in the capitalist sector. Public employees receive their salaries mainly through the taxing authority of the state, and this is a source of tension and conflict between these employees and workers in the capitalist sphere. A recurrence of "tax revolts" and "fiscal crises" can place the two groups in different political camps.

The conclusion I would like to draw from these observations is that the division between the publicly and the privately employed intelligentsia is important and ought to be further analyzed. Today, we can witness a swing toward right-wing political views in the advanced capitalist world, with criticism directed toward state expenditure, public-service production, social welfare, public bureaucracy, state ownership, legislation, and market control. We are now observing a struggle concerning the public sector between those who defend it and those who want to transfer some of its activities into private hands. The outcome of this struggle is very important for the development of capitalism and for the future of the intelligentsia.

My guess is that the public sector will not only survive but expand, although there may be temporary declines or rather slow growth in the coming few years. What, then, will a long-run expansion mean for the intelligentsia? Public-service production is a system with centralized planning. It can be seen as a skeleton of a planned economy, although the state has no direct control over the base of material production in society. One can at least regard it as an embryo that may grow into something more. This could open up the door for a new and possibly more decisive role for some layers of the intelligentsia. However, this embryo rests upon a capitalist economic structure that will determine its conditions for development.

George Konrád and Ivan Szelényi have argued that the intelligentsia under state-monopoly capitalism cannot form a class because of the operation of (1) the mechanism of representation in the political sphere and (2) the capitalist control of the basic material production.[11] While it is true that elected bodies are placed above the bureaucratic agencies that carry out the various public activities, it is nevertheless well known that the autonomy of bureaucratic apparatuses is considerable. This is, in fact, a major problem for the parliamentary political system.[12] Tensions and conflicts will continue to evolve around the distribution of power between elected bodies and the executive apparatuses they are supposed to command. The second aspect concerns the relations between capital owners and the professional-managerial groups they employ. I will deal with this issue at a little more length.

THE OWNERSHIP AND CONTROL
OF THE MEANS OF PRODUCTION

The economies of modern Western countries are still largely controlled by capitalist owners. There have been many attempts to show that employed managers and technical experts are continuously acquiring more power at the cost of the old-moneyed bourgeoisie.[13] However, even if there has been something like a "managerial revolution," ownership relations continue to be of decisive significance for understanding what occurs in the sphere of production.

The split between ownership and management in large corporations is a complicated matter. The power exercised by managers is at least formally delegated by owners, but, as is always the case with delegation of power, conflicts may arise. For example, there can arise differences of opinion between stockholders and managers about how much money should be made available for dividends and investments respectively. Such conflicts, however, seem to be quarrels within the family more than anything else. The mechanisms of market competition and profit requirements do not leave much room for managers to maintain policies in opposition to owners. Conflicts of the type just mentioned may also appear both within the managerial strata and among owners. Furthermore, there are many interconnections between the two groups. Top managers are themselves often stockholders or in a similar way tied to the company where they work.

This is not to say that the managerial and technical intelligentsia in the capitalist sphere of production are completely subordinated to the propertied class. It is necessary to distinguish between "formal" or "legal" ownership and "real" ownership and control of the means of production. This is the point of departure for Gouldner's criticism of those who argue that legal public ownership of the means of production in the Soviet Union tells us very little about the real control of the economy, and who at the same time make a great fuss about formal ownership in the United States.[14]

Although I think the distinction between formal and real economic ownership is very important, I am not sure that Gouldner makes the correct point about it. The economic structures of the Soviet Union and the United States are fundamentally different, making simple comparisons difficult. It is easier for capitalists to control their companies, even if they have to employ relatively autonomous professionals to take care of the tasks of management, than for the masses of people in the Soviet Union to control their highly centralized and closed economy. A vital difference is that a capitalist system has stronger mechanisms of impersonal economic self-regulation, that is, market competition and profit, while a planned economy is directed through a political process that leaves more room for the discretion of decision makers.

The distinction between formal and real ownership and control is, however, of central importance for any analysis of capitalism. Many changes in the economic structure can be fruitfully studied in the light of this distinction. There exists in some countries a large and expanding state ownership of the means of production. Although a certain proportion of state property does not necessarily change the fundamental structure of the economy, it does take up room from the traditional bourgeoisie—provided, of course, that state-owned production is a matter of profitable business, since otherwise it is generally of no interest to capitalists. When the state takes over a company today, the reason is often that the company is bankrupt and that numerous jobs are threatened.

Another aspect of ownership change is that unions, pension funds, and other noncapitalist organizations increasingly enter the stock market in order to have a share in the profits and power usually reserved for the capitalist class. In this context one can mention the legislation for wage earners' funds recently passed by the Swedish parliament. The question for us here is what these changes in ownership structure mean for the intelligentsia. I think these new types of more anonymous ownership may leave more power to the professional-managerial groups who carry out the actual work of planning and management in the economy. This is not to say, however, that the old bourgeoisie has already been degraded.

The existing ownership structure in Western capitalism is probably the most serious obstacle to any power aspirations of the intelligentsia. In the economic and political struggles at hand, the traditional bourgeoisie is perhaps losing ground. The complex combination and transformation of social forces, involving a decline of the petty bourgeoisie and the industrial proletariat and a growth of the middle strata and the intelligentsia, may undermine the position of the capitalist class. Together with the working class and other wage earners, the intelligentsia may use the state as an instrument for cutting the power of capital owners. In such a transformation, the intelligentsia has an opportunity to come out a winner. This is no more than a hypothesis, but it turns our attention to the role and strength of the intelligentsia in the field of trade-union and political activities.

THE ROLE OF UNIONS AND POLITICAL ORGANIZATIONS

In discussing the future role of the intelligentsia, one may ask whether it is organized or is on the road to organizing itself as a stratum or class "for itself." There are certainly those who deny that anything of this kind is under way.[15] To me the question is still unsettled, but since I believe that the intelligentsia is more than a simple servant or instrument of capitalist power, I recognize its potential for a more articulate self-representation. A highly significant aspect is, however, that the intelligentsia may promote its position without very much separate organization. Some of the points that follow will touch upon this possibility, but I also want to offer a few other remarks.

First of all, the members of the intelligentsia are to a certain extent organized in trade unions, but there are large variations in this respect between countries, sectors, branches, regions, types of enterprise, etc. The level of unionization may be considered one indication of the degree of autonomy that various occupational groups have attained. Professional unions are often very strong because their members are the monopolistic owners of specialized knowledge and skills in demand on the labor market. They are, therefore, in a powerful position when salaries and work conditions are negotiated. Furthermore, professional unions sometimes play a political role far beyond simple trade unionism. There are many historical examples showing that they have influenced the outcome of political conflicts. What I want to emphasize here is that the intelligentsia has already achieved a degree of self-representation. There is no reason to believe that its organizations will be weakened in the future. On the contrary, one would be surprised if they did not grow stronger.

Second, in the culture of critical discourse and the ideology of professionalism there is an element of universalism and a commitment to the social totality. As Gouldner points out, the privileged educational and social roles of the intelligentsia "are often defined as entailing an obligation to the collectivity as a whole."[16] He mentions, for example, that teachers are often regarded as "representatives" of the whole society and as "guardians of its national traditions." The intelligentsia may thus speak in the name of everyone. This can at times provide a way (and perhaps the most effective way) for it to pursue its own aspirations. In other words, one must carefully observe the issues around which various professional groups organize. Judgments and arguments cannot simply be taken at face value. Instead, one must look beyond ideology to see its relation to the social struggles in society.

A third aspect is the intelligentsia's political representation in the party system. The general problem of political representation is complicated in many ways. Political parties usually try to win support from large segments of a population and, therefore, may develop rather vague programs that appeal to several social classes and groups. Thus, they are often far from being pure class organizations. To what extent, then, do existing political parties articulate and support the different demands of the intelligentsia, not only in words but also in deeds? In discussing this question, I would call attention to the fact that the intelligentsia is often overrepresented within political parties. Its proportion among party members may be greater than its share of the population, but—more important—it usually has an even stronger over-representation in the higher levels of the organizational structures of political parties. Moreover, members of the intelligentsia have the advantage of possessing educationally acquired abilities, which provide the basis for their disproportionate influence over the program, the day-by-day political questions, and the inner life of the organization. These aspects must be taken into account when political representation is analyzed. I do not believe that po-litical activists with intelligentsia occupations or background sim-ply represent themselves in politics no matter what context they enter, but I do feel that they often leave a specific mark on what they do. The experiences of New Left politics since the 1960s are instructive in this respect.

Finally, one element behind the political role and strength of the intelligentsia is that it is to a large extent located in the state apparatuses and in the media. These are favorable positions for influencing political and ideological struggles without having to resort to parties or trade unions. The members of the intelligentsia are the experts and the informants, and therefore they often de-fine problems and suggest solutions. They have a key role in shaping the whole cultural context in which political and ideolog-ical issues arise and are settled.

Still, one must not forget that disagreement over political and other issues is very common within the intelligentsia. The battles between different groups are sometimes fierce and even an-tagonistic. This has to do with the fact that the intelligentsia is not only heterogeneous but is also cut across by the struggles of the main class forces in society. It is thus necessary to be aware of both dividing and unifying factors. Bourdieu has noted that within a given field there are always battles between defenders and challengers—between orthodoxy and heresy—but that at the same time the adversaries usually all defend the field as such.[17] For example, in the field of higher education we can find many intense controversies over various issues, scientific questions, educational methods, allocation of resources, organizational problems, etc. If the system of higher education is attacked from outside, however, it will generally be easy to achieve unanimity, even among passionate opponents.

CONCLUSION

The future of the intelligentsia in modern capitalist society is a question of the future of capitalism itself. Even though capitalism seems today to be stronger than it has been for a long time, there are tendencies indicating important changes in the present social and economic structure. In this paper I have offered some ideas about the changes that may be expected. The most significant result of these transformations will perhaps be that the social and economic position of the top layers of the intelligentsia is enhanced. This does not mean, however, that we will soon have a ruling class of intelligentsia in modern Western society. In order for that to occur, capitalism itself would have to be drastically restricted, and that will certainly take time.

NOTES

1. Alvin W. Gouldner, *The Future of Intellectuals and the Rise of the New Class* (Macmillan, 1979); Barbara and John Ehrenreich, "The Professional-Managerial Class," in Pat Walker, ed., *Between Labor and Capital* (Harvester Press, 1979); Nicos Poulantzas, *Classes in Contemporary Capitalism* (Humanities Press, 1975); Stanley Aronowitz, "The Professional-Managerial Class or Middle Strata," in Walker, ed., *Between Labor and Capital*; André Gorz, *Strategy for Labor* (Beacon Press, 1967); Serge Mallet, *Essays on the New Working Class* (Telos Press, 1975); and Erik Olin Wright, "Intellectuals and the Class Structure of Capitalist Society," in Walker, ed., *Between Labor and Capital*.

2. Gouldner, *Future of Intellectuals*.

3. Ibid., p. 8.

4. A good account of this distrust is given by Sandy Carter, "Class Conflict: The Human Dimension," in Walker, ed., *Between Labor and Capital*.

5. Wright, "Intellectuals and the Class Structure," pp. 203 et seq.

6. Ibid., p. 207.

7. Gouldner, *Future of Intellectuals*, p. 19 ff.

8. Ibid., p. 28 ff.

9. Göran Therborn, *The Ideology of Power and the Power of Ideology* (Verso/NLB, 1980), pp. 15–17.

10. See, for example, David V. Glass, ed., *Social Mobility in Britain* (Routledge & Kegan Paul, 1954); Jean E. Floud et al., *Social Class and Educational Opportunity* (Heinemann, 1956); Robert J. Havighurst, *American Higher Education in the 1960s* (Ohio State University Press, 1960); Pierre Bourdieu and Jean-Claude Passeron, *Les héritiers* (Éditions de Minuit, 1964); Pierre Bourdieu and Jean-Claude Passeron, *La Reproduction* (Éditions de Minuit, 1970); and Joan Abbott, *Student Life in a Class Society* (Pergamon Press, 1971).

11. George Konrád and Ivan Szelényi, *The Intellectuals on the Road to Class Power* (Harvester Press, 1979), pp. 76–77.

12. In Marxist theory this problem has often been underestimated due to a conception of the state apparatus as above all an instrument of ruling-class power. Weberian theory, however, pays more serious attention to the issue but tends to underestimate its relationship to the class struggle and the social contradictions in capitalist society. An interesting attempt to synthesize the different views of Weber and Lenin can be found in Wright, *Class, Crisis, and the State* (New Left Books, 1978), pp. 181–225.

13. See, for example, Adolf A. Berle and Gardiner C. Means, *The Modern Corporation and Private Property* (Macmillan, 1933); James Burnham, *The Managerial Revolution* (John Day, 1941); Adolf A. Berle, *Power without Property* (Harcourt Brace, 1959); John K. Galbraith, *The New Industrial State* (Houghton Mifflin, 1967); and Daniel Bell, *The Coming of Post-Industrial Society* (Basic Books, 1973).

14. Gouldner, *Future of Intellectuals*, pp. 13–14.

15. Aronowitz, "Professional and Managerial Class."

16. Gouldner, *Future of Intellectuals*, pp. 65–66.

17. Pierre Bourdieu, *Questions de sociologie* (Éditions de Minuit, 1980), pp. 113–120.

5

Intellectuals, Professionalization, and Class Relations

Edmund Dahlström

INTRODUCTION

Theories about intellectuals and dominant ideas in society are related to basic conceptions of the historical origin and development of capitalist society and its social structure. The first section of this essay deals with some fundamental notions about capitalist development and the role of intellectuals in this process.

"Social structure" here refers especially to the division of labor and social stratification into social classes. The rise of professional intellectuals is related to overall changes in the social division of labor in capitalist society (section two).

Some of the more controversial theories pertaining to the class structure of late capitalist society are analyzed in the third section, with special consideration given to the role of the intellectuals. New-class theory, with its assumptions about the coming rule of intellectuals in late- and postcapitalist society, is of crucial interest here.

The last section questions such assumptions of new-class theory and suggests an alternative interpretation of contemporary and future societal structures and class relations. It is suggested that forces exist in late-capitalist societies which countervail any power intellectuals may acquire and that an alternative is political options along the line of mass-legitimation and popular participation in knowledge development, with more consideration given to popular beliefs.

CAPITALIST DEVELOPMENT AND INTELLECTUALS

Two opposite lines of interpreting capitalist development have influenced the view of intellectuals and science in modern society.[1]

The *tradition of positive philosophy* (Saint-Simon, Comte, and Spencer) maintains that the development of science and its application in industry is the basis for societal progress, not only as a result of dominating and controlling nature but also through its ability to control a complex industrial society and to provide a new basis for social authority and political decision.

The *tradition of negative or critical philosophy* (Hegel and Marx) identifies reason with a nonscientific capacity to reveal the essential nature of man, society, and the material world and identifies progress with the discovery and expression of a rational essence rather than with the mere development of science and industry and their social consequences.

These opposite philosophies have influenced the two social-science theories that dominate our interpretation of late-capitalist development in the postwar period: the theory of industrial society and the theory of capitalist society.[2]

The theory of industrial society asserts a progressive change from traditional (preindustrial) to industrial society. Here it is claimed that the class conflict of early capitalism has been largely dispelled through the "institutionalization of conflicts" and increasing prosperity. The rise of the liberal-democratic state is an important factor in this transformational process, and progress in science is the key to development. In this theory, the middle class is seen as both a modernizing and a mitigating factor. Professionalization of this middle class creates a more collectivistic and altruistic culture, integrating all social classes.

In contrast, the theory of capitalist society assumes a fundamental contradiction between private expropriation and socialized production and a primary conflict between capital owners and wage earners. The middle stratum, which includes intellectuals, here represents an intermediate stratum between the conflicting main classes, forming a "contradictory class position." It is suggested that a large part of the middle stratum, including some intellectuals, suffers a degradation of its work and market in a process of proletarianization. The members of the middle stratum are divided among themselves in the struggle between capital and labor. A higher stratum is incorporated into capital interests, while the proletarianized parts are said to join the working class.

These theories have well-known ideological presumptions.[3] The theory of industrial society has its base in liberal-democratic ideology, in which the free market and private ownership are seen as the main forces of economic progress and the necessary conditions of democratic rule. The theory of capitalist society bases itself on a working-class ideology, proclaiming working-class control over the means of production and political rule as the highest value. The role of the state in the transcendence of capitalism has been a central point of disagreement between the main lines of socialistic thought.

A third alternative theory of capitalist society can be traced back to nineteenth-century populism and anarcho-democratic thinking. A contemporary version of this theory of self-reliance sees the development toward a large-scale concentration of production and political power in states and corporations in the First World and Second World as a threat to global welfare and as a source of class exploitation of the Third World.[4] The strategy of self-reliance proposes a higher degree of local economic self-sufficiency and local political self-management, implying a reduction of central professional-intellectual control and the increased power and participation of people at a local level.

THE DIVISION OF LABOR AND THE
PROFESSIONALIZATION OF THE INTELLECTUALS

Theories of industrial society have conceived of the existing division of labor in late-capitalist society as rational and legitimate, while theories of capitalist society have maintained that the capitalist division of labor reflects class exploitation: capitalists are said to seek control over the labor process in order to appropriate surplus.[5] Control of surplus (quantitative efficiency) and control of the labor process (qualitative efficiency) are said to be the main fields of controversy between capital and labor: capitalists seek to consolidate control over the labor process through management, and workers seek to resist this management of the labor process through collective actions. The resulting technical division of labor fragments labor tasks into repetitive operations and separates mental and manual work. However, wage earners are said to have managed to some extent to modify the division of labor to their advantage through collective and individual actions.

The struggle to control the labor process can also be said to include the struggle over the control of knowledge.[6] From this point of view, capital owners have sought to appropriate knowledge directly from productive labor (direct producers). The appropriation of knowledge from manual labor is thus not a rationally and technically determined, automatic process. Rather, it reflects class struggle and class relations. Here the "fetishism of intellectuals" may be regarded as a managerial strategy for controlling manual labor.

Here again, various forms of knowledge are systematized in the sciences and promulgated through education, processes that permit a more effective exploitation of labor. The development of a differentiated educational system generates a system of credentials in which knowledge and occupational groups (professions) seek to control access to particular places. The hierarchical structuring of credentials helps to sustain the intellectuals' claim that their labor is predominantly mental, requiring specific educational credentials, which in turn legitimate rewards and privileges.

A trend toward a polarization of the qualification structure can be noticed in the postwar period. However, views are divided about whether this has been in the direction of qualification or dequalification.[7] A large proportion of experts with a high degree of education tends to accompany a large proportion of very unqualified workers. This *bifurcation theory* assumes that the presence of very qualified employees requires that unqualified workers do unqualified work for them.[8]

The precapitalist and preindustrial division of labor had a corporative character, with estates, town municipalities, guilds, ecclesiastical communities, and universities. The creation and transmission of knowledge occurred within a system of corporate autonomy. Capitalism and industrialism broke up these corporate forms, but other institutions for the creation, coordination, and transmission of knowledge gradually emerged to replace them. A host of educational establishments grew, corresponding more or less to the different fields of the labor market. Professional organizations also emerged, claiming a knowledge and occupational monopoly over places in the labor market.[9]

Professions follow a strategy of closure through exclusion, usually having their rights recognized by public bodies. They create patterns of service relationships to clients and society, safeguard professional interests, maintain ethics and professional culture, and provide social control over their members at the same time that they enjoy a certain autonomy within these bounds. Professional self-regulation and independence (autonomy) varies from profession to profession and has somewhat different motivations and functions.

Traditional academic subjects can be described as scientific professions.[10] Some scientific professions lack a defined occupational area, and the cultivation and dissemination of their members' knowledge has been limited to the university. Other academic professions have strong attachments to practical institutional areas, and considerable knowledge development has occurred in these practical institutions.

The knowledge, information, and educational expansion in late-capitalist society has resulted in segmentation and fragmen-

tation. University disciplines create the basis for disciplinary segmentation, generating barriers for knowledge development over
disciplinary frontiers. The explosion of practically oriented institutions for knowledge development in different parts of society
has also contributed to a sectorial segmentation. Systems of
higher education and research have increasingly oriented themselves toward these practically oriented knowledge-producing requirements, involving the growing influence of corporations,
interest organizations, and public administrative bodies. Integrating knowledge and transcending knowledge barriers has become
both a more difficult and a more urgent task for universities.

The positivistic theory of industrial society sees the professions
as a means of transcending capitalism and class: according to one
of its proponents, "the class nature of professions has become a
peripheral issue in sociology."[11] More recent studies, however,
find professions reflecting changes in capitalism and its class
structure.[12] From this point of view, the collegial free professions
were typical of early capitalism, while the "bureaucratic professions" are more dominant in late capitalism. However, there has
always been considerable variation among professions in their
subordination to bureaucratic steering and managerial control.
The subordination to administrative steering is in some cases
more formal than real (e.g., in universities and hospitals.)[13]

Of the two opposite views of the professions, the proletarianization theory and the postindustrial theory, both have failed to
properly conceptualize the professions.[14] The subordination of the
professions cannot be compared with the subordination of the
working class: professionals still control the product of their labor.
But there has also been a decline in the professional's control of
the goal and direction of his or her own labor. This is partly due
to a decline of the self-employed professional. With this in mind,
it can be shown that postindustrial theories are inclined to over-
estimate the power and autonomy of professional groups.

CLASS RELATIONS AND INTELLECTUALS

The vertical division of labor constitutes a basis for social
stratification with regard to people's access to what appears

desirable in society in the form of power, material privileges, prestige, spiritual purity, education, and welfare of different kinds. Objective stratification matches subjective processes. Those who have the same amount of privileges, power, and education and the same standard of living tend to socialize with one another, communicate with one another, develop common systems of belief and similar life-styles, form collectives, and organize themselves and act collectively.[15]

Class structure is generally assumed to relate to broader historical formations, determined by encompassing structures. There has been a clash between two opposite views of class: one view emphasizes its objective, structural determination, and the other focuses on class consciousness and class struggle. There is a tendency today to transcend this opposition with an integrated approach.[16] Here, economic, political, and ideological conditions are said to structure the realms of class struggle, and these struggles are said to in turn affect the very conditions that structure them. The effect of this dialectical process generates a certain indetermination, since its outcome depends upon the dynamic interrelations between classes.[17]

Class struggle means exercising power. Elite theory is also concerned with power holders. But class analysis goes beyond the relations of power and takes into consideration the structural relations of economic, political, and cultural subsystems.[18] Those who have power have something more in common than power.

As Martin and Szelényi show in their contribution in this volume, different class theories emphasize different power resources of significance for class formation: control of the means of production and possession of human capital (education and skills) in the labor market, welfare resources, and political power. Class-forming conditions have also varied historically. Political and military power was the main class determinant in feudal society, while the control of capital in the market system is the basic class-forming factor under capitalism.[19]

Class theories assume a relationship of dominance and exploitation between classes. Historical studies show a complicated pattern of class rule, with coalitions of class fractions and limited control of the dominating class over the state.[20] Marx found in

Bonaparte's France that the bourgeoisie "in order to save its purse must lay aside its crown." Perry Anderson shows how the nobility under absolutism could only "make sure of their dominance by agreeing to deposite power with monarchy." Ralph Miliband observes of the experience of the bourgeoisie in both Italy and Germany under fascism that "having helped the dictators to rob all other classes and notably the working classes of any semblance of power, they found their own drastically curtailed and in some areas, notably foreign policy, altogether nullified." This kind of historical evidence should make us wary in generalizing about historical periods and of postulating simple relationships of class domination.

New-class theory maintains that intellectuals are the up-and-coming ruling class in late-capitalist and/or state-socialist societies.[21] As other essays in this volume have stressed, this new class is characterized by a culture of critical discourse (CCD), which is said to integrate a technical intelligentsia with humanistic intellectuals. The possession of "cultural capital" is the basis for power, income, and common class interest. Professional organization is its weapon, and the educational system is its reproductive basis (see Bengt Furåker's contribution).

As can be seen from these essays, there are different opinions about the prospects for intellectuals in late capitalism. In an earlier work, Konrád and Szelényi assert that the power of the intellectuals in late-capitalist countries is limited by capital owners' control of the means of production and elected representation in the political system.[22] The professional control of cultural capital is for them not a sufficient basis for class power and class rule. The road to intellectual class power is instead dependent upon the establishment of "rational distribution," as in state-socialist societies.

The amount of societal power we ascribe to intellectuals depends upon the functions that we attribute to the ideological-cultural subsystem in relation to other parts of society. The dominant-ideology theory assumes that dominant ideas steer and integrate total societies.[23] I am inclined to agree with critics of this theory, who find other, more important integrating forces in the political, economic, and everyday-life fields.[24] However, the legitimating effects of dominant ideas should not be neglected.

These are mobilized to bolster the sectional interests of hegemonic groups, where sectional interests are represented as universal and contradictions are denied or transmuted, and where the present is seen as natural and necessary (i.e., reified).[25] But these ideologies, in Mannheim's sense, should not blind us to the power of countervailing utopian beliefs and their impact on social criticism and countermovements. In such cases, alienated intellectuals may side with the exploited and lead revolutionary movements.[26]

SOME QUESTIONABLE POINTS OF NEW-CLASS THEORY

As Martin and Szelényi point out in their essay, new-class theory assumes a gradual weakening of the old class (the moneyed bourgeoisie) in late capitalism: an intelligentsia of managers is assumed to take over the power in private corporations, interest organizations, and public bureaucracies. But the theory of "managerial revolution" which lies behind this has been questioned in several studies.[27] There is no convincing evidence for the assumption that professional managers have interests different from those of capital owners (see Furåker). Managers carry out a policy geared to capital accumulation, and the conflict between employers (capital owners and professional managers) and wage earners continues even after the supposed managerial revolution. Structural conditions of the market limit possible interest formations and force enterprises "to accumulate or die," whether they are led by capital owners or by professional managers.[28]

There is a growing consensus among sociologists, in a broad range of critical approaches, that the basic contradictions and conflicts of capitalism prevail even in late capitalism.[29] Recent Swedish studies confirm the picture that the contradictions and conflicts between capital and labor permeate the society, with a stratum of white-collar workers in a middle position.[30] The predominance of such conflicts does not preclude other conflicts—between country and town, centrum and periphery, regions, ethnic groups, educational strata, age groups, and genders. The history of capitalism in Europe is the history of intricate cleavage-structures.[31]

There has been a differentiation of the middle strata into a deskilled white-collar group and a group of more qualified intellectuals called by some the "service class."[32] This service class can be said to have taken over such functions from capital owners as supervisory, planning, administrative and commercial functions.[33] The service class belongs at the top of all the hierarchies.

We can also observe a change in capital ownership. Impersonal-institutional-private ownership has to a larger extent replaced personal-private ownership. Institutional owners have delegated such "capital functions" as "conceptualization, reproduction, and control of capital" to the new service class. This implies that this service class has become the functionary of capital, not of capitalists.[34]

As mentioned earlier, the control of surplus is one important source of exploitation found in different modes of production.[35] Late capitalism includes personal-private ownership, institutionalized-private ownership, and public ownership. The state has taken over the function of appropriating surplus and realizing capital in state-socialist countries. At the same time, as Furåker points out, intellectuals have a more dominant position in public ownership and impersonal-private ownership than in personal-private ownership.

Statements concerning the power of intellectuals in late-capitalist society require a careful consideration of the role of intellectuals in different institutional areas, with different modes of production, different political subsystems, and different cultural-ideological institutions. This requires a clearer delimitation of intellectuals and a differentiation of groups of intellectuals with respect to interest-and-power relations.

Studies of universities, disciplines, and professions have not provided evidence to support the theory that the culture of critical discourse integrates intellectual substrata and elite groups, generating common class interests.[36] Although market interests do provide the basis for unionization and collective bargaining (a point developed by Furåker), they also create conditions for competition and fragmentation between professions and disciplines. Social contradictions reinforce these conflicts and the fragmentation between intellectual strata and elite groups, a point made also by Häyrynen in his contribution to this volume.

Cornelis Disco (in this volume) endorses the theory that intellectuals possess cultural (symbolic) capital, which serves as a source of income and power in the market and production system, offering an analogy to the old class's possession of moneyed capital. There are, however, some very important differences between cultural capital and moneyed capital, differences that make the comparison look like a poor metaphor.[37] Skills and knowledge are not exchangeable and transformable, as is moneyed capital. A wage earner's knowledge is subordinated to an owner's goals, according to the labor contract. There is also a large variation in the control of knowledge development in different professions. The assumption of an analogy (taken from the specific conditions of early capitalism) between the old class's dominance and the new class's dominance is a doubtful overgeneralization.

The dominant belief system of late capitalism depends upon ''democratic'' mass-legitimation as indicated by demand on the market, votes in elections, popularity in the mass media, and support in social movements and organizations. This ideology postulates that consumers, voters, members, and citizen-clients are ''sovereign.''[38] However, reality deviates from such ideals. Professional intellectuals may become dominant (a ruling class) when subsystems become perverted in comparison to ''perfect conditions,'' and intellectuals may exploit rather than serve people. This generates an ambiguous attitude toward intellectuals in late-capitalist societies. There are other sources in state-socialist countries for the legitimation of a new intellectual class, where notions such as ''scientific socialism,'' ''dictatorship of the proletariat,'' ''the vanguard party,'' and ''correct lines'' dominate discourse.[39]

People have begun to question the professional's role in, and contribution to, late capitalism. This criticism concerns professionalism's dequalification, pacification, fragmentation, isolation, degradation, and subordination of man as consumer, student, patient, and client.[40] The professions are criticized for preventing people from developing their own knowledge, insights, and even health through their own activity. The professions are accused of deciding norms, needs, how problems are to be solved, and what is best for man. Specialists such as technologists, economists, administrators, marketers, teachers, doctors, journalists, and lawyers have developed a system of guardianship of the citizen.

The notion that intellectuals are on the road to class power implies a deterministic view of the future of late capitalism. To my mind the issue is much more open. There exist possibilities for structural change along the lines of self-reliance and possibilities for reducing exploitation by means of democratization of the production-and-market system, the political system, and the cultural-ideological system.

This requires that popular beliefs be taken as a point of departure for the development of knowledge and that nonintellectual people be mobilized more often in critical knowledge-developing processes.[41]

NOTES

1. R. Badham, "The Sociology of Industrial and Post-Industrial Societies, *Current Sociology* 32 (1984): 1–136.

2. A. Giddens, *Sociology: A Brief but Critical Introduction* (London: MacMillan & Co., 1982), chap. 2. The typification of development theories of late capitalism is used in ideal-type manner. Badham, in "The Sociology of Industrial and Post-Industrial Societies," has correctly noted that the two typologies are difficult to apply to many social-science contributions.

3. E. Dahlström, *Bestämmande i arbetet: Några idékritiska funderingar kring arbetslivets demokratisering* [Critical throughts about democratization of the labor process] (Gothenburg: Department of Sociology, 1983).

4. J. Galtung et al., *Self-Reliance: A Strategy for Development* (London: Bogle L. Overture, 1980); B. Hettne, *Development Theory and the Third World* (Stockholm: SAREC report no. 2, 1982); M. Friberg and J. Galtung, *Krisen* [The crises] (Stockholm: Förlaget Adademilitteratur, 1983). Similar thoughts have been presented by authors with socialist backgrounds: R. Bahro, *Die Alternative: Zur kritik des real existierenden Sozialismus* (Cologne–Frankfurt am Main: Europäische Verlagsanstalt, 1977); and A. Gorz, *Adieux au proletariat au de la du socialisme* (Paris: Éditions Galilée, 1982).

5. A. Giddens, "Power, the Dialectic of Control and Class Structuration," and G. Mackenzie, "Class Boundaries and the Labour Process," both in A. Giddens and G. Mackenzie, eds., *Social Class and the Division of Labour* (Cambridge: Cambridge University Press, 1982).

6. A. Sohn-Rethel, *Intellectual and Manual Labour* (London: Macmillan & Co., 1978); N. Abercrombie and J. Urry, *Capital: Labour and the Middle Class* (London: George Allen & Unwin, 1983), pp. 72–103.

7. E. Altvater, "Kvalifikation och yrkesutbildning," in *Jämlikhetsmyt och klassherravälde* [Qualification and vocational education, in: The myth of equality and class rule] (Lund, Sweden: Bo Cavefors, 1976); K. A. Nielsen, *Kvalifikationsstruktur Klassestruktur* [Qualification structure and class structure] (Copenhagen: Kurasje, 1976).

8. P. M. Blau, *Inequality and Heterogeneity: A Primitive Theory of Social Structure* (New York: The Free Press, 1977).

9. I. Hellberg, *Studier i professionell organisation* [Studies in professional organization] (Gothenburg: Department of Sociology, 1978); G. K. Gyarmati, "The Doctrine of the Professions: Basis of Power Structure," *International Social Sciences Journal*, 27 (1975).

10. J. Ben-David, *Science as a Profession and Scientific Professionalism: Explorations in General Theory in Social Science* (New York: The Free Press, 1976).

11. J. Ben-David, "Professions in the Class System in Present-Day Society," *Current Sociology* 12 (1963–64): 246–298.

12. M. S. Larson, *The Rise of Professionalism: A Sociological Analysis* (Berkeley, Los Angeles, London: University of California Press, 1977).

13. T. C. Holliday, "Professions, Class and Capitalism," *European Journal of Sociology* 24 (1983): 321–346.

14. C. Derber, "Managing Professionals: Ideological Proletarianization and Post-Industrial Labour," *Theory and Society* 12 (1983): 309–341; C. Derber, ed., *Professionals as Workers: Mental Labor in Advanced Capitalism* (Boston: G. K. Hall, 1982).

15. E. Dahlström, *Klasser och samhällen* [Classes and societies] (Stockholm: Prisma, 1971), chap. 2.

16. Anthony Giddens has developed a class theory that tries to transcend subjective and objective class theories: A. Giddens, *The Class Structure of the Advanced Societies* (London: Hutchinson University Library, 1973). Göran Therborn has advocated an integrating approach: G. Therborn, "Den nymarxistiska klassanalysens uppkomst och problem" [Origin and problems of neo-Marxist class analysis], *Häften för kritiska studier*, no. 2 (1983). A convergence of views is also found in Erik Olin Wright's review of Giddens's critique of Marxism in the *New Left Review*, no. 138 (1983): 11–35.

17. Abercrombie and Urry, *Capital*, pp. 128, 158.

18. T. Bottomore, *Elites and Society* (London: C. A. Watts & Co. Ltd., 1964); T. Bottomore, *Classes in Modern Society* (London: George Allen & Unwin, 1965).

19. A. Giddens, *Power, Poverty and the State, A Contemporary Critique of Historical Materialism*, vol 1. (London: Macmillan & Co., 1981), chaps. 3, 4, and 5.

20. F. Parkin, *Marxism and Class Theory: A Bourgeois Critique* (London: Tavistock, 1979); K. Marx, *The Eighteenth Brumaire of Louis Bonaparte* (London: George Allen, 1926), p. 74; P. Andersson, *Lineages of the Absolute State* (London: New Left Books, 1974), p. 41; R. Miliband, *The State in Capitalist Society* (London: Weidenfeld and Nicholson, 1969), p. 73.

21. A. W. Gouldner, *The Future of Intellectuals and the Rise of the New Class* (New York: Seabury Press, 1979); C. Disco, "The Educated Minotaur: The Sources of Gouldner's New Class Theory," *Theory and Society* 11 (1982): pp. 799–819.

22. G. Konrád and I. Szelényi, *The Intellectuals on the Road to Class Power* (Brighton: Harvester Press, 1979); I. Szelényi, "Gouldner's Theory of Intellectuals as a Flawed Universal Class," *Theory and Society* 11 (1982): pp. 779–798; I Szelényi's "The Intelligentsia in the Class Structure of State Socialistic Societies," in M. Burawoy and T. Skocpol, eds., *Marxist Inquiries: Studies of Labour Class and Status* (Chicago and London: University of Chicago Press, 1982).

23. N. Abercrombie, S. Hill, and B. S. Burns, *The Dominant Ideology Thesis* (London: George Allen & Unwin, 1980); G. Therborn, *The Ideology of Power and the Power of Ideology* (London: Vervo/NLB, 1980).

24. E. Dahlström, "Kan sociologin förtöja kulturanalysen?" [Can sociology integrate cultural analysis?], in U. Hannerz, R. Liljeström, and O. Lövgren, eds., *Kultur och medvetande* (Stockholm: Akademilitteratur, 1982), pp. 141–155.

25. A. Giddens, *Central Problems in Social Theory* (London: Macmillan & Co., 1979), chap. 5.

26. K. Mannheim, *Ideology and Utopia: An Introduction to the Sociology of Knowledge* (London: Routledge & Kegan Paul, 1954), pp. 173–236.

27. M. Zeitlin, *Classes, Class Conflict and the State: Empirical Studies in Class Analysis* (Cambridge, Mass: Winthrop Publishers, 1980), chap. 1; A. Broström, *MBLs gränser—den privata ägnderätten* [The limits of labor law—private ownership] (Stockholm: Arbetslivscentrum, 1982).

28. E. Dahlström, *Bestämmande i arbetet*.

29. A. Giddens, *Central Problems in Social Theory*, chap. 2; A. Giddens, *Power, Poverty and the State*, chap. 10; C. Offe; *Strukturprobleme des kapitalistischen Staates* (Frankfurt am Main: Suhrkamp Verlag, 1975); E. O. Wright, *Class Crisis and the State* (London: NLB, 1978). Several papers presented at the Nordic workshop on Intellectuals, Universities, and the State express a similar view on late capitalism: for example, B. Furåker (in this volume); and B. Lindensjö, "The Perceptions of the Welfare State in Various Intellectual Groups" (ms.).

30. W. Korpi, *The Working Class in Welfare Capitalism* (London: Routledge & Kegan Paul, 1978); J. Stephens, *The Transitions from Capitalism to Socialism* (London: Macmillan & Co., 1979); U. Himmelstrand, G. Ahrne, and L. Lundberg, *Beyond Welfare Capitalism* (London: Heineman, 1981); G. Therborn, *Klasstrukturen i Sverige 1930–80* [Class structure in Sweden 1930–80] (Lund, Sweden: Zenit Förlag, 1981); R. Liljeström and E. Dahlström, *Arbetarkvinnor i arbete, hem och samhällsliv* [Working-class women in work, home, and civic life] (Stockholm: Tidens Förlag, 1981).

31. S. M. Lipset and S. Rokkan, *Party Systems and Voter Alignment: Cross-National Perspectives* (New York: The Free Press, 1967); S. Rokkan, "Nation Building, Cleavage Formation and Structuring of Mass Politics," in S. Rokkan, *Citizens, Elections, Parties* (Oslo: Universitetsförlaget, 1970).

32. Abercrombie and Urry, *Capital*, pp. 124, 152–153; D. L. Johnson, ed., *Class and Social Development: A New Theory of the Middle Class* (London: Sage, 1982), pp. 246–257.

33. F. Croner, *Angestellten* (Cologne: Kiepenhauer and Wirtsch, 1982), chap. 2; R. Dahrendorf, "The Service Class," in T. Burns, ed. *Industrial Man* (Harmondsworth: Penguin, 1969), pp. 140–150; J. H. Goldthorpe, *Social Mobility and Class Structure in Modern Britain* (Oxford: Clarendon Press, 1980), chaps. 1, 2.

34. Abercrombie and Urry, *Capital*, pp. 124–153.

35. J. E. Roemer, *A General Theory of Exploitation and Class* (Cambridge, Mass., and London: Harvard University Press, 1982), chap. 7.

36. B. Bruce-Briggs, ed., *The New Class?* (New York: Columbia University Press, 1979).

37. W. Korpi, *The Democratic Struggle* (London: Routledge & Kegan Paul, 1983), pp. 14–18. Some of my arguments here agree with arguments found in the papers by Martin and Szelényi and by Furåker in this volume.

38. G. Hernes, *Förhandlingsekonomi og blandingsadministration* [Bargaining economy and mixed administration] (Oslo: Universitetsförlaget, 1978).

39. C. E. Lindblom, *Politics and Markets: The World's Political and Economic Systems* (New York: Basic Books, 1977), pp. 237–275.

40. I. Illich, *Celebration of Awareness: A Call for Institutional Revolution* (New York: Anchor Books, 1971); N. Christie, *Hvis skolen ikke fantes* [If school didn't exist] (Oslo/Copenhagen: Universitetsförlaget, Christian Ejlers Förlag, 1971); D. Gannik and L. Launsö, "The Isolation of Health Services in Society: Development and Consequences," *Acta Sociologica* 21 (1978): p. 209 ff.

41. I have presented some ideas in this direction in E. Dahlström, *Samhällsvetenskap och praktik* [Social science and praxis] (Stockholm: Liber Förlag, 1980), chap. 4.

6

The Modern Intellectual:
In Power or Disarmed?

Reflections on the Sociology of Intellectuals and Intellectual Work

Katrín Fridjónsdóttir

INTRODUCTION

The relationship between intellectual work and power in society belongs to the classical questions raised in understanding the role and function of intellectuals in societal development. Complex and problematic as it is, this relationship has fascinated intellectuals and inspired them to analyze and reflect on their own role in this development. There are few subjects that lend themselves so well to combining existential self-reflection with historical, sociological analysis.

Recently, the role and status of intellectuals and the relationship between intellectual work and power have become intensely debated topics in social science. They stand at the center of various contributions to theories on postindustrial society, modern class analysis, reflections on the proletarianization of intellectual work, and, above all, theories of intellectuals as a "new class." Much of this debate is recorded in this volume. The theoretical approaches are diverse, reflecting the theoretical diversity in professionalized social science today. What unites them is that they all address the complexities of societal development in the industrialized world, concentrating their analysis on the increased role of knowledge (both theoretical and technical) in this development.

As to the attempts to define and categorize intellectuals and their social ("historical") function as a class in late-industrial society, the most interesting attempts rely on a radically revised Marxist class theory.[1] The concept of the new class is, however, also found in works on "postindustrial society," most often written by neoconservatives. The new class is here not a class in the Marxist sense of the word, that is, a category of workers with a common material situation and relationship to the means of production and therefore a common goal. What unites the new class, according to neoconservatives, are qualities of properties rather than of property, and the new class is here conceived of as a category of people united by the fact that they are all carriers of advanced "knowledge."

The societal background—that is, the transition to the postindustrial society—is viewed as radically changing not only with respect to its economic structure (the transition from industrial to service economy) but also, and above all, with respect to its "ideological" structure, as a consequence of the explosion of higher education. In the theories of postindustrial society, the new class seems to be a class in an otherwise "classless" society, populated by educated people, where some (the new class) are more expert than others.[2]

Theoretically more sophisticated are the attempts to "revise" the scheme for classical class analysis (by such writers as Alvin Gouldner and Konrád and Szelényi) in order to make intellectuals the main actors of social change. There seem to be two lines of argument in current discussions related to their works. One type of analysis is based on a metaphor concerning "cultural" skills (a metaphor originally developed by the French sociologist Pierre Bourdieu to explain the cultural reproduction of class relations), based mainly on theoretical knowledge: *ownership of cultural capital*. This attribute is said to unite intellectual workers around a common interest to valorize this capital. Another type claims that a common interest of a *teleological* nature unites intellectuals in the goal of taking control of the state against other classes. In both versions, intellectuals replace the usual (working) class referent as the main actors in a Marxist theory of social change.

It is not my intention to discuss the validity or implications of this revision of class theory or the theory of the new class as such. This is done rather well by other contributors to this volume. It must be admitted, however, that this theory, as well as the conflicting views about it, is one important inspiration for my own contribution. In pointing to the increasing number of highly trained, professional and intellectual workers in key positions in modern society, theorists of the new class have raised an important issue. This development, however, as also pointed out by Bengt Furåker and Edmund Dahlström, must be seen against the background of an increasing interdependence among different layers of power and administration. These layers subsume a great deal of what we call theoretical and technical knowledge today and should be seen against the background of the relationships among instances for power, administration, and the intellectual community itself and the training of intellectuals. Today we may better speak of the era of the ''professional expert,'' rather than of the era of the ''intellectual.'' However defined, modern intellectuals, including the professionalized expert, do not own the physical or cultural capital that anchors the contemporary social system. They are all workers inside this system, and to a certain degree they control only the mode of production of ideas in it. It seems doubtful that the policy analyst, the university professor, the writer, and the artist in modern society can all be said to hold positions of power, except, perhaps, in the relatively limited sphere of their own endeavors.

It is important, however, to analyze the *conditions* that shape their spheres and fields of endeavor in order to understand not only how these fields are connected to the larger social system but also their own internal conditions. For example, what about the economic and political conditions that shape the policy-analysis process, and what constitutes the conditions for knowledge production in the modern university? How are the processes of policy analysis and scientific work at the modern university related to mechanisms of power and social life at large? Such questions must be confronted before we can say anything about the power of the policy analyst and the university researcher. If we are going to say anything about the power of literary intellectuals, we must offer another example in order to take into consideration the structural condition of literary production.

Another topic that can be raised from the discussion of new-class theories concerns the "traditional" critical type of intellectual and the current conditions of that type of intellectual endeavor. The ideal-typical traditional critical intellectual includes the notion of always "questioning the truth of the moment in terms of higher and wider truths," as well as functioning as the critical voice of social conscience. As such, intellectuals are in a traditional sense the persons who have been entrusted with the task of not only conserving and transmitting but also molding and renovating the ideological and knowledge-based parts of culture. The process of intellectual development can thus be seen as a societal process of constant interpretation and reinterpretation and also of discovery. One of the consequences of societal development—the same development that has evoked the questions of the changing class structure as well as given rise to the sociology of intellectuals in its modern version—seems to be that this traditional role has somewhat eroded. At least, it appears to be performed under quite different conditions than when the idea of such a role was formulated. Perhaps we have to reevaluate the meaning and the importance of the category of the traditional intellectual itself as well as analyze its changing conditions. It might be fruitful to distinguish more clearly between a more traditional engagement of intellectuals (for example, in mobilizing societal movements, where intellectuals can play a special role) and other, perhaps more typically "modern" forms of the collective mobilization of intellectuals (such as those based on bureaucratic and state interests). When analytically separated, an interesting question arises about what relation exists in modern society between these two types of endeavors: the uneasy relationship between the mandarin intellectual and the more traditional intellectual. Do these two types tend to merge in a more harmonic way? A somewhat different approach includes asking *where*, and under what conditions, the mission of the traditional critical intellectual is performed today and then comparing this with those traditional conditions.

One way of describing the development of the intellectual endeavor in society and its changing conditions is to analyze the increasing professionalization of intellectual work and its consequences. However, this would not be enough if we wanted only to understand the complexities of intellectual work in modern society. Besides commenting on some past and present attempts to define the role of intellectuals and discussing the professionalization of the intellectual endeavor, I will also argue for a more cultural-sociological approach to the study of intellectuals and intellectual work. Of importance within such an approach are not only the social structure and intellectuals as a social stratum but also the content of ideas themselves.

SOME REMARKS ON THE BACKGROUND
TO THE CONTEMPORARY ISSUES

From Marx to Modern Class Analysis and
From "Clercs" to Civil Servants

Looking back over our intellectual heritage, we find that the word *intellectual* is historically connected with the concept of ideology. When introduced (in 1796, by Destutt de Tracy), *ideology* was used neutrally to designate a field of knowledge and, alternatively, as a general doctrine about ideas. If it was Napoleon who gave the concept its somewhat suspicious flavor (by calling his political rivals "ideologues"), it was Marx who gave the concept of ideology a definite normative and sociological meaning. One central theme in *The German Ideology* concerns the dependence of ideas and structures of thought on the social context, and, above all, on class interests in society. Here, ideology has the meaning of legitimizing an existing order and of concealing the real interests therein. Later, in *The Communist Manifesto*, Marx and Engels described intellectuals as more or less a section of the bourgeoisie, which, attaching itself to the working class, formulated the latter's ideas in written form.

Marx's aim in this analysis was merely political-theoretical. Soon after Marx, the relation between some particular form of consciousness and its social context became a problem for the *sociology of knowledge*. In this process of the "disciplinization" of the problem, contributions were made by both the politically engaged followers of Marx and the founders of academic sociology. In order to draw the boundaries for their new discipline (outward and toward other disciplines), both Emile Durkheim and Max Weber developed ideas about the role of knowledge and scientists in societal development.

In addition to the development of the sociology of knowledge, we have also witnessed several attempts to identify a *sociologically meaningful stratum of intellectuals*: those who formulate and work with ideas. It is reasonable to assume that writers such as Gramsci and Mannheim made such identifications primarily to find solutions to (different) practical problems: that of defining the means with which the working class could arrive at hegemony in society (Gramsci) and, in the sociology of knowledge, that of defining those who could be said to hold somewhat "objective" knowledge about society and nature (Mannheim). Their analyses are therefore rather vague and not suitable to application in the "hard" empirical analysis of occupations later favored by sociologists. Still, the question of how to define intellectuals has since become a favorite challenge to sociologists, especially within two of the field's subspecialties: political sociology and class analysis.

Alongside the development of the sociology of knowledge and the attempts to characterize intellectual workers and discover how their characteristics affect their social function, there is the recurrent theme of the traditional intellectual. This theme is an important part of our Western cultural heritage, where it is based on a view of the intelligentsia in society as a repository of moral and political values as well as of universal knowledge. According to this view, the social privilege of intellectuals is to seek an understanding of the social totality; therefore, it is their responsibility to defend the intellectual field of free speech and also to correct their fellow intellectual who might think otherwise. The theme is frequently expressed in reflective exposés written by intellectuals and addressed mainly to other intellectuals.

This theme can be found in, for example, Julien Benda's classical work on the treason of the ''clercs'' (i.e., intellectuals). The treason of the clercs consisted of accommodation to situational demands for certain ideas and ''truths.'' Among these ''treacherous activities'' was writing done in the service of political movements and parties.[3] Benda's theme reoccurs in Raymond Aron's criticism of his contemporary (Communist) party intellectuals, delivered in France in the mid-1950s. According to Aron, such intellectuals use ideologies as instruments for garnering access to the tower of power.[4]

The primarily moral argument of both Benda and Aron is based upon the view that the correct behavior for intellectuals lies in being an independent thinker. Such a thinker must choose between two main alternatives: being the mouthpiece of power for an interest group or staying critically independent, ''free-floating,'' in the Mannheimian sense.

Similar views of the role of intellectuals can be found in writings from the other (left) side, colored with reflections on the responsible, critical role of intellectuals, toward the ruling powers and their politics. Noam Chomsky's criticism of the *new mandarins* belongs to this type of reflection. Chomsky's criticism is aimed primarily at those social-science intellectuals who became mouthpieces of power and who used their qualifications to defend America's war in Vietnam. If natural scientists assisted in the war by developing the most effective ways of killing, the ''mandarinated'' social scientists helped to legitimate the war by giving the impression that it could only be understood by mandarin-experts.[5] A similar concept of ''new mandarins'' is *media celebrity*, formulated by Régis Debray in his recent work on intellectuals and power in French society. Debray's analysis is, above all, a historical and sociological analysis of the changing conditions of intellectual discourse.[6]

In the analyses of Chomsky and Debray we find reference to the *changing structural conditions* of intellectual work in its traditional sense. Structural conditions in the state and the power of the capitalist market are seen as forcing intellectuals into more "organic" relations. The breed of new mandarins is described by Chomsky as arising partly from the structural changes in American society and partly from within the intelligentsia itself. Intellectuals are seen as increasingly hired to run the welfare state and its affairs and, therefore, to become (state) *technocrats*. The rise of the *media celebrity* is seen by Debray as partly the result of the increasing *dominancee of the market* over intellectual discourse, regarding not only the form of this discourse but also its content. The rules of the commercial market for ideas is here said to be decisive. At the same time, both Chomsky and Debray view the traditional "responsibility" of the intellectual as both firm and unquestionable.

This ambivalence can also be found in the theories of intellectuals as a new class as formulated by Gouldner and by Konrád and Szelényi. At the same time, the "idea of the traditional intellectual" is rather important for them because it serves as a ground for establishing a new role for intellectuals in modern society. Gouldner points to the changing conditions of intellectual endeavors which secularization and the rise of a market for intellectual products brought forth. The intelligentsia, however, according to Gouldner, is united by a specific "culture": the culture of critical discourse. Although this discourse has to be marketed, it still gives its holders a certain amount of intellectual autonomy.

Konrád and Szelényi aim primarily at explaining the Eastern European social system and the role of intellectuals in ruling and administrating that system. Their work, however, also offers a historical analysis of the changing conditions and functions of intellectuals, in both the East and the West. They trace the historical background for this very far back in time, but some of the crucial events they refer to occurred during a definite historical period. This period was the era of competitive capitalism in Europe, when the traditional role of intellectuals seems to have gone through a radical transformation. From this time forward the intellectual lost part of his religious-mystical status and had to turn to the cultivation of the social goals of this world in addition to offering his skills for sale on the market. Following this, in modern capitalist societies intellectuals have been forced to make commodities of their knowledge and ideological skills. This is not the case in socialist societies, according to Konrád and Szelényi. In these societies (see Furåker in this volume), a special version of the traditional intellectual mission reemerges in the state bureaucracies, where state-employed intellectuals set the goals for societal development. This is a task that unites them teleologically and morally but, alas, also unites their interest in power and dominance over the rest of society.

Even though the analysis of the new class is probably not to be understood as the demise of the traditional intellectual, it offers a radical revision of their traditional mission. This revision is perhaps both rational and legitimate. Like the "event-generated anomalies" that have produced a dilemma for the class analyst trying to deal with the various and increasing numbers of intellectual workers while retaining the classical framework of class analysis, the complexities of societal development seem to have left very few—and scattered—islands for the traditional intellectual endeavor. This causes problems for the analysis of intellectuals in modern society. Some of this complexity has to do with the development of the market for intellectual ideas, some of it more directly with the professionalization of intellectual work. The latter is also associated with industrialization, the growth of science and technology, the development of the democratic order, and the growth of public administration, as well as with the development of the market for intellectual services.

MODERN SCIENCE AND THE PROFESSIONALIZATION OF INTELLECTUAL WORK

The usual definition underlying much of the sociological debate about intellectuals claims that an intellectual is someone qualified and accepted as qualified to speak on matters of cultural concern. This has led many sociologists to enumerate certain recognized professions in society as automatically qualifying as "intellectual." One such profession is the scientific one. This notion is hierarchical, since science is currently looked upon as a strong locus of cultural validation. Of relevance for the sociology of intellectual work, however, is both the context of scientific-knowledge production in modern society and the role of science in shaping the conditions of intellectual work in general.

The emergence of the concept of intellectual work as separated from other endeavors is one central aspect of modern culture. Thus, the increase in the numbers of people working mainly with their intellects itself represents an important aspect in historical development: the social division of human activities into intellectual and manual labor, thanks to the ingenuity of the former and the increased productivity of the latter. In this development, modern science and the social organization of scientific work have played an important role in addition to having been part of this development.

From the beginning, the birth and growth of modern science required the separation of "rational," discursive, logical thought and acts of abstraction from other mental endeavors. Aspects of mental activity could thus be distinguished from mere contemplation of the world, both good and evil. Philosophy came to constitute the greatest part of this "disciplinized" human knowledge, until science was (gradually) organized into separate "disciplines." Although it is not always so different from other ways of acquiring knowledge about the world, we can say that modern science is a specifically organized way, united in its epistemological rules and arranged in separate, disciplinized cognitive structures.

A prerequisite for the social organization of scientific knowledge is an institutional organization that could validate the principles of disciplinary authority as well as insure its social relevance. The current organization of science, which developed primarily in the nineteenth century, corresponds to a need for establishing science as autonomous and independent from society while at the same time being a prerequisite for the more effective use of science by society. Although functionally separate as a social unit, science is an integral part of the societal system. The "scientification" of society must be seen as a reciprocal process that includes the socialization and politicization of scientific knowledge.[7] Through this process science has been both disciplinized and professionalized, contributing to the professionalization of intellectual work in general. In this respect science, including its place and function in modern society, is rather fundamental to our understanding of the development of intellectual work as a whole.

An important event in the historical journey of mankind toward the scientific world and of special importance for the understanding of the birth of numerous modern intellectual professions is the institutionalization of social science and the founding of the social-science disciplines. The establishment of the social-science disciplines meant drawing boundaries, not only between the various disciplines themselves but also between political philosophy and science, between the normative and the scientific, and between the political ideologist and the social scientist. One of the founders of modern social science, Max Weber, formulated the task of the social scientist as primarily describing and explaining the structure of society and the process of social change but not intervening in political matters.[8] Weber thus indirectly pointed to the future situation of the modern intellectual: the very idea of social science moved the habitat of the universal-qualitative system of ideas from the sociopolitical arena into the seemingly neutral universe of science and universities.

The establishment of social science also forms the historical background for the creation of the modern professional intellectual. This professional could now on take a distinct place in the stratum of intellectual workers as a professionally trained intellectual whose training and education was academically controlled and even standardized. This arrangement was a precondition for social engineering, professional policy analysis, and related intellectual work.

Of course, a similar process took place in all the sciences. Discipline and professionalization are but two mutually dependent processes in the development of the social organization of scientific knowledge. A precondition for the social use of science is that it be at the same time partially "liberated" and given a certain autonomy vis-à-vis society. Science must, in other words, be allowed a certain degree of "inner professionalization" and discipline if it is to function as superior knowledge in the service of society. Besides fulfilling its social task of increasing knowledge, science professionalizes and also supplies the core means for the rationalization of society, including the division of labor, both intellectual and manual.

In the field of scientific work, the process of professionalization turns the scholar into a mental worker, an employee in academia or research institution. This process calls for a certain specialization as well as for certain social expectations, such as how one should act toward society itself. At the same time that the professional scientist is an organic intellectual in relation to the utilization of his knowledge in the sphere of society related to his research area, he is expected to regard his position and prospects primarily as a career within this disciplinary specialty.

The process of professionalization in fact seems to operate in rather similar ways in other spheres of intellectual life. One of the foremost "free" intellectual activities, literary criticism, has now (at least in the developed Western world) become the almost exclusively professionalized activity of predominantly academically trained persons. As argued by Debray, not only the form but also the content of this activity is controlled by those who dominate its market relations of production: the owners of journals and other media.[9] At the same time, the literary critic who fails in "catching the new fashion" in cultural criticism is not likely to survive long in his or her "profession."

Professionalization also operates in the spheres of politics and state administration. The acquisition of political power and its form of argumentation seems to have become a highly professionalized business, with an internal (bureaucratic) division of labor. Also, like the literary critic, the professional politician (in all political parties) is now more often than not an academically trained person, more or less specialized in his or her skills. Perhaps more striking, the sphere of policy and state administration has become a narrow professional specialty.

To emphasize these tendencies is not to say that the "traditional" characteristics of the intelligentsia are not correlated with modern political or scientific skills. They probably are. Likewise, the professional expert in state administration might very well be a critical intellectual, but he is definitively not expected to behave like one in his role as an expert. It is important for the analysis of intellectuals and intellectual work in modern society to view these tendencies as mirroring structural changes that have taken place during the course of "modernization," profoundly changing the relationships between intellectual work and the surrounding society. In addition, it is important to analyze the specifically modern form of intellectual work.

One can of course question whether professionalization and specialization are to be regarded as the "natural consequence" of the development of modern society, the complicated structure of which requires the same kind of specialized, vertical and horizontal division of intellectual work required in all other work. In order to answer this question, we need to look behind the appearance and into the essence of this side of societal development. This development appears common to all industrialized societies, but it does not take the same form in all societal contexts. The structure of ideological and knowledge utilization is determined by a broader context, which shapes the social need for a given service. There must, in other words, exist a "client" for intellectual, professionalized service if it is to become professionalized, just as there must be a demand for the scientific-professionalized behavior of the applied practitioners if they are to become academized. Such a client is a societal product, created in a specific socioeconomic history and ideological climate.[10] The problem field delimited by the process of professionalization of intellectual work should, therefore, be analyzed through a closer look at the different social and cultural contexts in which intellectual work is carried out, as well as at the content of the ideas inherent in different intellectual work and the social values held by those occupational groups that are engaged in intellectual activities.

CONCLUDING REMARKS CONCERNING THE SOCIOLOGY OF INTELLECTUALS AND INTELLECTUAL WORK

Theories of a new class of intellectuals bring out several important issues in contemporary society and in social science itself.

One issue is related to the basis of class theory. The dilemmas that tend to emerge in an attempt to deal with intellectual work within the framework of classical class analysis perhaps do not imply a total revision of this classical scheme. However, rather than centering the arguments on why, how, and if intellectual workers constitute a class, it might be as fruitful to look at other features of the intelligentsia. Rather than focusing on their nonintellectual interests (to valorize their human capital, for example), we might do better to concentrate on the cultural and political life of this stratum. It would be fruitful to look at the life-styles and attitudes of intellectual workers and, above all, at the qualitative aspects of their socialization in order to better understand their functions— as well as their relations to the class structure in society.

Another topic brought up at least indirectly by the theorists of the new class is related to the fate of the "traditional" intellectual, an idea that continues to have a hold on our intellectual culture. One of the consequences of the process of professionalization and specialization of intellectual work seems to be that this traditional sociocritical intellectual role is somewhat squeezed, on one side by disciplinized science and on the other by an increasingly professionalized polity. Since the ideas and values that the traditional idea of the intellectual crystallizes—not only among intellectuals themselves but also among a wider segment of society—are still so forceful, the erosion of the traditional role might be an important reason to analyze more profoundly its modern conditions.

These topics open up the more general question of the conditions of intellectual development in relation to societal development. It has been suggested that the professionalization of intellectual work is both part of and the result of the increasing rationalization and bureaucratization of modern society. Included in this development is the hierarchical organization of intellectual work, in which decisions are made from above and which is characterized by a horizontal compartmentalization that defines its proper areas of operation. The role of science was rather crucial in this development: here, the development of science can also serve as an illustrative case.

The disciplinization of abstract knowledge tends to give rise to relatively stable structures inside the context of scientific-knowledge production.[11] Part of these structural differences between disciplines can be explained by referring to the task division among the sciences themselves. In the course of their development, different sciences "react" upon reality by mirroring different aspects of it, giving it different principles of order. Parts of this order, however, are also "implicit," not only in the disciplinary structure itself but also in the social and cultural context. The general process of the demarcation of science from other intellectual endeavors as well as the process of the enclosure of aspects of reality must be looked at in relation to the function of science in modern societal development and against its broader context of utilization. The function of the technical and applied natural sciences and the relation to their context of utilization is perhaps the most obvious.

For the social sciences the context of economic-political development as well as of an ideological structure is probably of special importance in making up a broader "utilization context." For the humanities, the cultural climate as well as the ideological context probably define both the contents of these disciplines and the boundaries between them and other types of cultural and ideological activities in society to a greater degree than does the economic and technological structure of modern society. On the whole, most of the humanities and social sciences show somewhat more distinctive "cultural differences" in what is included and how it is dealt with than do the more "universal" and technostructure-oriented natural sciences. This might have some relevance for the understanding of intellectual work in general, since the humanities and social sciences seem to be the scientific activities most related to other types of intellectual activity outside science itself.

This suggests that there exist (besides a certain "uniformity" leading to "restrictedness") important cultural differences in the role and function of intellectual work. For example, there is a difference between the status and role of intellectuals in the East and the West. In Eastern Europe the transformation and modernization process, however fundamental it may be, seems to have left large pockets of traditional, high-status intellectuals who have, among other things, been responsible for dissent against Soviet rule and for the various changes that have resulted because of this. In the West, the comparable role of intellectuals seems to be a bit different, at least in appearance.

To conclude, while the processes of socialization, professionalization, and specialization of intellectual work can be regarded as somewhat general tendencies in the industrialized world, the specific result of the process in each society—and not only in different political contexts—is a unique mixture of cultural, political, and economic processes. In order to understand both its generalities and particularities, as well as the inner conditions of the development of intellectual discourse, I would like to propose that more studies be done which focus on the interior structures and development of intellectual life as well as on the social institutions within which it evolves. This should be done in a comparative perspective. Likewise, we need more studies that focus on the social conditions of different types of intellectual work as well as on the fields for the utilization of ideas and knowledge in different spheres of society. The meaningfulness and position of intellectuals can only be gauged in their social settings and measured in accord with the content of their ideas concerning the type of relationship that exists between the articulators and their societal context.

NOTES

I would like to thank Adam Westoby and an anonymous referee for valuable comments on a previous version and Ron Eyerman for comments on the language. This work has been supported by a grant from the Swedish Board of Higher Education.

1. A. Gouldner, *The Future of Intellectuals and the Rise of the New Class* (New York: Macmillan, 1979); G. Konrád and I. Szelényi, *The Intellectuals on the Road to Class Power* (Brighton: Harvester Press, 1979). See also I. Szelényi, "Gouldner's Theory of Intellectuals as a Flawed Universal Class," and C. Disco, "The Educated Minotaur: The Sources of Gouldner's New Class Theory," *Theory and Society*, no. 6 (1982). See also the contribution by Disco in this volume.

2. A representative for these theorists is the (once radical) social scientist Daniel Bell. See D. Bell, *The Coming of the Post-Industrial Society: A Venture in Social Forecasting* (London: Heinemann, 1974).

3. J. Benda, *La Trahison des Clercs* (Paris, 1927).

4. R. Aron, *The Opium of the Intellectuals* (New York: Norton, 1962).

5. N. Chomsky, *American Power and the New Mandarins* (New York: Vintage 1967).

6. R. Debray, *Le pouvoir intellectuel en France* (Paris: Ramsay, 1979).

7. K. Fridjónsdóttir, *Vetenskap och politik* [Science and politics] (Stockholm: Akademilitteratur, 1983), chap. 2.

8. M. Weber, ''Der Sinn der 'Wertfreiheit' der Soziologischen und Ökonomischen Wissenschaften,'' *Gesammelte Aufsätze zur Wissenschaftslehre*, Tübingen, 1968.

9. Cf. Debray, *Le pouvoir intellectuel*.

10. This is discussed by Sarfatti-Larson in her comparative analysis of professions in American society. A profession-to-be must standardize the production of professionals. This explains why higher education becomes such a necessary link toward professionalization. Moreover, the profession's ideology and standardized knowledge must conform to the social order. Dominant values put a constraint on the definition of professional competence. Thus, the structure of professionalization binds together ''a body of relatively abstract knowledge, susceptible of practical application, and a market—the structure of which is determined by economic and social development and also by the dominant ideological climate at a given time.'' M. Sarfatti-Larson, *The Rise of Professionalism* (Berkeley, Los Angeles, London: University of California Press, 1977), p. 40.

11. Cf. R. Whitley, *The Intellectual and Social Organization of the Sciences* (Oxford: Oxford University Press, 1984).

7

Mental Work, Education, and the Division of Labor

Adam Westoby

This paper addresses problems of characterizing modern intelligentsias indirectly. It outlines the changes in occupational structure and economic activity which mark the increasing importance of knowledge in social reproduction, sketching comparisons and contrasts with industrialization, and proposing—schematically—the significance of some microsocial mechanisms involved in the bureaucratic division of mental work. Its concluding remarks criticize ideas of knowledge as ''capital'' or as inhering in a ''new class.''

Its arguments bear on a number of questions discussed by other contributors: the distinctiveness, subdivisions, and cohesion of the higher educated, reviewed by Edmund Dahlström;[1] their political stances and potentialities; contrasts of ''technical'' with ''social'' knowledge; and the social renewal and extension of knowledge. Compression, however, means that others' arguments are introduced almost by allusion.[2]

OCCUPATIONAL SHIFTS

Two developments have paralleled each other in the twentieth century. The expansion of education has made schooling virtually universal, and higher education rather general, in industrially developed societies. Occupational structures have undergone congruent transformations in these societies. The proportion of jobs involving higher education has greatly increased, while physical labor accounts for a much diminished proportion of the total. Within these overall shifts, the "educated middle classes," living by salaried employment on the basis of specialist formal education, have grown from a very small to a sizable minority within the social structure. They form the core of what is meant by a "knowledge class," a "new class," and so on.

It is worth looking at these developments from the point of view of the long-term development of the overall division of labor. The growth of the educated middle classes stems from two combined aspects of economic development: the relative importance of their "outputs" has greatly expanded, while the productivity of their labor has increased only slowly, and their productivity *relative* to other forms of labor has thus declined. The effects amplify each other, and together they yield a great expansion of "educated labor" within both the labor force and society as a whole.

These assertions are easier to recognize than to prove, since they invite quantification but are applied to a portion of the labor force where the definition, not to mention the measurement, of "output" is extremely problematic. But comparisons are possible with the earliest great structural changes in society. Industralization saw the shift of a very large proportion of the population from an agricultural existence (preindustrial society) to manual wage labor in industry (industrial society). Now, increasingly, the shift is from manual to nonmanual and/or mental work and from the production of goods to services (post-industrial society).

Industrialization entailed an enormous magnification in the productivity of manual labor. It involved the almost total substitution of machine power for animal and human power and the subsequent transfer to machines of *control* over repetitive tasks that were simple enough, at any given stage in the development of technology, to be so transferred. The industrial worker thus became more and more a controller of increasingly sophisticated and expensive technology. The present phase centers on the application of a rapidly cheapening digital-computer technology, with machines (robots) that can imitate complex operations and that allow for an increasing range of characteristics in a changing environment. These machines are beginning to undertake tasks that previously required rather skilled manual workers.

Are analogous processes transforming mental labor? Only in part. The more routine it is and the more it involves formally standardizable operations, the more it may be substituted. For example, machine-readable information is now general in financial services and is on the way to becoming so in large-scale retailing. Electronic text-handling is rapidly replacing typing and, to some extent, document storage and transmittal. (The advent of reliable voice-inputting of text would threaten a further revolution in secretarial occupations.) But within other large areas of mental work, no such possibilities are imminent. In some, the pressures themselves are opposite. Many public-education systems, prodded by their teaching professions, have embraced as a long-term goal the *raising* of teacher-student ratios, and to this is added the relative growth of higher and postcompulsory education, with higher staffing levels. And, in many other areas, the element of judgment-flowing-into-response on the part of the human worker, along with the education and experience necessary for making these judgments and responses, rules out the automation of jobs' core functions.

Thus, while the numbers employed in routine manual tasks in manufacturing and agriculture shrinks, the numbers of teachers, technical and scientific workers, professional and administrative staffs of numerous sorts, writers and cultural workers, and so on rise. The occupational structure shifts in a manner comparably drastic to that which the earlier phases of industrialization saw. This is what is meant by "postindustrialism," and at its center is the growth of what is sometimes called the "knowledge class."

This shift results from two distinguishable processes superadded to each other: the relative *decline* in the productivity of the knowledge class, resulting mainly from the absolute increase in the productivity of manual labor, and the relative expansion of demand for their efforts. But both of these secular changes are complex. There is, first, the difficulty of comparing outputs over time when both their characteristics and their relative prices change greatly. Changes over several decades in the output of the manufacturing industry can be only very crudely conceived of as quantitative rises in productivity per employee. Much of what is produced in the most developed economies had no close relatives at the turn of the century. But this is only part of the problem of making analogous comparisons for mental labor. Economic theory suggests that if the relative productivity of a factor of production falls, the volume of it employed—and perhaps also its price—should diminish. I will return below to the connections among education, mental work, and earnings, but as far as volume is concerned there has been a relative increase in the numbers of people in "educated" work.

The reasons lie in the evolution of the total labor process, of which changes in manufacturing are only part. Take, for instance, an automated paper mill, costing hundreds of millions of dollars, which processes logs into newsprint twenty-four hours a day and is overseen by a small staff of cleaners and supervisors. Compared with earlier technology in the industry, this change is merely an extreme case of the general tendency in manufacturing to raise productivity through higher capital-labor ratios. But the improved capital equipment and associated systems themselves depend on increasing inputs of mental labor (for example, into research, design and development, and planning and administration). To provide these inputs, they depend on increasing expenditure and employment, education, training, etc.

Rising capital-labor ratios are one expression of a more general phenomenon that has been seen as the increasing roundaboutness of economic activity or as the rising proportion of embodied labor to direct labor. The initial industrial revolution also involved such a change. The application of machine power and heavy equipment to manufacture meant that an increased proportion of the labor force became employed in making producer rather than consumer goods.

From the shifts associated with postindustrialism we may draw out two general trends that increase the ratio of educated labor: first, its increasing share as an input, both as research and development and through the increasing relative weight of the control functions of organization and administration; and second, preceding these, the increasing proportion of labor which is employed (largely by the state) in maintaining and reproducing the laborers, the population, and the social organism (e.g., health and social services, education, and civil and social administration). Together, these trends mean that the production of both labor and other goods is becoming more and more intensive of educated labor. If, then, we speak of the rise of a knowledge class, it must be understood that its roots lie as much in production as in distribution or in control over it.

HUMAN CAPITAL

The members of a proliferating family of approaches to problems of the higher educated within the social structure base themselves on notions of "capital" (human, intellectual, cultural, symbolic—indeed, the phrase "human capital" has slid into more-or-less casual academic use). This is done, for example, by sociologists and social historians looking at cultural inheritance. They share, I think, family deficiencies, but in the context of economic development it is right to start with the more "economic" facets. These take concepts of labor and capital—the economics of the industrial revolution and the sociology deriving from it—and apply them to differences among workers arising from different educational preparations in the most technically advanced contemporary societies. The notion of human capital is shared by modern neoclassical economists and Marxist critics of Marxism (of which Machajski remains a good example).[3] This notion seeks to explain the higher earnings of the more educated relative to the lower earnings of the less educated. In each case the explanation is provided by theoretically endowing each educated worker with a portion of human capital. (Connected notions, such as "skill assets," seek to circumvent some of the problems associated with capital in economic theory.) In the eyes of the neoclassicals, this raises the productivity of their labor, which their earnings reflect, and human capital has thus been entered as a factor in production functions.

For Machajski, who denied the possibility of measuring individual workers' productivities, "intellectual capital" gave its possessors a share in the total social surplus along with the possessors of physical capital. Machajski provided both an elaboration and a critique of Marx, who, he held, accurately analyzed the exploitative relationships of capital to labor but only recognized the case of physical capital. Marx's category of "abstract labor" and his simplifying assumption that labor is all paid the same drew a veil over exploitation by intellectual capital, of which he was an ideological representative. (Machajski's resort to a purely distributive notion of intellectual capital is echoed by, for example, Alvin Gouldner, who cites Fisher's neoclassical definition of capital as a socially enforceable claim on an income stream.)[4]

The two approaches, though logically distinct, entail similar predictions concerning the economic effects of the expansion of qualified "brainworkers" as a proportion of the work force. Other things being equal, this implies a fall in the earnings of the highly skilled relative to those of the less skilled: in the first case because the marginal productivity of human capital declines, and in the second because a greater number of intellectual capitalists must share their fraction of the social surplus. If such falls have not occurred this would, again, be for similar reasons: in the first case because techniques and patterns of final demand have changed so as to raise the demand for educated labor by at least as much as its supply has increased, and in the second because technical progress has increased the total social surplus available to "intellectual capitalists" by an amount sufficient to prevent the portion from going to any one recipient of it falling (and, perhaps, because intellectual capital's share of the total social surplus has increased).

LABOR

The two approaches also have wider things in common. Both attack the question of educational differentiation from the point of view of labor and the social relations into which it enters. The higher educated produce and/or are paid more through their labor, thus establishing for themselves a different place within the economy, and their social differentiation begins from this. They live better, freer lives; reproduce and extend from generation to generation their command over culture; have richer, more varied and autonomous patterns of consumption; and acquire the social and political skills to establish hegemony, often almost a monopoly of actual power, within political processes very broadly defined. The argument, or argument-description, starts from labor and its characteristics (theoretically amalgamating it with a portion of capital) but makes its way into areas of psychological and/or social life which are not especially closely connected with labor. Is this, indeed, the best starting point?

"Labor," as a central category of social thought, was a by-product of the industrial revolution. Wage-labor came to be employed in interchangeable ways and in large aggregates. For industrial workers, labor time came to be separated from leisure, and its duration came to be internally structured to a far greater degree than had been the case for previous laboring classes. The factory hooter at each end of the shift severed the periods when the economy claimed the worker from those when (within the limits of his income and the law) he was his own master. Internally, labor power (measured by duration in time) was forced to adapt to the rhythms of the machine, the factory, and in due course to the scientifically designed labor process. Physical fitness, stamina, dexterity, and attention were required of the worker; complex intellectual operations or judgments, still less the expression of attitudes or sympathies, were not. The vacuous "freedom" of the worker in his leisure time was the obverse of his detailed enslavement during working time—unlike the situation of artisan or peasant, for whom the line between labor and leisure was far more blurred and who worked or relaxed according to the seasons, the weather, and the work to be done, remaining responsible for a wholer task. Above, and regimenting, the army of industrial wage workers—or biological machines—was a thin stratum of technicians, managers, and so on, assisted by foremen.

The concept of abstract labor, and of labor power as the commensurable essence underlying the calculi of values, expresses this model of industrial society in one of its purest forms. Two questions arise from it. First, how widely did it ever hold true? This, though important in itself, has only an indirect bearing on the category of "labor" in social thought; theory has inertias independent of realism. Raphael Samuel has argued that the British industrial revolution gave rise to a myriad of new skills to replace those it destroyed—mainly in making and servicing the equipment on which the process workers were employed; what "deskilling" meant was the displacement of earlier, more integrated, skills.[5] Perhaps what "abstract labor" reflects is also industrialism's urge to confer on workers the features it most values in machines: interchangeability, reliability, invariance over time, etc.

The second, more important, question is: How much can such a category of labor form the explanatory starting point for social differentiation today? Here it is clear that the concept has been eroded both from within and without. Internally, a very high proportion of work is now not closely disciplined by industrial tempi. It involves reflection and judgment, imponderable before being pondered, in order to define and execute its tasks. To bind it to a closely predetermined sequence of operations would at best drastically reduce its effectiveness and at worst lead to technical or operational catastrophes. The professional, it has been observed, is paid for his intentions, not his results. But the softening of external discipline which this implies now extends to a very large proportion of employees, not only in higher intellectual work but also in a multitude of operations, especially in services (the main growth area of less qualified employment). In services, the necessary combination of physical operations and planning, mental, and literary functions cannot be effectively substituted for by mechanical devices or bureaucratization. Delivery milkmen are a good case in point. For Britain, at least, these milkmen are now a larger part of the labor linking cow to consumer than are dairypersons.

BOUNDARIES OF LABOR TIME

Marx spoke not only of "abstract labor" but also of the quantum of it that was "socially necessary." That, too, presupposes a division between labor and nonlabor which is now often blurred. Consider a junior social worker, commuting an hour each way from a suburban home to a high-unemployment inner-city community center. On the train or bus he or she reads *The Guardian, New Society,* or another of the journals favored by the caring professions. Compare this social worker's activity with that carried out in mining villages, where wives put the kettle on at the sound of the pithead siren. Is the social worker's commuting "socially necessary"? Rather clearly, it is. If, in some vast thought-experiment, we removed the time and resources absorbed by transportation to work, the economic-geographic arrangements of society simply could not persist.

Not only the physical activity of commuting from home to work but also the social worker's mental activity is socially necessary. Reading keeps him or her in touch with the content, vocabulary, concepts, and metaphors of a body of knowledge and opinion which is, in one sense, professional but which also extends into the general culture of the social worker's stratum. While few of the items read would, if omitted, greatly affect this or that operation of this person's work (with reports of legal or administrative changes being a possible exception), taken as a whole this reading *is* "socially necessary." Without a familiarity with the news as presented in a "serious" newspaper (with focus in particular areas) and without some background reading in more specialist publications, the social worker would operate in his or her medium considerably less effectively. The same applies to a large proportion of government officers, to much of middle and upper management in the private sector, to teachers, to many of those in the social-service professions and to a number of their paramedical relatives, to public relations personnel, and, of course, to members of the media themselves. It is not only the poorly literate who have difficulty functioning in society. The inability to participate adequately in a (focused) area of general culture produced *for* you and offered *to* you, but not by you, is also, for an increasing proportion of the population, a basic handicap.

This need has in turn generated an industry around the media which is concerned with the popularization and predigestion of ideas for those who use them in employment. And, for those whose life-styles require the regular consumption of information, the time and effort needed to identify and retrieve relevant information from the much larger competing flux must be added to the time necessary to digest it. "Internal" and "external" erosion flow into each other. Externally, the division between working and leisure time breaks down for an increasing proportion of mental or cultural workers. Time spent with newspapers, books, television, and even with the plastic and performing arts feeds into the working process. Take it away and that process itself would suffer significant interference. *On* the job, a large proportion of time is spent in conversing, waiting, and arranging or on other activities not closely determined from outside. Supervision cannot be precise because what is done is too various, ill defined, and irregular. Close supervision worked when workers were closely integrated adjuncts of machines. Since parts of the machine system were endowed with a will to act and fallibility, discipline was necessary in order to prevent malfunctions on their part from interfering with the overall process. As one moves farther from this model it becomes less possible (a) to control according to fixed, repetitive criteria, and, consequently, (b) to allocate labor in accordance with a calculus of labor time expended. The more that supervision is of a "loose-rein" variety, the greater becomes the importance of directing labor according to tasks and goals rather than to expenditure of time.

Another way of expressing this development is that living labor is now reabsorbing its "labor of supervision"—a function severed from many workers in the industrial revolution. Automation and computer control mean that operations that can be supervised according to explicit, repetitive criteria are done far more cheaply by machines than by persons. What remains are more unpredictable tasks. The "return to craft methods" does not generally involve individuals producing directly for the market; much employment remains organized in large agglomerations. But it does entail a return in the sense that the individual worker must have rather generalized goals and tasks set and then must be permitted a wide choice in how, in what sequence, and through what subgoals these are realized. This results primarily from technique, not from social relations, and therefore imposes broadly similar stresses on both planned and market economies.

There is a similarity with workers in highly automated industrial processes: the worker does not contribute continuous activity but rather attention and readiness to take action when automatic systems alert him. Such a worker is "on duty" rather than "at work." His inactive time is nonetheless necessary for effective performance. This he has in common with the least-supervised mental workers (such as university teachers), whose slack regimens and ample time for relaxation are (whatever the appearances) essential to the job and resistive in the extreme to administrators' pleas for closer accountability. More generally, efforts to improve the productivity of secretarial-administrative-clerical workers by boosting the time spent in handling cases or typing relative to that spent in discoursing or drinking coffee generally fail—despite the impressive promises of time and motion studies—to boost output correspondingly. The attempt to eliminate "wasted time" generates indifference, slowing down, falloff of quality, and more frequent repetition, which go a long way to counteract it. All of this follows from the difficulty of defining and enforcing detailed goals/tasks.

WORK AND THE PERSON

This makes it sound as though the modern mental worker gets the best of both worlds: a return to the autonomy and pride in work of the preindustrial craftsman—retrospectively celebrated by both conservative and socialist critics of industrialism—together with salaried employment and shelter from the market currents that buffeted traditional artisans. But the comparison is illusory, arising from overgeneralized description. Most preindustrial crafts had their *deformations professionelles*—failing sight, bent back, tannin poisoning. Does modern, loosely supervised mental work deform the human animal less? Physically, yes; the Dickensian office, being so inefficient, is a thing of the past. But psychologically? From an evolutionary point of view, man is distinguished by adaptability, and the largest part of this is now psychological. Erect posture and the opposable thumb were the keys to the birth of technology, but language, literacy, logic, and fertile and flexible analogical thinking now hold the center of the stage. Whether the loosening of supervision and the internalization of goals within mental work constitutes a realization or a cramping of human personality is not a straightforward question.

Gramsci was an enthusiast of Taylorism, not only (as Lenin was) because it raised productivity but also because, since it was so repetitive and reduced to such simple, "atomic" operations, it required minimal attention. The worker in the "scientific factory" could thus apply his mind to other things, becoming thoughtful, cultured, intellectually and spiritually autonomous: a "philosophical gorilla," nonchalantly attached to the machine. The image is a little farfetched. But we cannot even begin to think about it with respect to much mental work, which absorbs the worker's psyche and fragments it according to the goals at hand, whatever his intrinsic interest in them or the manner of their fulfillment. It is the worker's resistance to more complete appropriation of his psyche by the job which forms the chief barrier to streamlining such work. And, more generally, the friction imparts particular distortions to his view of the larger whole of which his goals form a part.

Yet subdivision of the larger task often coexists with requirements for higher education and extended experience in performing its parts. Mikhailovsky, a searching critic of the enthusiasm shown by Herbert Spencer (and, later, by the Russian Marxists of the 1890s) for progressive differentiation and specialization, nonetheless thought an increasingly detailed *technical* subdivision of labor was very desirable. What he felt was so wrong was that each partial operation should be the permanent lot of one or another worker, the technical division of labor becoming frozen as its social division, turning the individual into a will-less "toe on the foot" of the complex social organism. Mikhailovsky's advocacy of an all-sided life moving between specialized *forms of labor* was certainly different from Marx's vision of a peripatetic hunter-philosopher in a plentied and laborless future.

While Mikhailovsky's project might once have been conceivable for much agricultural and industrial labor, it is certainly utopian for the modern occupations that require protracted formal education and long, sophisticated work experience. An increasing proportion of investment into individual psyches tends to entrench the technical division of labor as social. And Durkheim, who saw the industrial division of labor as more friend than enemy of individual personality, nonetheless stipulated rather tight conditions for the potential benefits of "organic solidarity" to be realized: that the individual worker consciously interact with his fellow workers and their needs and have a clear view of their common goals—conditions only very imperfectly met in much "educated" mental work.

The relationships of the modern educated worker to his employing organization partly parallel those of the "out-worker" during incipient capitalist industrialization. While the worker retained his skills and his control over the immediate shape of the labor process, the craftsman no longer worked directly for the end-user (i.e., the market or client). The "putter-out" decided on the overall purpose (the product) and distributed it; later, he came to provide the materials. The shift from "putting out" to full proletarianization as wage labor in larger workshops was a subsequent development, in which the capitalist extended his external control over the ends of work to internal control of labor processes and opened the way to a more developed division of labor within a unified organization, the factory.

Most educated workers today are employed by large organizations with elaborate internal divisions of labor, although the fact that what they process is generally information and documents may mean a greater dispersal of workplaces. (With cheaper and more powerful means of transmitting information, another regression toward the protoindustrial "out-worker" may emerge as employers economize on office rents by encouraging remote- or home-working.) Overall, however, the increasing division of labor is not heading back toward factory-style control. Though the pressures for it are omnipresent, the subjective obstacles to it also prove to be technical ones. While purposes and criteria may be defined, results (and the time necessary to achieve them) frequently cannot be: this follows from the specialized—or professional—division of intellectual labor.

BUREAUCRACY

The general social form that has evolved for raising the efficiency of mental labor is bureaucracy. Social and cognitive constraints combine in it to produce psychological (and some political) effects. Bureaucratization is the proletarianization of intellectual work but is limited to its exterior, not interior, control. Whenever an element of judgment is central which—no matter how mundane—cannot be standardized so as to be determinate, the human worker, and the elements of education necessary to judgment, are irreducible. The most that can be achieved is routinization—a key ingredient of bureaucracy. A rational division and redivision of tasks among operatives provides each of them with a more routine, faster-working process and thus raises the efficiency of the whole. As a technical advance this should not be compared to mechanization, still less to autonomation, but rather to the primitive division of manual labor brought within one organization, as in Adam Smith's pin factory. The individual worker—or unit—is made to place each case within the general category and to handle it according to predetermined principles. Where handling the category (or categorizing a case) exceeds the worker's competence, he passes it to a higher level, where more elaborate categories are applied to more varied and complex cases. The study of the general flow of cases (and of the flow of their failures to correspond with existing rules) is integrated with devising and modifying the rules as "policy," itself subject to bureaucratic organization. The system is "rational" in both of Weber's senses: impartial, and hence more efficient. However, to put it very simply, the scope for improving efficiency is limited by the operatives. Bureaucracy does not involve the replacement of living labor by machinery. Past labor can be substituted for present labor only to the extent that it can be embodied and preserved in organizational structures and routines.

Bureaucracy has epistemological (or at least cognitive) as well as social and economic dimensions. One of its principles is the division of knowledge according to degree of generality or abstractness: the more senior workers deal with the more general, the less senior with the less so. Rules for general categories apply also to the subcategories within them. In practice, however, the knowledge of the more senior figures, who formulate the principles, is largely indirect: hence the central, ruling illusion of bureaucratic organization, that (as Marx put it in his critique of Hegel on the Prussian bureaucracy) "the top entrusts the understanding of detail to the lower levels, whilst the lower levels credit the top with understanding of the general, and so all are mutually deceived."[6]

Feelings and motivations

We may perhaps recognize within the abstract mechanics of bureaucratic labor one source of the blend of radical alienation with deliberated compliance which often characterizes the educated classes. Bureaucracy can act in a way similar to that of Lewis Feuer's conflict of generations, renewing the "ideologization" of the young in conflict with their seniors. Middle and lower functionaries are already equipped by initial education for the higher posts they aspire to. What separates them are those infuriating intangibles of time and experience. They are wedded by avocation to the worldview that rational bureaucratic organization can accomplish most things. Credentialed official status already sets them off from the mass of the population, who are objects, not officers, of bureaucracies. Yet their day-to-day experience is dominated by the showering down of irritants, problems, and delays, mainly due to the fact that the general rules enunciated above them fit, but only very imperfectly, the specificities of the cases they handle. This has two sometimes simultaneous effects.

One effect is that it grinds and smooths the personality, defusing emotions, tempering frustration, inducing a more detached view of others and their motives, and encouraging convenient hypocrisy or fudging. This erosion and reshaping of the psyche is an essential part of the "experience," which may be acquired slowly or quickly but which is vital to most forms of bureaucratic promotion. However, the cascade of imperfect experience, in wearing down the flinty juvenocratic surfaces, can also strike sparks. The bureaucrat's sense of autonomous expertise within his own domain is easily magnified, engendering the feeling that those at the top are incompetent or, worse, that the organization—and perhaps the society of which it is part—is subject to fundamental malfunction, and that if only those who really understood matters were in charge, things could be revolutionized for the better. The structure of bureaucracy asserts itself as a necessary illusion: the knowledge and control of complex processes, which can only exist as socially divided, *appear* to those who handle them through forms of knowledge that have grown up around the single knower. Their compartmentalization thus appears as a defect of rationality—rather as, seen up close, the fragmentation of a mosaic may appear to be a general blemish.

Of course, fragmentation and its frictions are real, not merely illusory problems, and all bureaucratic organizations include or develop means of compensating for them. Perhaps the most important is the committee: a forum in which departmental perceptions and interests are reconciled, grievances are ventilated, feathers are both ruffled and smoothed, individuals and their ambitions are selected and assessed, and, more formally, in which goals and principles of the right degree of generality and ambiguity are evolved and made binding. The precise character of committee arrangements within systems of divided intellectual labor naturally varies with many factors: the extent of specialization among the functions that are to be coordinated and the importance of the creative and unanticipatable within them, the organization's ethos of authority and its mechanics of career development, and the degree to which the organization's objectives are complex, multiple, ambiguous, changing, and determined outside itself.

Bureaucratic hierarchies and committee arrangements are only two examples of the machinery through which the social division of intellectual work is organized. But they are central (what bureaucratic administration fundamentally *means*, Weber held, is the domination of knowledge),[7] and together they suggest the extent of psychic molding involved. Its two principal sides are a pronounced, frequently very narrow, specialization and an equally pronounced formalization and homogenization of communications and relationships. (There is an analogy with the heightened specialization of industrial labor, achieved only by the general circulation of the one purely formal and homogeneous commodity, money.)

The need for integrable psychological shapes engendered by the division of intellectual work takes active as well as merely selective forms. The human appetite for direct, substantial, emotionally charged relationships with others, continuously bred—through the family, for example—even into the educated population must be blunted and reconciled to the needs of organizational life. Hence the provision of, as well as specific training for, organizational lubricants: education, conditioning, sometimes therapy, for the "interpersonal relations" (the phrase itself testifies to the reification of others and relationships with them) which are widely experienced as opaque and threatening.

Such sensations, united to frequently narrow specialization, exacerbate the individual's feelings of dissatisfaction with his or her actual situation. The alienation of intellectual workers is not necessarily less than that of those in more routine tasks, but it takes different forms. While the process worker sharply counterposes work to leisure and seeks escape from the former into the latter, the higher intellectual worker's wishfulness is directed more toward those posts he perceives as kindlier to his preferences and autonomy and as more open in scope—that is, generally more senior. Thus, affective pressures cohere with the cognitive sources of bureaucratically engendered radicalism in a general tendency toward upward escapism.

Microeconomic mechanisms complete the functional picture. The modern division of intellectual work, like any other division, requires not only principles of functional design and appropriately formed human types but also specific means of meshing the individual's efforts into the overall process. As with most modern forms of labor, the basic link is the individual wage. But again there exists a limitation, within the "technical" characteristics of the work: the difficulty of defining and measuring performance. Labor is a commodity, but unlike with any other commodity, the buying and using of it are not separable but are part of the same process; labor is active in its own sale. In much manual work, control of the labor activity and purchase of the labor power can be linked together in a more direct way, since generally its functions are more easily conceptualized, checked, and measured, and payment can be geared to them. Piecework is the quintessence of these possibilities, but many forms of labor supervision and discipline embody them. The division of the more complex forms of intellectual work, however, is different, since most "outputs" cannot be known in advance (if the results of intellectual labor could be known in advance, it would not be necessary). Gearing the employee's activity to the purchasing of his labor must therefore be less direct, not via results but through ex post facto assessments of competence, efforts, intentions, and their more-or-less subjective (if highly formalized) validation—credentialism, referees, staff reporting systems, and so on. There thus emerges, superimposed on the pay system, the promotion system as the typical framework of incentives facing the individual worker. Microeconomic structures, reinforcing the epistemological itch to substitute oneself at the central levers of command, align themselves with the conditions of bureaucratic escapism and radicalism.

At the root of economic theories of human capital lies the well-known correlation of income with level of (initial, formal) education. The widespread existence of hierarchies of pay and promotion, corresponding to hierarchies of (at least imputed) knowledge and competence, offers an alternative viewpoint on this—and, perhaps, on the incompleteness of the correlation and the increased significance of age at the higher educational levels: the gradient of the cross-sectional mean age-earnings profile is typically steepest for tertiary education and peaks latest, in late middle age.

The effects of promotion systems, contrasted with explanations based on the idea that additional education raises the productivity of individual workers by providing them with extra human capital, lead to an interesting question: How far should pay increments arising within promotion structures be considered as the distribution of part of a social surplus? (It should be added that within centrally planned economies affluence turns less on money income and more on nonmarket forms of distribution—forms that are also institutionally aligned with bureaucratic status.) Within a highly integrated division of labor it is difficult to test directly the notion that individuals' earnings differences reflect the marginal productivities of their labor. However, the system of incentives and promotion *is* socially necessary in order to elicit satisfactory performance from individual functionaries—including not only performance of their immediate responsibilities but also, in an adequate proportion of cases, assimilation of the experience and loyalty needed for more senior positions. Promotion practices themselves testify to the inseparability of labor's characteristics from the wider mental and spiritual life of the laborer.

CONCEPTS

Study of the modern educated middle classes is now conceptually congested. The competition among concepts suggests that none has yet succeeded in establishing a secure niche; not only is there overcrowding but competing ideas also interpenetrate and overlap. Reviews of the field are untidy and tend to be unsatisfactory taxonomies of concepts.

Thomas Söderqvist has urged that microsociological studies be designed to investigate how knowledge enters into individual relations and, in particular, the nature of "knowers'" domination over those who know less (of professional over client, priest over believer, etc.). More generally, he has reminded us in this of the important principle that micromechanisms and macroconcepts should cohere.[8] May we not apply this (with other principles of conceptual selection) among the various descendants and modifications of the idea of "human capital" which now contend? To the economic version first advanced by Machajski have been added variants—distinguishing symbolic, cultural, intellectual, technical, and other types of capital—which attenuate the link with higher earnings and stress different types of knowledge, educational advantage, noneconomic social relations, and so on. Yet even among the more attenuated versions (such as Ivan

Szelényi and Bill Martin's)[9] the call is to be heard from an integrated theory of capital, which would draw money capital and forms of symbolic capital within one framework.

The prospect is tempting. In its favor are the several points in which such "capital" resembles the capital accumulated during industrialization: it is the present embodiment of past, "dead" activity; it represents the private appropriation of social effort; possession of it is the basis of a socially recognized stream of income and other benefits; and it enhances the capacities of labor. Also in its favor is the fact that it engenders among its possessors both mutual competition and a certain esprit de corps vis-à-vis the rest of the world. But these characteristics are not peculiar to capital: it shares them with socially produced private property of many sorts. And a noticeable esprit de corps is also characteristic of a number of noncapitalist propertied classes. The force of treating individual specialized knowledge as capital, therefore, must be found elsewhere.

If notions of human capital are to be more than a metaphor, they must bring it within the same (or a congruent) theoretical framework as money and physical capital, showing that the same or analogous microsocial processes are involved. And here the real difficulties begin, since the basis of capital as a *distinct* category is the separation of the laborers from the nonhuman means of production, the freeing of both into the market, the appropriation of a social surplus through command of the means of production, and, thus, the self-moving and unbounded accumulation of value, the ground of the technical and social transformations wrought by modern capitalism.

The same distinctive characteristics do not apply to human capital, in any of its variants, and it is difficult to think of analogous ones that would permit the integration of both forms of capital within a single analytical framework. There is no market in human capital as such; it cannot be separated from labor. True, it exhibits continuous accumulation, but this is not of the same type, nor is it capable of the same phenomena of concentration, as conventional capital.

We may be warned, perhaps, by attempts to convert the notion of capital to fit communist or socialist societies in "state" capitalism. Here, too, the problems that capital goods are not exchanged (except technically) and that capitals do not compete have elicited various surrogate devices—for example, the argument that national capitals compete not economically but through arms competition. But in such conversions what disappears is precisely the coherence of macrosocial concepts with microsocial mechanisms and their structures of motivation, which is what gives capital and its related concepts their force.

Of any dynamic macrosocial model it may be asked, How does the expanding self-reproduction of the system form the basis of a historical transformation? Accounts of conventional capitalist industrialization are all, in a sense, "demand led": factory manufacture is more efficient than, and thus expands to supplant, existing forms of production. Capital's expansion creates the proletariat it requires, largely from the rural population. The change cannot be understood just as a change in the ratios of existing occupational categories: industrial wage-laborers and capitalists are defined by relations that are both technically and socially new.

Similarly, with what we call (in shorthand) the advent of "knowledge society" and the "new class," the change in occupational proportions is more symptomatic than fundamental. The underlying transformation consists not simply of a shift in the proportion of people who have specialized knowledge but also of the new centrality of the structures of socially objectified knowledge—a point registered from different angles by various writers (for example, Richta et al.'s view of science as the main productive force, or Daniel Bell's account of knowledge as the "axial principal" of postindustrial society).[10] Society's self-reproduction centers increasingly on the use of its collective cognitive equipment. This includes renewing, updating, modifying, extending, preserving, and retrieving knowledge—and (since the social sphere endures while individuals are finite) preparing other people to undertake these activities. Their increasingly specialized character corresponds not only to the increasing coverage and complexity of theoretical knowledge but also to the progressive "crystallizing out" and internal subdivision of knowledge-handling and controlling functions, largely corresponding to the spread of bureaucratic organization. As social knowledge ramifies, an increasing proportion of the effort spent on it, much of it as paid employment, is directed "inward" rather than at its "applications" (although, as the change progresses, the distinction is of diminishing use).

Education is part of the internal renewal of social knowledge. Paid work teaching others is only one fraction of the social effort that goes into it. An increasing period of early life is spent in learning. In addition, as Weber reminds us, much knowledge of formal organizations is of structure, procedures, precedents, and so on and is acquired during adult life; gaining it must also be included in the time costs of social reproduction. Such forms of learning are increasingly being separated into the institutional forms of in-service training and continuing education, and the social effort required for them—along with the other functions of "maintaining" knowledge mentioned above—is increased by the fact that this knowledge is continually being added to and changed.

The transformation arising within and from the knowledge structure of society is, however, clear in static terms, without analyzing the effects of its dynamics. The growing proportion of human effort devoted to renewing the operating knowledge, and the limited scope for raising its productivity, imposes considerable strains. These are, however—crudely speaking—compensated for by one of the results (or by-products) of social knowledge: technical advances in material production. These free labor for the growing sectors, analogous to the effects of the modernization of agriculture in allowing urbanization.

Can the expansion of social knowledge be conceived of as the accumulation of a form of capital? And, its corollary question, can differential access to and facility with parts of it be conceived of as individuals' capital? Only, I think, as metaphor. It would be possible to list many basic points of difference. Knowledge, as intangible and universal, can only give rise to stretched and imperfect property rights. It cannot assume a full commodity form, and its circulation and expansion cannot rest fundamentally on exchange. New theoretical knowledge, for example, supplants and modifies the existing stock directly, not through devaluing it. And as far as the structures of motivation facing the individual "capital" are concerned, any similarities are superficial: to the essentially quantitative, unbounded expansion of money capital corresponds the qualitative and finite life, education, and career of the individual.

Of course, society's economic and cognitive relations *do* interpenetrate and mutually color one another. But this permits the import only of analogies. The antithesis of social and individual is central to the social structuring of knowledge, too, but here it takes forms *sui generis* to the ways in which it orders its diversity—forms that are only beginning to be investigated. The social division of knowledge, for example, also has its historical turning points, its "revolutions," but their main grounds lie in specifically cognitive (or linguistic) "technologies" (e.g., generalized alphabetic literacy, printing, or electronic communications). By a gentle irony, the attempt to analyze the knowledge structure of modern societies by attributing to the individual "capital," and related ideas of class membership, ignores Marx's caution that man cannot be understood as "squatting outside society."

POLITICS

For many writers (Bahro, for one, is an exception), questions of social structures and groupings have been dominated by discussion of criteria (education, forms of capital or of social closure, cultural or political dispositions, Bourdieu's theoreticizing, or Gouldner's culture of critical discourse) for demarcating or at least defining an intelligentsia grouping—in the limiting case, a constitutive (in Cornelis Disco's sense)[11] class-for-itself. The preoccupation with criteria of inclusion-exclusion reflects in part a lack of agreement on what the essential relations are, and in part a natural curiosity as to the social future coupled with the habit of thinking that changes arise from the conflicts of antagonistic groups.

This leads naturally to a concern with political proclivities. The rise of salaried- relative to self-employment among the higher educated, the exterior control of the goals of their work, and the sheer increase in their numbers has led to talk of their "proletarianization." And (though the argument of increasing misery is not deployed) the suggestion often stands that the educated classes could pick up the factory proletariat's traditional baton. The stress is on political radicalization through economic blockage and the experience of social subordination.

Views of the new-class, by contrast, tend to see its trajectory as following that of the revolutionary bourgeoisie. Machajski's expectation was that the educated strata would first ally with an established capitalism, then (through socialism, state ownership, and bureaucratic offices for the educated) supplant it as recipients of the social surplus. This sense persists in most usages, though it is often joined with the suggestion that the new class is "new" in having appropriated radical political initiative.

Hence, two different—and, in a sense, opposite—social and economic conceptions frequently lead to similar political predictions. One stresses the subordinate, prescribed character of much intellectual labor, the other its urge for dominance on the basis of rationality and expertise. As I have suggested above, these are features that, far from being mutually exclusive, tend within many systems of organizing intellectual work to mutually require each other. While many accounts present bureaucracy and radicalism as opposites, there is much evidence to suggest their symbiosis. Thus, for example, Lenin's early exegesis of his principles of party organization[12] depicts a well-formed pyramid, staffed by "intelligenti" and structured by committees. In this pyramid, instructions go downward and information flows upward. Modern organization theorists would find its problems instantly recognizable (these same problems appalled Russian revolutionaries at the turn of the century, not least by making a routine of their ethical calling). The example reminds us of how difficult it is to meet Szelényi's wish to explicate intelligentsia orientations toward capitalism and the market according to their type of symbolic capital. Pro- and anticapitalist attitudes—no less vehement for being hypothetical—sharply clashed and alternated among the Russian intelligentsia from the 1870s on. Although industrial development, accelerating sharply in the 1890s, undoubtedly swelled "technical" relative to "cultural" symbolic capital (to use Szelényi's terms), it is very doubtful that this produced a greater spirit of compromise toward money capital. Insofar as this *did* occur, it might be identified with the rise of liberalism, led by Struve (a quintessential case of "cultural" symbolic capital) in the early 1900s. But the differences between the support of the intelligentsia for the liberals, the socialist revolutionaries, or the social democrats (or, for that matter, the latter's two factions) correlate very poorly with "technical" versus "cultural" activity.

The example, and its problems, also remind us of the methodological division thrown into relief by Szelényi's "teleocratic" tendencies (which are generally political before they are redistributional) and, more generally, by subjective phenomena among the higher educated.[13] When viewing the higher-educated strata as a whole their dispositions tend to be explained functionally, or by group or class social interests. When, however, the focus narrows to sections of the higher "cultural intelligentsia" (from which, incidentally, almost all students of the subject are drawn), there is a striking turn to subjective interpretation—for example, toward the history of ideas, with social conditions providing the premises, but not the outcomes, of mental life. Of course, the distinction between the two approaches is less clearcut than I have summarily implied, but it is real, and they are some distance from satisfactory fusion. To establish the notion of a new class, for example, would seem to require not just social homogeneities but also efforts at collective self-definition. One could counter that the importance of mediating functions inhibit these, but this raises the question of whether knowledge and controlling functions are not now too deeply dispersed and diverse to define a distinct grouping.

Lastly, the study of the educated strata must come to grips with a paradox. The growth in their numbers is just one expression of society's increasing abundance of theoretical knowledge, leading to such conceptual suggestions as "surplus consciousness." But it has not led—as one might have supposed—to more love of abstract knowledge for its own sake. Although it is increasingly available, almost as a free good, the final demand for it has scarcely exploded.

Athenian intellectuals, living in a society in which practical knowledge led directly to personal and civic prosperity, readily accepted the idea that the ultimate purpose of knowledge was happiness. That attitude persisted in the tense relation of revelation to reason in the Western church, and continued into the industrial revolution (e.g., as the association of self-education with early socialism). Nowadays, however, despite the expansion of theoretical knowledge, attitudes toward it are overwhelmingly instrumental, a circumstance that underlies much cultural pessimism. One cause, at least, lies in the fact that modern knowledge is more socially divided and indirect. Today the Renaissance polymath is an impossibility, and the number of fields in which the individual can hold a candle to intellectual institutions diminishes; even philosophy has become subject to professionalization.

The better educated are certainly no exception to the general instrumentalization of knowledge. But neither should one look to them for a cure: their emergence is more effect than cause of the restructuring of society's knowledge. And, fortunately for them, they have too little cohesion to accept collective responsibility.

NOTES

1. Dahlström's contribution in this volume.

2. This paper has benefited greatly from discussions throughout the workshop at which it was originally presented.

3. The fullest account of Machajski's ideas is in Marshall S. Shatz, "J. W. Machajski and 'Makhaevshchina,' 1866–1926: Anti-intellectualism and the Russian intelligentsia" (Ph.D. diss., Columbia University, 1968).

4. Alvin Gouldner, *The Future of Intellectuals and the Rise of the New Class* (London: Macmillan & Co., 1979).

5. Raphael Samuel, "Workshop of the World: Steam Power and Hand Technology in Mid-Victorian Britain," *History Workshop* no. 3 (Spring 1977).

6. *Contribution to the Critique of Hegel's Philosophy of Law* (1843), in Marx-Engels, *Collected Works* (London: Lawrence and Wishart, 1975), pp. 46–47.

7. Max Weber, *Economy and Society*, vol. 1 (Berkeley, Los Angeles, London: University of California Press, 1978), p. 225.

8. "Informationssamfundets konfliktstruktur: fra makrosociologi til fölelesmaessig interaktion," in T. Söderqvist, ed, *Informationssamfundet* (Arhus, Denmark: Philosophia Förlag, 1985).

9. Szelényi and Martin's contribution in this volume.

10. Radovan Richta et al., *Science at the Crossroads* (White Plains, N.Y.: International Arts and Sciences Press, 1969); Daniel Bell, *The Coming of Post-Industrial Society* (London: Heinemann, 1974).

11. Disco's contribution in this volume.

12. "A letter to a Comrade on Our Organisational Tasks," in *Collected Works* (Moscow and London, 1961).

13. Szelényi and Martin's contribution in this volume.

8

Socialism and the Educated Middle Classes in Western Europe, 1870–1914

Carl Levy[1]

INTRODUCTION

This paper summarizes one of the main areas of study in an Open University project that is currently drawing to a close. We have sought to examine how far, and in what ways, the membership and activity of the educated middle classes shaped the development and policies of a range of European socialist and labor organizations during the period 1870–1914. In this paper I shall concentrate on a cross-national examination of the social composition of the socialist parties of four Western European case studies (Britain, France, Italy, and Germany), allowing myself occasional glances eastward to Russia and westward to North America.[2]

INTELLECTUALS, INTELLIGENTSIA, AND VARIETIES OF NATIONAL SOCIAL FORMATIONS: THE INHERITORS AND THE MERITOCRATS

It might be best to dispense with the ever-present controversy over the usage of the word *intelligentsia*. By now it is common-place to separate the Eastern intelligentsia from national groups of Western intellectuals. Thus, many writers differentiate the Eastern intelligentsia from the Western intellectuals by tracing the diverse occupational and cultural patterns allowed each respective group.

The argument goes like this: Western feudalism gradually disintegrated through the subversive influences of isolated urban cultures. The clerisy passed through an intermediate stage of patronage by liberal or enlightened despots, but finally modern intellectuals became dependent on a market economy that guaranteed them productive and socially integrative work. In the East, however, civil society was, to quote Antonio Gramsci, gelatinous: lacking independent and countervailing sources of power and income, the state became all-powerful, a rich civil society was missing, and the intelligentsia remained isolated from the Asiatic state but equally distant from the lower orders. A part of the intelligentsia finally secured its social and psychological moorings in the late nineteenth and early twentieth centuries by discovering its transformative/teleological vessel in the small, compact, but fast-growing proletariat (after an early generation had sought similar salvation via the peasantry). The proletariat became its agent of modernization, an unconscious agent, a form of human dynamite to demolish the edifice of the Asiatic state. From being a cowed or disorientated stratum, this section of the intelligentsia, to paraphrase George Orwell, inherited the Asiatic state's whip and held it very firmly over the proletariat's head. Those intellectuals became the founders of a new class: the destruction of all countervailing powers—because of the decimation of revolutionary workers during the Civil War, because of foreign intervention and successive famine, and because of the purges of errant colleagues and rebellious peasants—laid the foundations for this new class to create a self-perpetuating political apparat.[3]

The general outlines are well known. I would argue only against such a sharp demarcation between Eastern and Western intellectuals during the period covered in this paper. I would also emphasize that there were crucial differences in the evolution of various Western national intelligentsias. A final related objection concerns an irritating stages-of-history mentality (on the part of Marxists, ex-Marxists, and non-Marxists alike) which pervades discussions of social history of intelligentsias and remains dominant in related studies of postindustrialism. Such an attitude, I believe, obscures rather than illuminates the complex relationships among Western intellectuals, national state formation, and the development of local capitalist-market economies.

It is accepted procedure for both Marxist and non-Marxist historians to divide the industrial revolution into three stages: coal, iron, and steam (1780–1900); chemicals, electronics, and internal combustion (1900–1945); and services, microtechnology, and nuclear power (1945 to the present). If we follow this division too strictly we will finish off with a functionalist history of "educated labor" rather than one that stresses the subjective cultural history (*mentalité*) and independent political weight of the professionals.

The industrial revolution would have never occurred—or at least would have occurred at a much slower pace—if a series of service revolutions (in banking, mass communications, retailing, and professionalization) had not been present during its initial stages. So one may argue that a very crucial "service revolution" took place during the seventeenth and eighteenth centuries which had as much to do with the advent of industrial society as did the great agrarian and technological revolutions that accompanied it. Furthermore, it was the explosion of the ancient professions out of their medieval ghettos which signals the dawn of the modern world. Talcott Parsons is certainly correct when he claims that "the development and increasing strategic importance of the professions probably constitutes one of the most important changes that has occurred in the occupational system of modern societies."[4]

Hence, professionalization has an ancient tradition behind it. Before industrialization, the triad of "divinity, law, and physic" symbolized the limits of its world. Very few people ever actually met lawyers or doctors; only priests were present in everyday life. While the triumph of the scientific method over humanism, religion, and magic may have allowed for the creation of new professions, it should not be argued that science devastated its opponents. The new scientific professions, based on empiricism and mathematical certainties, employed humanism as their lingua franca. Professionals were bred, and to a certain extent still are, in institutions dominated by a prescientific ethos.

In addition, the scientific method—at least in its more unrefined, materialist variations—was not unknown before Galileo, Newton, and Descartes. Carlo Ginzburg's exalted Friulian Miller and Christopher Hill's Lollards are proof of this. The self-educated artisan remained the scientific revolution's sleeping partner until our own times.[5]

I am trying to approach a complex problem of definition, but I fear that if we are to understand the subjective and objective qualities that created the modern professional, we shall have to write an unresolved history of fractured consciousness. The problem should at least be borne in mind.

Urban intellectuals have a very long memory. As Gramsci explained (and I think that even though he was thinking of a very specific Italian case, we can safely include other Western European states), they "feel the continuity of their category and their history, the only category which has had an uninterrupted history."[6] Pierre Bourdieu and Jean-Claude Passeron continually stress the "legacy" that makes up the consciousness of the French professional intellectual:

> The constellation of attitudes which was codified in the seventeenth-century ethic of *hônnete homme*—and is not so far removed from the ethic of the "literary gentleman" in the Confucian tradition—owes to the historical permanence of its function the ease with which it has been able to perpetuate itself, at the cost of a few re-interpretations, despite the changing of the classes placed in the dominant position. Consider, for example, the primacy of manner and style; the value attached to naturalness and lightness, conceived as the antithesis of pedantry, didacticism or effect; the cult of the "gift" and the disparage-

ment of apprenticeship, the modern reformulation of the ideology of "birth" and contempt for study; the disdain for specialization, trades and techniques, the bourgeois transposition of contempt for business; the attention devoted to nuances and imponderables, perpetuating the aristocratic tradition of "refinement" and expressed in the subordination of scientific to literary culture and artistic culture, still more conducive to the indefinite niceties of the games of distinction; in short, all the ways, declared or tacit, of reducing culture to the relation to culture, in other words, of setting against the vulgarity of what can be acquired or achieved a manner of possessing an acquirement whose whole value derives from the fact that there is but one way of acquiring it.[7]

It is worth noting in passing that America may be an entirely different case, where from the beginning the modern middle classes have dominated cultural and academic traditions. It goes without saying that both British and German intellectual life was dominated by the ethos dissected in *Reproduction*.[8]

To sum up, as we investigate the intelligentsias of Western Europe, we should not forget the unresolved battle between the intellectual's aristocratic *habitus* and "on-the-job" scientism.

FORMATION OF WESTERN INTELLIGENTSIAS AND THE RISE OF MODERN SOCIALISM: 1830–1900

Throughout late-nineteenth-century Europe, the modern usage of the word *intelligentsia* became widespread. The late Georges Haupt traced the passage of a Russian conception of a *revolutionary* intelligentsia through its dissemination by Western colonies of Russian political émigrés.[9] This distinctive usage found widespread acceptance among the first generation of populist-cum-anarchist socialists. These yearnings were best expressed by Errico Malatesta, the famous Italian anarchist who joined the Italian International in 1871 after abandoning medical school at the University of Naples and apprenticing himself as an electrician and gas fitter. He was not alone, but he was perhaps one of the few Italian *narodniki* who remained a manual worker (with occasional stints as a revolutionary journalist), until he was placed under house arrest by Mussolini when he was nearly seventy-five years old. He recalled:

> labour was declared a social duty for everyone and . . . the condition of the workers was considered the only one compatible with a truly human morality, and many Internationalists coming from the middle classes, in order to be coherent with their ideals and to better approach the people, began to learn a manual trade. We saw in the working class, in the industrial and agricultural proletariat, the great factor of social transformation, the guarantee that it would really be done for the advantage of everyone and would not give rise to a new privileged class.[10]

But this notion of a *narodniki* intelligentsia was not without alternative formulations. Indeed, local conceptions of an intelligentsia merged with older, more rooted traditions of the university-trained professional, and these were adopted by a broader but related stratum commonly known as the new middle class.

Thus, when we turn to the most well-known notice of their coming of age—the *Manifesto of the Intellectuals*—launched by Zola and other literati during the Dreyfus Affair, it is instructive to note how its usage and its very wording betrayed a quite different type of intelligentsia than that which the Russian or Italian *narodniki* had envisaged. First, this manifesto was a distinctly French phenomenon, harking back to the Revolution, but certainly reinforced by the important intervention of artists, poets, and writers in the revolutions of 1830, 1848, and, to a certain extent, 1871. The sacred principles of 1789, a vague social republicanism shading into outright collectivism, and an underlying spiritual high-mindedness defined the boundaries of the signatories' worldview. Honest work, anticlericalism, and a secularization of daily life were their first principles, usually joined with membership in the Freemasonry. There was a distinctive Parisian connection among certain *grande écoles* (the *École Normale*, above all), the middle and upper levels of the republican anticlerical bureaucracy, and literary politicos. No one had the slightest intention of abandoning Paris's literary salons for the workshops of Belleville. At most, one would very shortly find a band of intellectual guerillas (led by Sorel) who would unmask their pretensions but remain firmly implanted in the same milieu.[11]

The British intelligentsia at the turn of the century was of quite another sort. Britain's social history since industrialization had been marked by peculiarities that distinguished it from its Continental neighbors. An intelligentsia did not appear on the scene until the last decade of the nineteenth century. Intellectual life in Britain was marked by an informality unknown in the rest of Europe. Britain was the pioneering industrial nation, and, more important, it lacked the centralizing bureaucracy and standing armies that preceded large-scale industrialization on the Continent. British capitalism was, in fact, placed within a political superstructure largely controlled by a traditional rural elite that had established itself as capitalist farmers, dispensing with a mass peasantry and equally capable of digesting or perhaps seducing most of its radical educated critics. Britain lacked the state-created intelligentsias of post-Restoration Europe who, outpacing economic growth, faced serious underemployment and played important roles in the revolutions of 1830 and 1848. This lent the British ruling elite great cohesion, but it eventually also retarded the modernization of its pell-mell capitalist economy.[12] "The bureaucrat," Eric Hobsbawm writes, "the technologically and scientifically trained manager or businessman, even the office worker, or for that matter a national system of primary, secondary and higher education were commonplace in Germany and France from the early nineteenth century, but not in Britain."[13] If Britain lacked Jacobin or *narodniki* intelligentsias, it did possess a less numerous and more decentralized educated class—commonly known as the professionals—who played significant roles in social movements even before the emergence of Fabianism in the 1880s. They were not, of course, the mass semiemployed stratum that Schumpeter described in *Capitalism, Socialism and Democracy*, nor even the nascent Hegelian new class discerned by Alvin Gouldner in pre-1848 Europe.[14]

Recent historical work has uncovered the pervasive influence of the upper and lower layers of the educated middle class in popular radical or reforming movements throughout the century. It was (in chronological order) the utilitarians, the radicals, the "educated" Chartist leadership, Harold Parkin's "forgotten class of middle-class professionals," Arnold's "lights of liberalism," the more radical positivists, and, finally, the men of letters who founded the socialist organizations of the 1880s and 1890s. These individuals—and this is a British peculiarity (with, perhaps, analogies in Scandinavia and America)—were usually Dissenting Protestants who found a ready audience among trade unionists and artisans raised in a similar tradition of debate and self-improvement.[15]

But when the British accepted the term *intellectual* in the 1890s, it was meant to negate this specific tradition of political activism. As Thomas Heyck has persuasively shown, the largely literary British intelligentsia assumed an ascetic, detached, and largely apolitical conservative vocation. Only at its fringes did a bohemian or romantic assault on Victorian respectability occasionally lead such individuals as Edward Carpenter, Oscar Wilde, and William Morris to socialism. More emblematic, perhaps, was the haughty pessimist George Gissing.[16]

The appearance of a discussion of the Italian and German intelligentsias in these countries' newspapers in the 1880s and 1890s was usually associated with the problem of underemployment or unemployment of university graduates. In Italy, the mismatch between an abundance of humanistic *laureati* and a distorted labor market did pose real problems, but it cannot be easily proved that unemployed intellectuals were the significant force behind the massive intervention of university graduates in the three generations of Italian socialists who lived before the war. Malatesta's generation threw in their lot with the workers and peasants for complex reasons of psychological displacement. The second positivist generation approximated the French *Normaliens*; socialism was an extension of successful professional lives. The last generation of syndicalist university professors did not differ socially from the positivists (indeed, in this case we are discussing political rather than biological generations). Here, however, we do find a lower-middle-class stratum of underemployed syndicalist journalists who may well have been motivated to enter politics for complex reasons of status disequilibrium and related feelings of "social homelessness."[17]

In Germany, intellectual underemployment became less serious when the Bismarckian state initiated its *Gründerkapitalismus*.

However, there remained the higher status afforded to classical *Bildung* which isolated the technically educated middle class.[18] In both Italy and Germany, the humanistic middle class and its university intelligentsia retained their dominance by assuming the roles of guardians of the national language and, indeed, at least before unification, of nation builders.

Germany and Italy were both young nation-states composed of a bewildering number of local subcultures; both were societies rent by regional, social, religious, and class cleavages. James Sheehan has shown that the *Gebildeten* dominated the preunification German liberal nationalist movements "precisely because in a society without an extensive communications system, without national markets, a national press, or unified political institutions, professional relationships, and above all, the nexus of the state's bureaucratic institutions (were) of great political significance for the development of supralocal personal and political ties."[19] In Italy, a *classe dei colti* (university professors, lawyers, *liceo* teachers, architects, journalists, etc.) had been Italy's spiritual and (locally) effective political ruling class for centuries. Professionalism predated nineteenth-century capitalist-induced credentialization movements. Its accompanying status and monetary rewards had been operative since the rise of communal civilization. It had been intellectuals and priests (true organic intellectuals), not a national market or a nation-state, which had lent the peninsula a sense of unity for more than 400 years. And the Risorgimento's shock troops, as Clara Lovett has shown in an excellent prosopographical study, were largely young university graduates of the *ceti medi*. In a country where less than 10 percent of the population spoke the national language in 1861, an educated middle class was bound to play a role far greater than their actual numbers would suggest.[20]

If these factors link the German and Italian cases, there were also important differences, which we have already hinted at. During the preunification movement, both the *Bildungsbürgertum* and the *classe dei colti* hated the aristocrats but feared and despised the lower orders. But whereas the *Bildungsbürgertum*, especially the vast majority of university professors and state functionaries, were easily integrated into Bismarck's expansive, revised version of the Prussian civil-service state, the Italian state remained a weak reed to lean on. It did not create an effective bureaucracy or educational system, nor did industrialization spread in Italy as rapidly as it did in Germany. Long-lasting alienation from the tarnished results of the Risorgimento affected sections of the *ceto dei colti* and turned some toward socialism as a form of populist salvation at first, and later, more important, as a strategy of modernization and national integration. Besides, the Italian Catholic elites, unlike the Junkers, opposed the new state, and as a result the ruling elite of modern Italy was extremely thin. What we witness is a bifurcation of the *classe dei colti* into rulers and *sovversivi*. Usually after a few years of decades of ''crowd management'' many of the latter would join and reinforce the former. Mosca and Pareto did not have far to look for their notions of circulations of elites.[21]

Perhaps a more significantly numerous and socially buoyant new middle class had greater importance within the post-1870 European socialist movement. This more prosaic middle or lower-middle class was growing very rapidly within all four nations. Even in Italy the university professors would have found it difficult or impossible to communicate with the rural and urban working class, which joined the PSI (Italian Socialist Party) without the mediation of a *ceto di frontiera* that had an immediate relationship with the lower classes. Throughout Western Europe the lower-middle class combined an admiration of modernization with a profound respect for the precapitalist classical humanism that university socialists embodied. Next we shall summarize the class typologies of Western European international socialist parties, and then we shall define the ''intelligentsia socialism'' of the new middle classes.

SOCIAL COMPOSITION OF SOCIALIST PARTIES: 1890–1914

The peculiar mixture of individuals from the lower-middle class, university-trained middle class, and self-educated *artisanate*, or working class, within our four socialist parties have to be understood in light of their widely varying social weights and national histories. As we have mentioned, the importance of university graduates in Italy—not only during the *Risorgimento* but also in their role in the formation of the post-Risorgimento state and the organization of the largely illiterate *braccianti* rank and file in the PSI, a mass party in formation—is clearly of a different order than that of the English university stratum. The influence of the latter on the labor movement was felt indirectly through a network of regionally based socialist groups or via the Fabians. These were not (at least until 1910) largely composed of university graduates but rather of self-made middle-class intellectuals whose higher education after public school (with the striking exception of the lower-middle-class Webbs and the middle- and upper-class "new women") was followed by the London circuit of night schools and self-improvement discussion circles.

Furthermore, for at least a half century before its neighbors, Britain possessed a massive popular movement of trade unionists directly connected to civil society. Foreign observers were impressed with the ability of the British labor movement to create an impressive network of cooperatives and trade societies by the middle of the nineteenth century. These were capable of producing a leadership largely autonomous of middle-class intellectuals (even if close and long-lasting ties did develop between the previously mentioned professionals and the trade unions' "civil service"). One need only recall the deep interest that the trade-union movement produced in the exiled European intelligentsia living in London before 1914. "The Trade Unions," wrote the Webbs in the famous conclusion to *The History of Trade Unionism*, "offer the century-long experience of a thousand self-governing working-class communities." And Bernstein, Lenin, and Sorel all studied the movement and the Webbs' theoretical work very closely indeed.

The major British socialist party, the ILP (International Labour Party), was a relatively small one (with 30,000 members at its height) that gained influence through an alliance with Lib-Lab trade unions whose members were counted in the millions. The party activists were a composite of lower-middle-class individuals and self-educated workers. With the exception of a few pioneer high intellectuals, however, the ILP did not afford the university graduate much scope. Its Methodist and secularist roots were deeply anti-intellectual and certainly were not a comfortable nesting ground for Continental-type theoreticians. These usually migrated to the SDF, the smaller Marxist party, or remained tied to the Fabians, but more likely than not they allied themselves with radical-liberal collectivists who shunned the white-collar salariat for more exclusive circles of "dinner-table think tanks."[22]

In France, as we have seen, the centralized state and the inherent *"étatisme"* of the Jacobin tradition produced a variety of socialist ideologies whose main tenets were nonetheless defined with respect to the legacies of the French Revolution. The bloody aftermath of the Commune of Paris had destroyed a generation of self-educated socialist and radical artisan leaders, and university graduates after 1870 played important roles in both the statist and antistatist camps. The educated middle classes were predominant within the anticlerical and republican culture that served as a common ground for most of the French Left. Even in workerist anarchism and syndicalism the "enlightened" classically educated journalist/lawyer, attracted to notions of libertarian education, dominated national and local organizations. In four of the five parties that defined the splintered socialist movement before the creation of the unified socialist party (SFIO), university-trained journalists and free professionals held almost undisputed sway. And even in the openly workerist Allemanist party (POSR), intellectuals such as Lucien Herr, the famous socialist librarian of the *École Normale*, were not without their importance. The Independent Socialist parliamentary group, led by Jaurès and other *Normaliens*, is the most extraordinary example of the dominance of high intellectuals in the French political socialist movement.[23]

The SPD was the largest socialist party, and in 1910 its membership exceeded the combined total of the other European socialist parties. It has long been pictured as a party in which a self-educated bureaucracy, undergoing a process of *embourgeoisement*, was the chief political actor. Since the appearance of the impressive, if ahistorical, study by Robert Michels (an intellectual who was active in the Italian and German socialist movements), we have been accustomed to imagining the SPD as a great oligarchical machine. More recently the party has been described as a subculture in which the isolated urban working class created institutions parallel to those of Wilhelmine Germany's and was effectively "negatively integrated" into broader German society.[24]

Two points should be made. First, as Dick Geary cogently argues, deradicalization theses imply that there existed a golden era of unsullied radicalism. In fact, from the beginning the SPD favored a reformist strategy, even if its ideologists wrestled over how the socialist revolution would come about. In addition, the machine was never as monolithic as many commentators like to imagine. Recent work shows that the party was a composite of locally rich regional and municipal groupings; that trade-unionist officials, like their British contemporaries, did not readily listen to the socialist ideologists when their conclusions threatened daily pragmatism; that internal debate was vigorous; and finally, and perhaps most important for our argument, that the working-class rank-and-file and trade-union officialdom were largely unaffected by the Marxist texts produced by the intellectual elite. Surveys of workers' libraries and the memoirs of leading trade-union officials show that the books that made them politically aware were few in number: Bebel's vulgarization of positivist Marxism, *Women under Socialism*, Bellamy's technocratic utopian projections, and Lassalle's pamphlets (to the eternal discomfort of Marx's shade) were perhaps the most popular strictly political reading. But this was overshadowed by a steady diet of "penny dreadfuls" and occupational manuals.

So where did the much-studied German socialist intelligentsia come in? Ideology served to bind the party's intellectual elite to what Guttsman calls its functionaries' democracy, that is, the middle- and lower-level clerks and minor officials who by 1910 could be numbered in the thousands.

The SPD university graduates experienced a uniquely uncomfortable life in comparison to their French or Italian contemporaries. Michels readily recognized the difference. The German university intellectual who declared openly for socialism had his career abruptly terminated. Since civil-service jobs were prohibited to socialists, many university graduates were forced to become journalists or lawyer/journalists. More than 30 percent of the SPD's editors were academicians suffering interruptions of their first careers. Furthermore, socialists originating from the *Bildungsbürgertum* were unceremoniously ostracized from all aspects of polite society. For Michels the strain was too much; he found succor at the University of Turin. This state of affairs contrasted sharply with our other three cases where formal liberal rights were granted, at least, to the educated middle class.

The case of Italy is perhaps the diametric opposite of the German case.[25] Here, the university graduate, especially the previously mentioned second and third generations, could retain great prestige at the university and could even increase their standing in certain sections of polite society through their political activities, while simultaneously mingling with the lowest strata of rural society. It was a phenomenon that fascinated the chastened Michels when he wrote his useful if uneven study of the Italian educated's relationship with the labor and socialist movements.[26]

Besides journalism, another avenue of influence for the German university intellectuals was the party school. Anyone who has read Nettl's magnificent biography of Rosa Luxemburg will recall how she and others gathered around Franz Mehring and used their stints at the Berlin school to polish up their radical theories before a select group of trade-union officials and socialist-worker students. Their educational methods rather than their specific ideological direction influenced moderate and radical students alike.[27]

Finally, the German socialist *Bildungsbürgertum*, at first, did play a predominant role in the socialist *Reichstagfraktion*, but this diminished as trade-union and party funds allowed socialist-worker and trade-union candidates to contest unsalaried Reichstag seats.

In Germany, the free professional or intellectual journalist retained an overwhelming importance for the first generation of "heroic" socialists. One could mention famous examples: Liebknecht, from a family of high civil servants (descendants of Luther) or Von Vollmar, the southern reformist university aristocrat. Standing above all these individuals was Lassalle, the flamboyant authoritarian intellectual whose popularity, forged by his famous defense of Countess Hatzfeld, cannot be underrated.

Although we cannot do justice to the fascinating subject of working-class authoritarianism in this paper, it is worthwhile to make a few general remarks. In early workers' movements the notion of an alternative "good" and "pure" nobility, or regal elite, which would replace the present corrupt crew, was widespread. We all think of the popularity of Father Gapon, but there are many examples in Western Europe. Fergus O'Connor, the Chartist leader, was afforded regal triumphal welcomes when he toured the north of England in the 1840s. The criminologist Enrico Ferri was welcomed with hysteria by his Po Valley *braccianti* followers seventy years later; they greeted him with a round whose words claimed that the good professorial demagogue had "invented socialism." Michels, one of the first students of the subject, exaggerated the extent of working-class hero worship and made the fatal mistake of lifting phenomena linked to specific historical conjunctures onto a timeless plane. If one wants to identify the point at which the semianarchist Michels began his evolution toward being an ideological spaniel of *Il Duce*, it is probably here that one should start. In any case, it might be more fruitful to consult Bernstein's fine account of Lassalle (1893), which stresses the specific historical conditions that gave birth to hero worship. The development of working-class self-education and the availability of party finances tempered the worship of "regal" free professionals in Germany. The Lassallian parliamentarian cast in the mold of the rhetorical Italian or French socialist gave way to the "machine man," perhaps best exemplified by Fredrich Ebert. A glance at the widely varying social compositions of the socialist *Reichstagfraktion* and that of the Italian *Gruppo Parlementare Socialista* tells the story.

In 1903, of thirty-three socialist deputies in the Italian Camera, twenty-nine were university graduates, among whom were found nobility and *haute bourgeoisie*. Only two were lower-middle class and two skilled working class. Contemporaneously the SPD had eighty-one deputies, of whom thirteen were university graduates, fifteen lower-middle class, and fifty-three working class (more likely than not, trade-union officials). If nearly 88 percent of the GPS were university graduates, only 16 percent of the German deputies were. Of twenty-four graduates in the GPS, nine were professors, three times the total for the entire Reichstag.

Very few full-time professional organizers or trade unionists were found in the GPS and associated independent socialist groupings in the Camera before 1914. They could be found within the local socialist subcultures of the Po Valley, especially in the socialist communal governments that predominated in Emilia-Romagna. In Rome, however, the free professional, the professor who was also a deputy editor of a socialist newspaper or theoretical journal—the part-time player—was the rule.[28]

The mass base of all socialist parties during this period derived not only from the manual working class but also from a particular type of worker. First there were skilled textile workers, printers, locksmiths, artisans, and even a smattering of "preindustrial" political shoemakers—at least in the Mediterranean countries. They were members of the respectable, self-educated working class who carried with them an older, craft-based radicalism. However, they shaded into a new wave of skilled machine operators (lathe operators, turners, precision toolmakers, engineers, and engine drivers) who were attuned to the scientific and technocratic socialisms being synthesized by various intellectual currents.[29] (I say *socialisms* because the adjective *scientific* was not restricted to the Marxists; indeed, the Fabians, in their famous anti-Marxist *Essays*, used it proudly, and so did Italian positivists, and so for that matter did a later generation of revolutionary syndicalists. Even the Catalan anarcho-syndicalists were attracted to the vision; one glance at their political pamphlets, with hymns and paeans to turbines and futuristic libertarian smokestack utopias, shows that the so-called utopians and the Marxist scientists had a great deal in common.)

The worker socialist was easily identified. An observer of a Chemnitz factory in 1891 noted that worker "public opinion" concerning industrial questions was molded by a few skilled worker activities. The whole work force stood under a certain, undefinable pressure, and the threads of this silent influence came together in the hands of certain characteristic personalities. These "elite socialists" were the nodal point for thousands who grouped themselves around them. In Germany the division expressed itself between skilled workers with less physically demanding work and recently arrived rural laborers who were under an increasingly demanding tempo of rationalized production timetables. Robert Roberts, a former resident of a particularly

down-at-the-heels Salford slum, recalled that the ILP relied upon
similar social types in the north of England who were considered
to be the "cream of the working-class society."

> In factory and workshop they were very often the most skilled
> and knowledgeable hands doing work to the highest standards,
> not to suit an employer but to satisfy their own integrity. They
> wanted nothing but what was earned: but that they demanded
> and would fight for. Active members of choirs, cycling and
> walking groups, socialist Sunday Schools or Methodist Chapels,
> readers of Ruskin, Dickens, Kingsley, Carlyle and Scott,
> teetotalers, often, strait-laced, idealistic, naive, they troubled
> and disturbed the liberal voting artisan, made him feel that his
> preoccupation with mere pay issues of the day was pitifully in-
> adequate when a whole new society waited to be born.[30]

During the early 1900s, throughout Italy's industrial triangle
skilled engineers barely one generation away from guildlike car-
riage makers formed the proletarian backbone of the Turinese or
Milanese PSI. The archetypal individual was proud of his professional dignity (la fierezza del mestière), read the Origin of Species, at-
tended the local Università Popolare and went to the light opera,
admired German technology and hated the Kaiser, and loved the
Russian Nihilists and voted for Turati. "The socialist worker,"
recalled one official of the FIOM (the metalworkers' union), "is
conscious of being the protagonist of a new history which begins
with him."[31]

Second, in certain working-class or rural wage-worker communities where communitarian feelings outlived the collapse of older
paternalistic hierarchies, socialists could gather support. When industrial organization or the cruel logic of the world capitalist mar-
ketplace disintegrated an old or sheltered world, such workers
could rapidly be radicalized. Thus—and this example is perhaps
the most striking for its numbers of recruits to socialism—the braccianti of the Po Valley, the miners of the South Wales valleys, the
wine-growing peasants of the Var, and the protoproletarians (the
worker peasants) of the Urals entered socialist politics.

Conversely, in the Ruhr's mines and steel mills paternalism
reigned until immigrants arrived around 1910; federations of

moderate miners controlled the Northnumberland colliers until the courts threatened even these unions' inviolability. The "yellow unions" in France had more members than did the vastly exaggerated syndicalists, and only the war and the Popular Front government really made inroads in this powerful paternalism. Finally, in Italy the great southern peasant masses remained locked in a system of poverty and local terror which turned them into envious and, later, bitter enemies of the *signori*: the hated ones, the industrial workers of Turin and Milan who earned more in one day than some of the peasants saw in several weeks.[32]

In all four countries the semiskilled workers (where they existed) were singularly difficult to recruit for socialism, but it was the vast pools of urban and rural poor whom socialist organizers (with the striking exception of the *braccianti*) wrote off in scarcely veiled outbursts of disgust and fear.

The Germans called them the *lumpen proletariat*, the British "the roughs," the French *les classes dangereuses*, and the Italians *le classe pericolose*—and this was in their more restrained moments. When their imaginations got the better of them, they called the poor "pauper bandits," *la feccia* ("the scum"), or simply criminals. Keir Hardie, explaining ILP recruiting strategy, could be speaking here for any number of skilled-worker trade-union officials or lower-middle-class socialists throughout Western Europe:

> It is the intelligent well-off artisan in Great Britain who responds to the Socialist appeal, and it is the slum vote which the Socialist candidate fears the most.[33]

But working-class strength was, of course, severely limited, not the least because of the very low rates of unionization prevalent throughout Europe. Even in Britain and Germany these rates did not exceed 35 percent, and in France and Italy they hovered around 10 percent, while the socialist and syndicalist trade unions had perhaps 7 percent or 8 percent of the organized on their membership rolls. It may be argued that local, rich lower-class cultures in France and Italy mobilized in far greater numbers. Certainly the *Bourses de Travail* and the *Camere del Lavoro* could mobilize far greater crowds than actual membership would warrant one to believe. Even more significantly, these local organizations, which were often run by anarchists and syndicalists, would throw away first principles and get workers to vote in a political socialist city government so as to guarantee their financial subsidy.[34] However, these electoral and direct-action mobilizations were sporadic. Without greater national consistency, socialists relied on another social group to provide continuity and institutional cement.

Between the university intellectuals and the skilled working class lay socialists from new middle-class or less sharply defined "middling-class" backgrounds. Their influence, like that of other social classes, was determined by specific national historical and cultural legacies. In Germany the white-collar middle class—the *Angestellte* and *Beamte*—were separated by law, custom, and psychology from the manual workers to a greater degree than were British clerks and, certainly, leftist French public *employées*. As Kocka had shown, the very words used to describe the German white-collar workers betrayed the precapitalist corporate mentality they largely adopted. Even so, many party functionaries in the SPD came from small master- and petty-clerking families, and the large number of socialist tavern keepers (a central political and social institution for the party's grass roots) made some inroads into what was commonly believed to be an antisocialist class of small shopkeepers. As Blackbourn notes, the long-standing argument that the SPD suffered from *embourgeoisment* through a growing artisanal and petty-entrepreneurial middle-class vote can be turned around to mean that these classes were not as resolutely antisocialist as is commonly believed.[35]

In France and Britain two types of lower-middle-class groups penetrated local and national socialist politics. First, there were the "middling-class" representatives. They hearkened back to presocialist conceptions of the people (*le peuple*); latching onto older myths, what Birnbaum calls the struggle of *le peuple contre le gros*. This is also what Stedman Jones, Neale, and E. P. Thompson identify as that long-standing battle of "the free-born Englishman" against the "Thing," the "Corruption," a holy war against the city of London, the established church, and the rural but plutocratic aristocracy. In Britain such individuals might be Dissenting Ministers, especially Congregationalists and Primitive Methodists; small masters and north-of-England shopkeepers; and local journalists, schoolmasters, and schoolmistresses. (Although teachers straddled old and new, they were at once incorporated with older radical virtues and "proletarianized" as organized white-collar workers after the 1870 reforms.) In France and Italy, local socialist parties would more likely than not be populated by small-time lawyers, journalists, *instituteurs*, pharmacists, and *maestri*.[36]

The second group included many diverse modern white-collar occupations. All became socially significant with the arrival of mass industrialization, especially with the growth of factory size, modern civil services, and the expansion of financial and other tertiary services.

The Fabians identified this group as *nouvelle couche sociale*, a term borrowed from the French radical politician Gambetta, who basically meant what an earlier generation of Victorians called the industrious classes: clerkdom, of course, but also shopkeepers and small- and medium-sized entrepreneurs, more akin to a middling class. The Fabians, being scientific socialists, honed down Gambetta's definition and lent it a distinctively modern flavor. The group included, Stephen Yeo explains, "would-be metropolitans, de-racinated, 'exiles' in search of a home." Their natural home was in the area of the *social* rather than the merely political (e.g., social work, social science, socialism, and social control). They were, Hobsbawm pithily wrote many years ago, "independent women, often earning their own livelihood as writers, teachers, and even typists . . . self-made newspapermen and writers, civil servants, political lecturers . . . clerks and professional men."[37] "They were the type of being," an anonymous Milanese pamphleteer wrote in 1880, "who did not really belong to the bourgeoisie or the proletariat" *enti fuori-classi*. In the 1890s an English labor newspaper sketched the portrait of just such an entity, Mr. Forest:

> Mr. Forest was a man of wide and catholic sympathies; he was equally at home in the SDF, Fabians, ILP, Labour Church, pleasant Sunday afternoons and trade unionist platforms. He

would go into a park single-handed, get on a stand at a street corner and speak to the promiscuous passers by. His was an intensely missionary nature. With a substratum of belief in revealed religion he hated the artificiality of the churches and raised frequent protest at missionary meetings against the folly of attempting to convert the heathen abroad while the heathen at home was shamefully neglected. He hated intensely the commercial calling, for which he had to earn his livelihood and more than once he threatened to give it up and go into the world to work with his hands.[38]

But these brief impressions do not give this protean group its full justice. My particular fascination is with a certain gray area of former workers, would-be journalists, and skillful machine men who might have working-class roots but who were born late enough to enter the first wave of new white-collar workers. We might take the brutal example of Benito Mussolini, the hero of the younger self-educated workers, a first generation to grow up in the jerry-built industrial suburbs of Milan and Turin. Mussolini was a Romagnol *maestro* and a would-be poet and sociologist (or at least such were his dreams), but he made his career as a fire-breathing journalist. Like so many other practitioners of labor journalism, he combined a modern style copied from the American press with a socialist message. He hated physical labor, as any self-respecting member of the *classe dei colti* would. He called forth the holy proletarian crowd (even in his revolutionary socialist phase Le Bon was his bible) to unleash the *giornate rivoluzionarie*, although not very far from the surface he detested the readers to whom he appealed for support.[39]

Less dramatically, Keir Hardie and Ramsay MacDonald also inhabited the gray area (although they were not pathological gangsters like Mussolini). Both were Scottish and illegitimate and eventually made their ways to the great metropolis; both came from great poverty; and both sought respectability in their own ways but were ultimately individuals cast adrift in the urban hubbub. Hardie made his ascent from collier through self-taught journalism (a common avenue in Britain; Robert Blatchford was its master). MacDonald was a pioneer organization man. He made his career *through* the first socialist organizations with the assistance of the Liberal party, after having gained the requisite skills as a Birkbeck night-school student. Gray-area inhabitants were quintessentially social mediators, usually attracted to crowd psychology as a trick of their trade and as their vocational and personal philosophy. They usually mixed with trade-union officials (not always easily, but differences were eventually sorted out). This last group would not have made its ascent from manual labor if the politics of socialist parties had not called forth a necessary division of labor. Members of this group were the Legiens, Hendersons, Buozzis, Bondfields, and Jouhauxs. They were tough reformists who knew how to control the rank and file, especially during periods of radicalization (such as the prewar syndicalist revolts and the postwar council and shop-steward movements). They possessed a knowledge of industrial conditions and working-class life in that intimate way that the "grays," the lower-middle class, or the university socialists could never hope to acquire.[40]

"INTELLIGENTSIA SOCIALISM": AN ATTEMPT AT A PORTRAIT AND DEFINITION

In the course of this paper we have noted the connection between the rising new educated middle classes and the parallel formation of nationally based socialist organizations founded on ideologies purporting to be scientifically socialist. In order to flesh out a provisional definition of intelligentsia, socialism, and its ideology, I suggest four unifying themes: productivist positivism (including its Marxist variants), socialism as pedagogy, socialism as religion, and socialism as national integration. These themes arose from a specific cultural force field that Yeo's words, quoted earlier, so brilliantly illuminate. In short, we are describing the still little-investigated binominal socialism/sociology. Before we turn to this ideological framework, a few words should be said about the political and cultural ground rules that strengthened the position of the educated middle classes within socialist parties.

Electoral Strategies

Adam Przeworski has recently shown that almost immediately from their debut on the national scene, socialist parties were forced to pitch their propaganda to middle-class voters. This was caused by several interrelated facts of political life. First, suffrage was restricted in Italy, Great Britain, and France. Until 1912, Italian suffrage was formally restricted by literacy requirements. In Britain and France, residential requirements disenfranchised many migratory workers. In Germany, the three-class Prussian voting system weakened Bismarckian male suffrage, and in any case the Reichstag's power was clipped by the Junker bureaucracy, the military, and the Kaiser. In all cases women were excluded from electoral participation on the national level. Because of this, and also because the other socialist parties never achieved the mass membership of the SPD, the French, British, and Italians opted for a cadre-party strategy. Maurice Duverger defines a cadre party as one with a small but active membership whose main aim is electoral success and which must thereby draw on the sympathy of nonparty members who sympathize with the aims of the party.

In these three cases, radical-liberal groupings and parties frequently established local or national alliances with socialist election machines. The *nouvelle couche sociale* was particularly adept at fusing the modernizing bourgeoisie and the industrial proletariat around local "gas-and-water" socialist programs. The socialists promised to modernize the infrastructure and rationalize technical education, and in some places this was enthusiastically supported by industrialists. The SPD, on the whole, is a different case, as the National Liberals were firmly attached to the antisocialist coalition. Attempts at creating electoral pacts with Progressive Liberals in 1912 merely drove their supporters into the arms of the antisocialist bloc. But on a limited regional basis, things could be different. Southern German socialism approximates other European experiments.[41]

Education/Self-Education

If these political limitations on working-class participation within socialist parties increased the value of middle-class investment within intraparty and parliamentary/electoral party activities, another set of parallel barriers created an implicit, and at times explicit, hierarchy within the European socialist movement, which was reinforced by the cultural capital of the socialist-educated middle classes.

Socialist parties have served as educational institutions in their own right, offering members a range of political and other instructions. In important part the weight of the educated middle class within them has been due to this ability to supply and support this education, both directly and through popular journalism and party schools. At the same time educational activities formed a "filter" in which politically active workers were selected for leading roles.

Concurrently there existed a zone of persistent tension between educated scientific socialists (again, not always Marxists) and workers' attempts at self-education and self-expression. Marx looked upon self-educated worker-philosophers with ill-disguised contempt, and he was not alone. The workers were meant to inherit German philosophy, not, like Proudhon or Dietzgen, to construct their own brand. Similarly, Lenin found Bogdanov's, Gorki's, and Lunacharsky's experiments with cultural party schools dangerous, not only because—like some hardheaded Western reformists—he feared worker graduates would be unsuitable for boring agitational work but also (and perhaps more important) because he felt that the conception of "proletarian culture" threatened the monopoly of knowledge which "bourgeois renegades" were supposed to dole out. And this, too, was not restricted to Bolshevik intellectuals. Turati and Jaurès wanted workers to inherit good bourgeois lay schools, not proletarian universities; the leading German Social Democrats praised classical *Bildung*; and Gramsci felt that Latin grammar exercises would discipline the minds of worker students.[42]

Historical accounts of how the elusive battle between scientific cum classically educated middle-class socialists and worker autodidacts was fought would certainly substantiate the largely anecdotal or biographical evidence currently available. But we do not pretend to suggest that self-educated workers shunned the classical heritage; on the contrary. Still, there are tensions between the formally educated and the self-taught. Two periods that would serve as historical backdrops are the following:

(1) The 1890s, when a self-consciously locally based workerism founded on autodidactic culture (e.g., the French Allemanists, the *Partito Operaio Italiano*, the early Russian Economists, the north-of-England and Scottish labor clubs and "unions" or German educational clubs and localistic SPD party structures) confronted the formally trained metropolitan scientific socialists.

(2) The so-called Syndicalist Revolt (ca. 1910–1914), when forms of self-education (e.g., the Ferrer Schools, the Plebs Leagues, the *Bourses de Travail*, and *Camere del Lavoro* educational experiments, etc.) combined with worker antiofficialist (i.e., antiprofessional labor leaders) and antistate socialist intelligentsias in rather confusing "rebel movements." The fortune of the English notion of a new "servile state"—a marriage of the interventionist state (just flexing its muscles), big capital, and professional socialist/labor leaders—would be very interesting to trace. My own, albeit preliminary, investigations suggest that its imagery traveled quite rapidly around Europe.

In neither of these two historical examples should it be assumed that revolts against intelligentsia or official socialism were merely led by autonomous working-class producers. This assumption would be naïve and entirely counterproductive. Indeed, in the 1880s and 1890s the German *Jungen* (largely literati), the Morrisite socialists (also literati), or the guild socialists of the syndicalist revolt (literati and academics) lived in close and, at times, tense proximity with self-taught rebels, supplying them with ammunition but also being inspired by and learning from skilled workers and artisans.[43]

Another rewarding research strategy would be to chart the process by which socialist parties as bureaucracies created a new middle class of their own. Naturally, Michels is usually quoted in such a discussion. But we need to digest empirical and impressionistic evidence that reveals how manual workers experienced their transformation into white-collar workers via this well-known route. To this extent, it would be necessary to empirically ground Michels's speculations.

Of great importance is that existential break when one becomes one's own boss, when the ex-manual worker gains a certain control over personal time and enters the white-collar world. This could be accomplished by a content analysis of working-class autobiographies, triumphalist or otherwise, focusing not on evidence revealing the imperial or racist sentiments of ex-labor aristocrats but rather on those passages that document the ex-manual worker's *coupage* from his or her regimented working life. The white-collar worker's salary (even if initially modest) replaces the precarious wage packet. Work-time discipline is modified dramatically, and the potential for both geographic and social upward mobility takes a quantum leap. It might also be possible to test empirically to what extent socialist-party careers were a specialized form of social mobility linked to the universally noted generational shifts caused by increasing white-collar growth after 1870. To do so one might construct vast prosopographical portraits of a pre-1914 socialist party's national and local leadership through a careful coding of the available and abundant sociological facts found in various national dictionaries of labor biography.

Socialism as Sociology[44]

All of this still untapped information, I believe, could be interpreted through a theoretical focus that centers upon the marriage of socialism and sociology during this historical period. It is an area with which political sociologists, political scientists, historians of ideas, labor historians, and social historians have tangled, but we still lack the necessarily interdisciplinary and certainly difficult synthesis from discrete specialties.

Socialism as a sociology can be linked to seemingly universal determinants. The growth of state intervention in economic and social processes and the use of arbitration machinery for industrial disputes parallels the growth of socialism in this period and its progressive incorporation toward the machinery of government. This was joined to psychological, or at least subjective, requirements of intellectuals and, perhaps more important, of the broader middle-class and lower-middle-class socialists, who increasingly pressed for state intervention in the economy and in social life as a way to regulate industrial disputes and to solve the persistent problem of urban pauperism. Scientific socialism as a sociology erected a moral and political agenda, heightening the importance of specialists and/or articulate socialist spokesmen.

The educated middle-class socialist explained his or her "mission" by employing two philosophies (although at times this term might be too grandiose a way of expressing thoughts that were offshoots of high culture and popular vulgarization). There are many affinities between the educated socialist and nonsocialist middle classes, so what I shall say can be easily transferred to their political adversaries. These two schools of thought or mentality were not mutually exclusive in practice. Indeed, one reinforced the other.

(1) *Positivism* stressed the need for expertise, special training, and trained intelligence as prerequisites for the functioning of mass movements. The educated middle classes groomed themselves for this role. They drew sustenance from a desacralizing of tradition and the rapid expansion of the public sphere. Professionals (usually criminologists, anthropologists, lawyers, doctors, economists, and sociologists) were concerned with categorizing the living tissue of civil society. They were the champions of modernization, busily constructing sciences of social behavior and ethics.

(2) *Neo-Hegelianism* informed the discourse rather than the methods of most of the professionals. Professionals were, therefore, the brains, if not the direct leadership, behind socialist strategy (a position reinforced by their "neutral" positivism). A universalizing creed seemed to lend coherence to modern culture. Finally, sometimes only implicitly, political and/or voluntary organizations were envisaged as vehicles for realizing this aspiration. Put more mundanely, the professionals became the voice of civil society.

Socialism as religion, as a form of secular faith, thus combined an appeal to *solidarisme* or "social service" with schemes for the organization of society which substituted for traditional elites and capitalist entrepreneurs, a stratum of experts, and/or the lay clerisy. Examples can be found among the Fabians and the ILP, Bellamy and other American authoritarian utopia builders, the Italian socialist professors, and the French socialist elites.[45]

Closely related to this first formulation was socialism as a substitute for collapsing traditional hierarchies of social control and/or as a tonic to stimulate new integrative or heroic values, staving off plutocratic assaults on society's values. Both socialism as pedagogy (the masses had to be taught socialism and modern forms of political behavior) and socialism as a national integration (particularly strong in anticlerical and premodern French and Italian settings) are quite closely linked together. In their socialist phases, both Durkheim and Pareto reflected these concerns and advised national party leaderships in indirect but important ways.

Productivist positivism, or even productivist antipositivism, in the Sorelian case, seemed to underpin the three other themes. Put rather simply (the equation in all its variations was simplistic), socialism would create a healthy productive bourgeoisie that in turn would generate its "negators." This was particularly true in late industrializers like Italy (*la borghesia del lavoro* was the revealing definition bandied about), but ILP propaganda, Kautskyist Marxism, and a good deal of Russian Marxism also contained heavy doses.

We need to tease out and differentiate the various national and cross-national influences on these projects. For instance, if the Fabians shared with the German *Verein* marginalist economics and an explicit quest to justify economically the higher salaries of the educated, because of local conditions the Fabians succeeded in affecting ILP propaganda and the political educations of trade-union officials. The *Verein* were shut out from socialist politics even if they evinced sympathy for reforms not very different than those proposed by the SPD. Furthermore, it might be useful to see how extensively these various sociological socialisms were vulgarized. Following from recent studies of the dissemination of Marxism in Europe, it would be equally important to see how intelligentsia socialism traveled from one country to the next. We might follow the adventures of the term *nouvelle couche sociale* or the transmutations of the Fabian conception of a "rent of ability."[46]

Finally, and most important, we need to examine to what extent intelligentsia socialism can be related to the grander mission of the new middle classes, outlined by Foucault, Frykman and

Löfgren, Baumann, Elias, Stearns, and many others.[47] This mission sought to dissolve folk culture and disseminate popular culture; to routinize, control, and classify physical and mental human behavior; to advance technological rationalization and industrialization and inculcate the lower orders with punctual and predictable behavior; and to re-create the world in the image of the urban white-collar worker. These points might be slightly overdrawn. At its most sublime, intelligentsia socialism desired a return to communal values, the generalization of human friendship and love, and the reconciliation of the mental and manual through the humane usage of modern science. However, for every William Morris, there was an Edward Bellamy whose particular "religion of solidarity" had more in common with Bentham's ubiquitous panopticon than with the English artist's good and peaceful utopia.

SUMMARY

I have identified seven social groups within each national case's socialist movement: the university intelligentsia and literati; the traditional professional class; a new lower middle class of white-collar workers and semiprofessionals; trade-union officials, party bureaucrats, and elected representatives; a traditional middling class of petty entrepreneurs, shopkeepers, and artisans; the modern skilled working class; the semiskilled working class; and the unskilled urban and rural working classes/peasantries. The internal class dynamics of socialist parties can be partially illustrated by imagining them as educational hierarchies where knowledges (both traditional knowledge and knowledge as the outgrowth of the socialist project) validate the power of party members. One way to understand intelligentsia socialism is to uncover the extent to which institutionally created knowledge furthers an endogenous process of social closure, mimicking and feeding off more generalized exogenous trends in pre-1914 Europe.

Particularly important is the transmutation of socialist beliefs which occurs throughout Europe as socialist ideologies depart from a populist appreciation of commonsense knowledge of what is defined as "scientific socialism." Thus, Engels's and Kautsky's vulgarization of evolutionary Marxism, the Fabians' anti-Marxist scientific socialism, and Franco-Italian positivism are at once an attempt to validate the role of scientifically trained leadership over and against the "primitive democrats" and a rather conscious appeal to both traditional professional and lower-middle-class enthusiasts or full-time cadres and, perhaps more important, to a rapidly expanding group of elected officials and self-educated bureaucrats within national organizations.

The specific trajectories and weights of social actors possessing formal or party credentials or popular forms of knowledge were partially determined by existing national social cleavages. While labor historians seek to generalize about the political behavior of the organized working class by quantifying strike waves and demands arising from them, a similar method cannot be employed to capture the importance of credentialed individuals within socialist parties or the national labor market.[48] Indeed, it was the particular relationship of credentialed power to national language and literature which, paradoxically enough, causes so-called cosmopolitan intellectuals to exemplify national political cultures for psychological and market-related reasons. It is notoriously difficult to quantify cultural capital or to correlate the effects of economic cycles to the growth or stagnation of the educated labor markets or, for that matter, to generalize about the radicalizing or paralyzing nature of intellectual underemployment and unemployment. As Frank Parkin shows, credential-based social closure is not easily subsumed within a Marxist paradigm. Effective exclusionary strategies rely on monopolies of knowledge enforced by some sort of moral or coercive power that is not merely an appendage of the Marxist dualism of capital/noncapital.[49]

It might be argued that to the extent that the rate of growth of each national case study's white-collar strata affect positively or negatively the growth and character of socialism, there is in fact an indirect relationship between the expansion of the tertiary-section, levels of industrialization and white-collar participation. However, as we have noted, white-collar growth is mediated largely through extraeconomic factors, and certainly political behavior is refracted through older social cleavages. The state interventionism of precocious second-comers generates fast white-collar expansion. Power configurations, therefore, are a more fruitful area in which to initiate a search for cross-national variables. The most important variable was that of the particular relationships of civil society to the state and of these, in turn, to the university. Civil law rather faithfully reflected different national outcomes. First of all, primitive forms of policy-making were more easily nurtured in societies where pragmatic scientific traditions prospered, whereas administrative systems shaped by purely legal orientations were inimical to such growth. This divided the effects of Anglo-Saxon common law from Franco-Italian Roman legal cultures.

Anglo-Saxon common law furthered, to a greater extent, the continual development of popularly based voluntary organizations. Roman law was more obstructive, while the Russian legal code was positively lethal. Although a degree of self-parody is involved, by using this scale one can differentiate between English "unconscious laborist collectivism" on one hand and "rhetorical" and "scientific Marxist" Continental socialisms on the other.

State/church relationships posed further variations, which Weber and Gramsci appreciated. The well-known effects of the intimate relationship between the clergy and the faithful in sectarian Protestant England and Scandinavia on rich voluntary organizational networks are usually contrasted with undernourished Russian civil society, where state and church were identical. Anticlericalism in France and Italy countered clerically inspired associational activities and supplied the language and substance of a good deal of socialist politics. German associational life was widespread, although it is difficult to align an organized Protestant skilled working class with an English-style dissenting tradition. Protestantism tended to be either quietist or statist, and German organizational structures lacked English informality. Indeed, the socialist subculture was circumscribed by bureaucratic and guild traditions in which the state was heavily involved in setting rather strict limits on the ways in which voluntary organizations could grow.

Research will be necessary in order to flesh out a further series of variables and their causal relations, mentioned in passing in the narrative. These can only be listed here, as follows:

1. The relationship between educational systems, the formation of white-collar qualifications, and national traditions of credentialization and all three vis-à-vis popular cultural knowledge.
2. The scale of voluntary associational cultures in each national case study as correlated to the degree of white-collar trade unionization.
3. The effects of humanist culture and artisanal materialism upon emerging scientific techniques and forms of credentialed social closure.
4. The varieties and densities of social spaces where the university merged with popular movements. One might delineate Latin "coffeehouse" culture, to use Weber's phrase, and Anglo-Saxon "dissenting-club" culture as nodal points where various knowledges are circulated and cross-fertilized. Since the history of working-class clubs is well documented, monographic studies of the educated–middle-class café or club emphasizing its manifold roles as party university, labor exchange for intellectual workers, and unofficial power network within the party would fill out the equation.
5. Finally, all variables describing the state/civil society relationship could be compared to the degree of social distance experienced by educated socialists in their daily encounters with less-educated socialists. With all the striking similarities in intellectual problematics, the Webbs certainly felt closer to the labor movement than Weber did to the German Social Democrats.

NOTES

1. Dedicated to Dr. Elias Berg, Department of Political Science, University of Stockholm, Stockholm, Sweden.
2. Carl Levy and Adam Westoby, *Socialism and the Educated Middle Classes in Europe, 1870–1914* (Milton Keynes, England: School of Education, Open University, 1981–84).

3. The literature is vast. Representative samples are: A. Gella, ed., *The Intelligentsia and Intellectuals* (London and Beverly Hills: Sage Publications, 1976); R. J. Brym, *Intellectuals and Politics* (London: George Allen & Unwin, 1978); A. W. Gouldner, *The Future of the Intellectuals and the Rise of the New Class* (London: Macmillan & Co., 1979); G. Konrád and I. Szelényi, *The Intellectuals and the Rise to Class Power* (Brighton: Harvester Press, 1979).

4. For Parsons see T. Parsons, "Professions," in D. Sills, ed., *International Encyclopaedia of the Social Sciences*, vol. 12 (Glencoe, Ill.: The Free Press, 1968), p. 536. A general overview can be found in W. Prest, "Why the History of the Professions is not Written," in G. R. Rubin and D. Sugarman, eds., *Law, Economy and Society, 1750–1914* (Abingdon, Oxford: Professional Books, 1984); R. M. Hartwell, "The Service Revolution: The Growth of Services in Modern Economies," in C. Cipolla, ed., *The Fontana Economic History of Europe: The Industrial Revolution* (London: Fontana, 1973).

5. See C. Ginsburg, *The Cheese and the Worms* (London: Routledge & Kegan Paul, 1978); C. Hill, *The Intellectual Origins of the English Revolution* (Oxford: University Press, 1965).

6. A. Gramsci, *Quaderni del carcere*, Vol. II, edited by V. Gerratana (Turin: Einaudi, 1975), p. 769.

7. P. Bourdieu and J-C. Passeron, *Reproduction in Education, Society and Culture* (London and Beverly Hills: Sage Publications, 1977), p. 130.

8. For the American case see V. F. Calverton, *The Liberation of American Literature* (New York: Charles Scribner's Sons, 1932). For the German case see F. Ringer, *The Decline of the German Mandarins: The German Academic Community, 1890–1933* (Cambridge, Mass.: Harvard University Press, 1969); K. Jarausch, *Students, Society and Politics in Imperial Germany* (Princeton, N.J.: Princeton University Press, 1982). For the English case see M. Wiener, *English Culture and the Decline of the Industrial Spirit, 1850–1980* (Cambridge: Cambridge University Press, 1980).

9. G. Haupt, "Role de l'exil dans la diffusion de l'image de l'intelligentsia revolutionnaire," *Cahiers du Monde Russe et Sovietique* 19 (1978): 235–249.

10. E. Malatesta, *Scritti*, Vol. III (Carrara: Il Seme, 1975 ed.), pp. 329–330. This volume originally appeared in 1936 and the passage cited is from an introduction to a book published in 1928.

11. For the role of intellectuals and artists in French social movements during the nineteenth century and the early twentieth century see E. Herbert, *The Artist and Social Reform in France and Belgium, 1885–1898* (New Haven, Conn.: Yale University Press, 1961); T. Zeldin, *France 1848–1945: Politics and Anger* (Oxford: Oxford University Press, 1979); Zeldin, *France*

1848–1945: Intellect and Pride (Oxford: Oxford University Press, 1980); R. Debray, *Teachers, Writers, Celebrities* (London: Verso, 1981), pp. 17–59; L. Pinto, "Les Intellectuels vers 1900: Une Nouvelle Classe Moyenne," in G. Lavau, G. Grunberg, and N. Mayer, eds., *L'Univers Politique des Classes Moyennes* (Paris: Presses de la Fondation Nationale des Sciences Politiques, 1983).

12. On the "peculiarities" of the British see E. P. Thompson, "The Peculiarities of the English" (1965), in *The Poverty of Theory* (London: Merlin Press, 1978); Wiener, *English Culture*; M. Sanderson, *Education, Economic Change and Society in England, 1780–1870* (London: Macmillan & Co., 1983), pp. 47–48. For the problem of unemployed or underemployed intellectuals/bureaucrats on the Continent see L. O'Boyle, "The Problem of an Excess of Educated Men in Western Europe, 1800–1850," *Journal of Modern History* 44 (1970): 471–95.

13. E. J. Hobsbawm, "The Fabians Reconsidered," in *Labouring Men* (London: Weidenfeld and Nicolson, 1964), p. 267.

14. J. Schumpeter, *Capitalism, Socialism and Democracy* (New York: Harper, 1978), p. 153. For a full treatment by Gouldner see his posthumously published volume *Against Fragmentation* (London: Macmillan & Co., 1985).

15. For studies of British "reformist professionals" see R. Harrison, "The Positivists: A Study of Labour's Intellectuals," in *Before the Socialists* (London: Routledge & Kegan Paul, 1965); H. Parkin, *The Origins of Modern English Society, 1780–1890* (London: Routledge & Kegan Paul, 1969), pp. 252–270; V. Kiernan, "Labour and the Literate in Nineteenth-Century Britain," in D. E. Martin and D. Rubinstein, eds., *Ideology and the Labour Movement* (London: Croom Helm, 1979); T. Heyck, *The Transformation of Intellectual Life in Victorian England* (London: Croom Helm, 1982).

16. J. Goodie, *George Gissing: Ideology and Fiction* (London: Vision Press, 1978).

17. C. Levy, "Socialism of the Professors and Socialism of the People in Italy, 1870–1914," (MS, Open University, 1983).

18. Ringer, *Decline of the German Mandarins*; Jarausch, *Students, Society and Politics.*

19. J. J. Sheehan, *German Liberalism in the Nineteenth Century* (London: Methuen), p. 21.

20. For an initial study of the Italian *classe dei colti* see P. Macry, "Sulla storia sociale dell'Italia liberale: Per und ricerca sul 'ceto di frontiere,'" *Quaderni Storici* 35 (1977): 521–550. For Lovett see C. Lovett, *The Democratic Movement in Italy, 1830–1876* (Cambridge, Mass.: Harvard University Press, 1982).

21. For an acute study of the Italian case see P. Farneti, *Sistema politica e società civile* (Turin: Giappichelli, 1971).

22. For the Webbs see R. Harrison, "The Webbs as Historians of Trade Unions," in R. Samuel, ed., *People's History and Socialist Theory* (London: Routledge & Kegan Paul, 1981), pp. 322-26. The quotation from the Webbs is found in S. and B. Webb, *The History of Trade Unionism* (London: Longman, Green and Co., 1894), pp. 475-476. For the class composition of the socialist movement see S. Pierson, *British Socialism: The Journey from Fantasy to Politics* (Cambridge, Mass.: Harvard University Press, 1979). And for the class compositions of the Fabians see C. Levy, "Fabianism, the Nursery of Organised Socialism" (MS, Open University, 1983). For the Italian case see J. E. Miller, "Reformism and Party Organisation: The Italian Socialist Party, 1900-1914," *Il Politico* 8 (1975): 102-126.

23. For the role of intellectuals in French socialism see G. Lefranc, *Jaurès e le Socialisme des Intellectuels* (Paris: Editions Ouvrières, 1968); S. S. Gosch, "Socialism and Intellectuals in France, 1880-1914" (Ph.D. diss., Rutgers University, 1971); M. Meissonier, "Le Mouvement ouvrière francais et les intellectuels avant le première guerre mondiale," *Cahiers d'Histoire de L'Institut Maurice Thorez* 15 (1976): 12-34.

24. For an overview of these arguments see R. Michels, *Political Parties* (New York: The Free Press, 1962 ed.); G. Roth, *The Social Democrats in Imperial Germany: A Study in Working-Class Isolation and National Integration* (Totowa, N.J.: Bedminster Press, 1963); D. Groh, *Negative Integration and Revolutionär Attentismus* (Frankfurt am Main: Propylärn, 1973).

25. For Geary's argument see R. Geary, "The German Labour Movement, 1848-1919," *European Studies Review* 6 (1976): 297-330. On the reading habits of the Social Democratic rank and file see H.-J. Steinberg, *Sozialismus and deutsche Sozialdemokratie* (Hanover: Verlag für Literatur and Zeit Geschehen, 1967). For general accounts of Social Democratic culture see G. D. Steenson, *"Not one Man, Not one Penny": German Social Democracy, 1863-1914* (Pittsburgh, Pa.: University of Pittsburgh Press, 1981); V. Lidtke, *The Culture of Social Democracy in Imperial Germany* (forthcoming). A series of essays edited by Richard Evans contrasts broader working-class culture to the more narrowly defined Social Democratic culture. See R. Evans, ed., *The Culture of the German Working Class, 1890-1933* (London: Croom Helm, 1981).

26. For a brief account of Michels's relationship to the SPD see W. J. Mommsen, "Max Weber and Robert Michels: An Asymmetrical Partnership," *European Journal of Sociology* 23 (1981): 100-116. Michels's study of intellectuals and the Italian socialist movement is *Il fratelli proletariato e borghesia nel movimento socialista italiano* (Turin: Bocca, 1908).

27. For the Berlin party school see P. Nettl, *Rosa Luxemburg* (London: Oxford University Press, 1969 ed.) pp. 262–267; N. Jacobs, "The German Social Democratic Party-School in Berlin," *History Workshop Journal* 5 (1978): 179–187.

28. A comparison of German and Italian socialist parliamentary groups' class composition is found in H. U. Hesse, "Il gruppo parlamentare del partito socialista, la sua composizione e la sua funzione negli anni della crisi del parlamentarismo italiano," in L. Valiani and H. Wandruszka, eds., *Movimento operaio e socialista in Italia e in Germania del 1870 al 1920* (Bologna: Il Mulino, 1976).

For an analysis of Labor M.P.s in Britain see D. E. Martin, " 'The Instruments of the People': The Parliamentary Labour Party in 1906," in Martin and Rubinstein, eds., *Ideology and the Labour Movement*. For Bernstein's study see E. Bernstein, *Ferdinand Lassalle: As a Social Reformer* (New York: Scribner's, 1893). On the "machine man" Ebert see C. E. Schorske, *German Social Democracy, 1905–1917* (Cambridge, Mass.: Harvard University Press, 1955; 1983 ed.), pp. 116–145; D. K. Buse, "Friedrich Ebert and German Socialism, 1871–1919" (Ph.D. diss., University of Oregon, 1972).

29. A good summary of a vast literature can be found in R. J. Geary, *European Labour Protest, 1848–1939* (London: Croom Helm, 1981).

30. The German evidence is derived from P. Gohre, *Drei monate fabriksarbeiter, und bandwerksbursche* (Leipzig: F. W. Grunow, 1891), p. 102. The English observer is R. Roberts, *The Classic Slum* (Harmondsworth: Penguin, 1973), p. 178.

31. For working-class cultures in Italy see the summary by G. Bonacchi and A. Pescarolo, "Culture della communità e cultura del mestère all origini della resistenza operaaia italiana," *Movimento Operaio e Socialista* 3 (1980): 37–48. The FIOM official is Fernando Santi. See C. Castagno, *Bruno Buozzi* (Milan: Avanti!, 1955), preface (F. Santi).

32. Geary, *European Labour Protest*.

33. K. Hardie, *From Serfdom to Socialism* (London: George Allen, 1923), p. 26.

34. One famous "revisionist" essay dismisses the French anarchosyndicalist movement. See P. Stearns, *Revolutionary Syndicalism and French Labour* (New Brunswick, N.J.: Rutgers University Press, 1971). For more balanced accounts of French and Italian anarcho-syndicalism see B. Moss, *Origins of the French Labor Movement* (Berkeley, Los Angeles, London: University of California Press, 1976); G. Procacci, *La lotta di classe agli inzi del Secolo XX* (Rome: Riunit, 1970); A. Riosa, *Il sindicalismo rivoluzionario in Italia* (Bari: De Donato, 1976).

35. For Kocka see the summary of his work in J. Kocka, "Class Formation, Interest Articulation and Public Policy: the origins of the German

white-collar class in the late nineteenth and early twentieth centuries,''
in S. D. Berger, ed., *Organising Interests in Western Europe* (Cambridge:
Cambridge University Press, 1981). For Blackbourn see D. Blackbourn,
''The *Mittelstand* in German Society and Politics, 1871-1914,'' *Social History* 4 (1977): 409-433. For British clerks see G. Crossick, ed., *The Lower Middle Class In Late Victorian Britain, 1870-1914* (London: Croom Helm, 1977).

36. For the French case see N. Birnbaum, *Le peuple et le gros: histoire d'un mythe* (Paris: Grasset, 1973). For the English case see E. P. Thompson, *The Making of the English Working Class* (Harmondsworth: Penguin, 1968 ed.); G. Stedman Jones, ''Rethinking Chartism,'' in *Languages of Class* (Cambridge: Cambridge University Press, 1983).

37. S. Yeo, ''Towards 'Making form of more movement than spirit': Further thoughts on labour, socialism and the New Life,'' in J. A. Jowett and R. Taylor, eds., *Bradford, 1890-1914. The Cradle of the Independent Labour Party* (Leeds: University of Leeds, Centre for Adult Education, 1980), p. 84. Hobsbawm, ''The Fabians Reconsidered.''

38. The Milanese pamphleteer is quoted in R. Fede, ''Socialismo e litteratura,'' in various authors, *Prampolini e il socialismo riformista*, Vol. I (Rome: Mondo Operato Edizioni Avanti!, 1978), pp. 134-135. The English journalist was Joe Burgess in *The Workman's Times*, 14 July 1894.

39. On the young Mussolini see R. De Felice, *Mussolini il revoluzionario* (Turin: Einaudi, 1965).

40. See the points raised in R. McKibbin, ''Arthur Henderson as Labour Leader,'' *International Review of Social History* 23 (1978): 79-101.

41. On electoral strategies see G. Therborn, ''The Rule of Capital and the Rise of Democracy,'' *New Left Review* 103 (1977): 3-41; A Prezeworski, ''Social Democracy as a Historical Phenomenon,'' *New Left Review* 122 (1980): 27-58. Duverger's concept is explained in M. Duverger, *Political Parties*, 2nd Eng. ed., rev. (New York: Wiley, 1963), pp. 63-71, 101.

42. In general see Gouldner, *Against Fragmentation* (see n. 14). For France see W. K. Sewell, *Work and Revolution* (Cambridge: Cambridge University Press), 1980; J. Rancière, *La nuit des proletaires* (Paris: Fayard, 1981). For English see J. Ree, *Proletarian Philosophers* (Oxford: Clarendon Press, 1984). For the Bolsheviks and Bogdanov see J. Schurrer, ''Bogdanov e Lenin: bolscevismo al bivio,'' in E. J. Hobsbawm et al., *Storia del marxismo*, vol. 2 (Turin: Einaudi, 1979), pp. 495-546. For the German Social Democrats see Evans, *Culture of the German Working Class*. For Gramsci see H. Entwistle, *Antonio Gramsci. Conservative Schooling for Radical Politics* (London: Routledge & Kegan Paul, 1979).

43. See bibliography compiled by Levy and Westoby on education/self-education in the pre-1914 European socialist movement, n. 2.

44. The theme of socialism and sociology is pursued by Gouldner. See Gouldner, *The Future of the Intellectuals*; idem, 1985.

45. For Bellamy see A. Lipow, *Authoritarian Socialism in America* (Berkeley, Los Angeles, London: University of California Press, 1982).

46. For an overview of Second International socialism see Hobsbawm *Storia del marxismo*, vols. 1–2. For the theory of rent see S. Clarke, *Marx, Marginalism and Modern Sociology* (London: Macmillan & Co., 1982).

47. Bauman summarizes the theories nicely. See Z. Bauman, *Memories of Class* (London: Routledge & Kegan Paul, 1982). For a social historian's viewpoint see P. N. Stearns, ''The Middle Class: Toward a Precise Definition,'' *Comparative Studies in Society and History* 21 (1979): 376–396. See also the marvelous social anthropology of J. Frykman and O. Löfgren, *Den Kultiverade Människan* [The cultivated man] (Lund: Liberförlag, 1979).

48. P. N. Stearns, *Lives of Labour* (London: Routledge & Kegan Paul, 1975).

49. F. Parkin, *Marxism: A Bourgeois Critique* (London: Tavistock, 1979).

9

Socialism and Intellectuals in *Fin-de-Siècle* Vienna: Max Adler on the Relationship Between Socialism and Intellectuals

Lennart Olausson

INTRODUCTION

Around the year 1890 many intellectuals in Europe turned to socialism in order to find an answer to the social problems caused by the modernization of society. Some became increasingly involved in the workers' movements and Social Democratic parties. Most, however, turned to the right within a decade. In his paper in this volume, Carl Levy discusses how the educated middle classes influenced different socialist and labor organizations in the period around 1900. My concern with this problem (i.e., the connection between socialism and intellectuals) relates to the question of how a socialist at the turn of the twentieth century sought to convince intellectuals that because of their function in society they actually had an intrinsic interest in socialism. My example is the Austrian Social Democrat Max Adler, who, in his paper *Der*

Sozialismus und die Intellektuellen (1910), tried to promote ideological change among intellectuals in *fin-de-siècle* Vienna to win them over to socialism.[1]

The method I use in my paper, an analysis of what I will call ideological transformation,[2] is to concentrate upon what a person, an organization, and a party does in order to win people over to his or its own cause. In this case the main part of my analysis consists of a reading of Adler's text. I will also concentrate on the semantically oriented part of the work of ideological transformation. In order for such an analysis to be complete, one has to consider the practical and organizational aspects of political mobilization. Of course, for my own purposes I cannot completely ignore political, institutional, and cultural aspects. In this regard a few remarks are in order. Which political and intellectual features of *fin-de-siècle* Vienna constitute the background dimensions for my analysis?

The situation was, roughly, as follows. Toward the end of the century two mass political parties were forming. On the right was the anti-Semitic Christian Social party, with Karl Lueger as its dominant leader. On the left was the Austrian Social Democratic party, with Victor Adler as chairman. The political organization of masses of people was a new phenomenon. As late as the 1870s political life was dominated by small political clubs and the like. With the rapid industrialization promoted by the Hapsburg monarchy and the consequent expansion of the population of Vienna, one finds corresponding changes in the political life of the city.

The Christian Social party was a Catholic party. It can be further defined as a municipal conservative party, with strong anti-Semitic leanings. In the 1890s it grew very strong among the petite bourgeoisie and part of the working class in Vienna, and later it widened its base among the peasants in the countryside. A great deal of the party's success depended on the charisma of its leader. A mass party of Catholics, not unlike the Social Democrats, took to the streets and organized mass demonstrations. This shocked both the old hierarchies in the countryside and the Viennese liberals. The Social Democratic party also grew very quickly in the 1890s. It was influenced not only by German socialists but also by some particularly Austrian political issues and debates. The common question was, of course, the struggle for universal suffrage, while the dominant specific Austrian question concerned the national right of self-determination. The party was organized as a more-or-less miniature Communist International, where the different nationalities within the dual monarchy had their own organizations within the larger party. On the political level, the Social Democratic party fought for national self-determination within the Austro-Hungarian state.

Liberalism had reached its climax in the 1860s and 1870s. Toward the end of the century its influence had almost entirely been eclipsed. Both Karl Lueger and Victor Adler were former liberals. The crisis of liberalism was mostly a crisis concerning basic values, that is, rationalism and individualism. These values were beacons of social progress. The means or the road to progress was via science, education, and hard work. To these values we may also add the aesthetic. In the 1890s the heroes of the upper middle class were no longer political leaders but were instead actors, artists, and critics. The liberals in the middle class lost their interest in politics and turned to the arts, and they also turned to some extent to science.

The Social Democrats embraced many of these liberal values, which were attacked by different social strata in Austria. It was primarily the pan-German movement, with its strong anti-Semite leanings, which in practice stood for much of the criticism of the liberal values. This movement was also the one that had its strongest roots among students.[3]

It was in this political and intellectual milieu that young intellectual socialists formed their views of society, some of them becoming members of the Austrian Social Democratic party. My focus in this paper is on a special group formed at the beginning of the new century, the so-called Austro-Marxists.

This group was organized in 1904 around a series of studies called *Marx-Studien*. Within a few years the group also began a journal called *Der Kampf*. All the members of this group, including the most well-known—Max Adler, Otto Bauer, Rudolf Hilferding, and Karl Renner—had studied at the University of

Vienna, and all became doctors of law, with the exception of Hilferding, who became a medical doctor.

In the *Marx-Studien*, they published book-length studies in such areas as economics, the national question, the sociology of law, and philosophy. They tried to apply Marxism to new fields of study, and many of the problems they dealt with theoretically were the immediate political problems of the Social Democratic party.

The Marxism of the Austro-Marxists may be characterized by saying that this group viewed Marxism as an open system. They made efforts to use the theories of Marx in new fields and to relate his works to important topics in their own time, especially to neo-Kantian philosophy.

SOCIALISM AND INTELLECTUALS

My main point in the following analysis of the aforementioned book by Max Adler is to show how and what Adler did when he tried to convince the intellectuals of his time that they actually had an intrinsic interest in socialism. To his contemporaries these two entities—intellectuals and socialism—were seen as opposites, while to Adler it was a political necessity in the battle for socialism to win intellectuals to the cause of the working class. He believed that he could convince intellectuals of this by showing them the real meaning of *intellectual* and of *socialism*.

My approach is directed toward an understanding of *ideological change*, which means that I am interested mainly in the change in signification of some "ideologemes" that are important in this connection. This kind of analysis of ideological change is oriented toward the ideological struggle over the meaning of important symbols. These symbols can be things such as national flags, first of May, or concepts such as freedom, democracy, socialism, human nature, and social science.

In order to make my approach more clear I will offer an example. Adler notes that socialism is basically not a *worker's* movement, but a *culture* movement; and the movement of this culture consists precisely in this, that the socialism realizes the culture through the workers set in motion, that it moves the culture and the workers to here and will continue to move through it (page 50).

(im Grunde gar keine *Arbeiter*bewegung als solche, sondern eine *Kultur*bewegung; und die Bewegung dieser Kultur besteh gerade darin, dass der Sozialismus die Kultur durch die in Bewegung gebrachten Arbeiter verwirklichen, dass er die Kultur und die Arbeiter heranbewegen und durch sie fortbewegen will.)

Socialism is, according to Adler, something cultural and at the same time something related to the working class. He also argues that the workers are aware of this cultural movement in socialism. If we look at other places in Adler's book, we can find that socialism is a science (p. 42) and that socialism is the realization of a tendency in human nature toward unity—in Adler's words, toward *"Einheit und Harmonie"* (''unity and harmony'') (p. 75).

From this short analysis, we can construct the following scheme around which the subsequent discussion of Adler's ideological transformation work will be concentrated. What Adler attempts is to unite two sociologically different groups, the working class and the intellectuals, the latter being part of the middle class. He does this by changing the connotations of some ideologemes. Here, I think that it is also correct to call the social categories ''working class'' and ''intellectuals'' ideologemes, but of course at the same time they have their own very specific denotations.

	ideologemes	
	socialism	
	culture (*Kultur*)	
working class	unity in human nature (*Einheit und Harmonie*)	intellectuals
	science (of society) (*Sozialwissenschaft*)	

The prerequisite for Adler's project is that all the words that are central are more or less ambiguous and vague. In the following

I will show how Adler, by giving the ideologemes a partly new and more precise meaning, connects socialism with the working class on the one hand and intellectuals on the other. In this process he makes use of the ideologemes mentioned above, giving them new connotations. In the process he also changes the connotation of the two social groups (the working class and the intellectuals) themselves.

SOCIALISM

The Hapsburg monarchy, Adler says, is a capitalist society. It is divided into classes, where the dominant class struggle is between capitalists and workers. In Austria-Hungary, as in all capitalistic societies, the working class is the lowest class. The workers, by virtue of their class position, know their own intrinsic interests. At first, they can only subconsciously feel their interest, but when they begin to unite in struggle, side by side, this feeling becomes ever more distinct. With this one finds the emergence of class consciousness. It is at this point that workers can come in contact with socialism. Once they have done so, they never forget it. By means of this contact with socialism, in the meaning given to the term by Marx, the workers come to understand both their position in society and what to do in order to change that position. The workers are then part of the new society to come (p. 43).

When the proletariat liberates itself in this way, it is liberated not only from its economic chains but also from its "spiritual" (*des Geistes*) chains—that is, the private, economic view of work. Here, the working-class movement carries on its struggle in the interest of all human beings, for the common interest of human culture (*Menschheitskultur*). Through the development of the productive forces it becomes possible to make real a social organization that is compatible with the cultural interests of mankind. Socialism is, for Adler, connected with the working class, but it is also something more than this. It is in part the cultural content of *human* culture, but it is also more. Since the days of Marx, he argues, the scientific investigation of economic life has been possible (pp. 41–

42). Socialism is a science, and Marx achieved in the social field what Newton achieved in the physical. Marx was the founding father of *the* theory of society.[4]

This means that socialism will, in practice, order the whole of social and political life, arranging everyone according to this whole and putting each occupation in its proper place. The natural scientist, the engineer, the economist, the teacher, the doctor, the lawyer, the priest, the author, the artist—all these new and old professions must turn to social science—that is, to Marxism—to solve their theoretical problems and must embrace political socialism in order to solve their practical ones. Socialism is also a cultural movement, or *"Kulturbewegung,"* as Adler says. When he used this concept of *"Kultur,"* he did so as a man deeply involved with German humanism and with the German idea of the place of the humanistic university in society. *"Kultur"* is connected with education, or, more precisely, with *"Bildung."* It is through this *Bildung* that one develops a unique personality and through this becomes a member of the *"Bildungsbürgertum."* By means of such concepts, Adler seeks a form of solidarity which unites everybody into a spiritual community (p. 11).

"KULTUR"

If we look back in history, Adler notes, we can find periods when people were united through a common culture. He mentions the years around 1800 and 1848 as examples. In these two periods intellectuals were not separated from the rest of the population. After 1848, however, there appeared a widening gap between intellectuals and workers, with intellectuals coming under the sway of a bourgeois conception of culture.

The "ideologeme" of the "cultural" is central to Adler's discussion. It has a double connotation. On one hand it is a neutral concept in relation to class struggle in that it is related to human nature and the movement toward unity and harmony. On the other hand, it is very important for Adler to show that the conditions for the realization of the cultural in society are not classless. Under capitalism the cultural realm is not allowed to dominate. Instead, capitalism leads to its degeneration. Only socialism can facilitate this realization of the cultural in society.

Like the concept of the "cultural," "socialism" is also only vaguely defined in Adler's ideological transformation work. Ever since the concept first came into use at the beginning of the nineteenth century, there had existed a leftist and a rightist version, or connotation, of the term. It was not always easy to see the difference between them. To make my point clear, we can look at Marx, Lassalle, and Bismarck, all of whom claimed to be socialists. What unites them is an opposition to liberalism and a common subordination of the individual to the whole of society.[5] In the 1890s socialism came to be more and more related to the working class and to the Social Democratic parties. Socialism became more and more connected with ideas concerning the socializing of private property, especially the means of production. This is also where the difference between a leftist and a rightist socialism comes to the fore.

In order to understand how Adler tried to win intellectuals to socialism in *fin-de-siècle* Vienna, it is important to understand the rightist version of socialism as well. In Vienna this kind of socialism was very closely tied to a university academic tradition. One of the most important men in this connection was L. von Stein. He was also one of the first to make use of the term "socialism." For von Stein, socialism did not question the idea of private property—this was "communism"—but rather promoted a society in which everyone could develop himself in accordance with his own faculties.[6] Von Stein taught at the University of Vienna from the middle of the 1850s to the end of 1880. There, he influenced many students. One of his successors was the professor of law Anton Menger, who continued von Stein's tradition in a way. Menger wrote a book on the history of socialism and another on the social problems confronting Austria-Hungary. The latter book was discussed by Engels and Kautsky in *Die Neue Zeit*, where they coined the new concept "socialism of jurisprudence" (*Juristen-Sozialismus*) in order to reveal Menger's position.[7]

Menger was an Austrian "*Katheder-Sozialist*," and as such he tried to formulate theories about social issues and even to develop a sociology based on jurisprudence. We can also mention in passing that Karl Grünberg, the teacher of many Austro-Marxists,[8] studied under von Stein and Menger. With von Stein and Menger we find a rightist version of socialism that connects socialism not with socializing private property but with the development of culture. Obviously, Adler could make use of the connotations that von Stein and Menger had given the word *socialism* when he, in his turn, tried to give it some additional connotations. *"Katheder-Marxisten"* might perhaps be a suitable nickname for the Austro-Marxists.[9]

INTELLECTUALS AND SOCIAL SCIENCE

The first part of this essay revealed how Adler connected the working class with socialism. However, he also emphasized the connections between socialism and science, culture, and a tendency toward unity in human nature. In order to win intellectuals to his viewpoints, I think it was most important for Adler to establish the relationship between culture and socialism on the one hand and between science (*Wissenschaft*) and socialism on the other. He could thereby show that intellectuals actually had an intrinsic interest of their own in socialism.

For Adler, intellectuals were no "servants of the proletariat," nor did they have to try to subordinate the working class to their leadership. Both the working class and the intellectuals had an interest in socialism, but it was from different positions. Just as workers would not spontaneously grasp this, intellectuals would not either. Intellectuals did not understand what socialism really consisted of, nor did they understand that there was something there for them.

In order to understand Adler's strategy in solving this problem, we first have to make clear both the denotations and connotations of the word *intellectual*. The word has a history that is not as long as that of *socialism*. Nor are we here faced with a clear leftist or rightist version of the same concept. On the contrary, I think that "intellectual" is for the most part associated with liberalism and with *Bildung*. At the same time, "intellectual" has something insulting about it when it is used by either socialists or conservatives.

The connotations of the concept of "intellectual" are very complex. In the cultural milieu of Vienna we assume that the discussions in France, as well as those in Germany and Russia, in connection with the Dreyfus affair were of importance.[10] For the sake of simplicity, however, let us concentrate on the German usage. First, it is important to note that the term *"Intellektueller"* had its origins in the concept of *"intelligenz."* In turn, this concept was central in Hegel's conception of the *"Mittelstand,"* which was connected to the governmental and bourgeois intelligence. Von Stein, however, used the term in another connection than did Hegel. He saw the third estate (*der dritte Stand*) as a central concept, an estate composed of workers, capitalists, and the intelligentsia. It was the "Besitzer geistiger Güter," that is, the intelligence, that is most interesting here.[11] Vienna followed this connotation introduced by von Stein. The intelligent man was defined as the educated man, who differed from both capitalists and the unpropertied classes. To von Stein, intelligence characterized men who fought against the absolutist state.

We can say that Adler did for the Social Democrats on the left what had already been done for the right. Here we have the connection between socialism, culture, and science. Adler tries to give socialism other connotations, but he does more than that. He also has to give a positive meaning to the concept of the intellectual. This was a difficult task in the Social Democratic party of his time. Among Marxists we can find two different uses of *"Intellektueller"*: one is related to class analysis, and the other is related to a standardized, insulting usage.[12]

Most of the discussion about intellectuals occurred within the German Social Democratic party. Kautsky, its leading theorist, said that the intelligence was situated somewhere between capitalists and workers. One could, he argued, hope to win some supporters of socialism from this group, especially in times when people with a university education were threatened by unemployment. This was the case in the 1890s, and there occurred a debate in *Die Neue Zeit* about this problem. Kautsky argued that the unemployed university graduate belonged to the unemployed reserve army. In this case, one could even talk of a *"Proletariat der Intelligenz."*[13]

When we look for negative connotations of "intellectual," we can find these expressed by Bebel. In connection with the revisionist controversy, Bebel argued that one ought to be suspicious when dealing with a university graduate or teacher.[14]

SOCIAL SCIENCE AND INTELLECTUALS

The situation faced by Adler when he tried to win the intellectual over to socialism was that the Social Democrats needed support from other layers in society besides the working class. But the need for support from intellectuals was combined with great suspicion toward them. As for the intellectuals themselves, I think that the connotation of "socialism" in Vienna was vague enough to be attractive for the majority of those in this stratum of society. It was Adler's task to convince intellectuals that the working class and the Social Democratic party were their friends.

In order to do this, Adler had to show that there was an inherent opposition between capitalist society and intellectuals as a social group. To be an intellectual meant to be engaged in spiritual activity, where one should be left undisturbed and where one also had the possibility of participating in and gaining from the conception of intellectual as Adler conceived of it: workers of the mind. This kind of work demanded freedom, he argued, a freedom that was not compatible with capitalism. The conclusion that Adler draws from this fact is that intellectuals share no interest with capitalists, that is, they have no interest in perpetuating capitalism. Of course, he understood this not to apply to all intellectuals. Those who are employed by capitalists or are capitalists themselves have no interest in socialism, and the same goes for those who would defend the established order. The remainder of intellectuals, the dominant number, do not have any interest in maintaining established order by virtue of their social position. The problem is that this group in itself has very little influence.

As far as I can see, Adler tries to adopt both the definition of intellectual used by Kautsky and the one introduced by von Stein. But he draws conclusions that are different. He insists that many intellectuals could become followers of socialism. One need only show intellectuals, he says, that their class interest is the same as the content of socialism, which, in turn, is the same as the cultural interest of intellectuals. This achieved, one can win intellectuals over to socialism.

Even if Adler could succeed in convincing intellectuals that they have an inherent interest in socialism, this by itself would not be enough. He would also have to convince his fellow Social Democrats that intellectuals are not something for them to fear. The best way to do this is, of course, to show that Marx also believed this to be the case. Adler claims that Marx and Engels discussed this problem in the *Communist Manifesto*, where they argued that some of the ideologists of the bourgeoisie would leave their own class and join the proletariat. They would do this because of a theoretical understanding of historical development, which favored the working class. But it seems that Adler is not satisfied with winning this small group of the bourgeois to socialism. The most important characteristic of intellectuals, Adler says, is not their position between the dominating classes but their education. By "intellectual" he means all sorts of people who do spiritual work and whose work requires higher education. Adler's reason for emphasizing education instead of other characteristics follows from the premise that—for him—the important thing is to point to the relationship between intellectuals and socialism and, in this connection especially—and most important—to point out the scientific side of socialism.

I think we can find additional support for this interpretation of Adler's thought by looking at his scientifically oriented work. In 1921 he became, to my knowledge, the first Marxist professor of sociology. His chair was located in the faculty of law at the University of Vienna. The fact that Adler obtained this professorship at all is closely connected with the dissolution of the Hapsburg monarchy in 1918 and the formation of the first Republic of Austria.

It is not his work in the 1920s that is interesting here but rather the way in which he obtained this professorship. In 1907, the Viennese *Soziologische Gesellschaft* was founded by, among others, W. Jerusalem—a neo-Kantian philosopher—and Adler. Another Austro-Marxist, Karl Renner, also played an important part in this association. This sociological association had its forerunner in the *Sozialwissenschaftliche Bildungsverein* (educational union for social science) in the 1890s. Here, many radicals of *fin-de-siècle* Vienna could meet and discuss the social problems of the day.

It was students and teachers of jurisprudence who offered the radical critique of industrial society. And it was also in this faculty that Adler, Renner, and Bauer were registered as students. Renner and Adler became doctors of law in the 1890s. This small group of radicals and socialists worked together with another group of social reformers at the university. Most of the latter also came from the faculty of law, and so-called socialists of jurisprudence belong here. I think that these two groups were very important in forming the new kind of social science that was developed in Austria at the beginning of this century.

MARXISM AS SOCIOLOGY

Adler wrote a book on causal and teleological explanations, *Kausualität und Teologie im Streite um die Wissenschaft* (1904), in which he tried to show the kinds of foundations necessary for social science generally and for sociology in particular. He tried to provide an answer to the question, How is social science possible? It was a question formulated in Kantian form, but Adler tried to give it a Marxian content. Therefore, we can reformulate his question as this: How is Marxism possible as social science or as sociology? His answer shows that he found two conditions for this possibility. The first was the formal one, where Kant was important, and the second was the contextual one (regarding socialized mankind), a view of man formulated by Marx. These two conditions, I think, may be unified within the context of Adler's philosophy of history. In his view, social science and socialism have the same goal in history: to reach the classless society, which is a society without contradictions, a united society.

Adler also argued this point in a more philosophical way, basing his thought on Kant's philosophy. The fundamental kind of law relating to human life concerns its accordance to norms (*Normmässigkeit*). This means that human life has the highest ecumenical goal. Viewed psychologically, man manifests a living teleology toward unity. One finds this conception in all of human activity: logic, ethics, and aesthetics—that is, in thinking, willing, and enjoying. These formal and general sides of norms are, Adler says, the epistemological expression of the social side of human life. There exists a kind of inner conformity to law which, through man's intentional activities, becomes an outer causality. By such means we find

> the wonderful bond, that connects the world of values with any world of natural necessity, that the causality in the domain of social life is not any longer acting in a blind way, just as it no longer does within the organic domain, but *is determined through its imminent formal relations toward a fixed direction.*[15]

> (das wunderbare Band, das die Welt der Werte mit jener der Naturnotwendigkeit verbindet, dass die Kausalität im Bereich des sozialen Lebens nicht mehr blindes Wirken ist, so ist es schon nicht mehr im Organischen ist, sondern *durch ihre immanenten formalen Beziehungen nach bestimmten Richtungen determiniert ist.*)

STUDENTS IN VIENNA AS AN INTELLECTUAL MILIEU

In his discussion of intellectuals, Adler talks about professionals and students. It appears to be the latter group that captures his main interest. This interpretation is supported by the fact that Adler wrote his book to celebrate the fifteenth anniversary of *Die freie Vereinigung sozialistischer Studenten in Wien*. Adler had been the first chairman of this student union, and it was through it that many of the Austro-Marxists gained their first education in

Marxism. The student association itself emerged from an intellectual circle called *"Heiligen Leopold,"* a name deriving from that of an inn at which they used to meet. There was also another circle of younger students called the *Veritas* whose meeting place was the famous coffeehouse Griensteidl. It was the meeting place of writers, artists, and politicians. Here they could meet and talk not only with fellow Austrians but also with many of the Polish and Russian refugees who had found their way to Vienna. In the beginning of the 1890s the young students were mostly apolitical. During the course of the decade, however, they became politicized, particularly in their regard of German nationalism. The *Freie Vereinigung* was not very successful in recruiting students. Rather, it was the anti-Semitic and rightist organizations that were more successful. Political awakening among students focused on the question of language and on nationalism. Thus, it was detached from the working-class struggle for universal franchise and the solution of social problems.[16]

What position did the students and the university have in society, according to Adler? It seems that Adler saw the cultural, scientific, and other intellectual spheres as existing above and beyond class struggle. He saw in the universities the organizational means to bring these fields together and, moreover, to bring them forward. However, he thought this was possible only in an ideal situation, not in the university of Vienna as it then existed. When criticizing the universities of his own day, Adler distinguished between their formal, outer freedom and their inner freedom. If this inner freedom, the real idealism, could survive within the university, it would have been possible to move beyond bourgeois ideology to the cultivation of inner spiritual freedom and self-education. But this inner freedom had disappeared from the university under the pressure of outer freedom and reality.

Consequently, according to Adler, if the Social Democrats were interested in attracting students, reforms would have to be made within the educational sphere. He had in mind reforms that were adjusted to scientific and philosophical interests instead of to the interests of capitalist society. For Adler, it is the duty and responsibility of scientists to oppose this society; failing this, they are in fact giving up their task as intellectuals.

The university system in the Hapsburg monarchy had changed substantially by the end of the nineteenth century. Technical colleges and similar institutions were organized into the university system. Here, one can see that different reforms were made in order for the universities to be adapted to the new economic and political demands. The adjustments were combined with an attempt to renew the autonomy of the universities, but such autonomy was not used for the purposes Adler sought. Instead, one can see how an authoritarian professorship continued to dominate the entire structure of higher education, especially at the University of Vienna.[17]

Adler wanted the students to be as students had been in 1848. At that time, he says, students were freedom fighters. In the revolution of 1848 students were the first to fight. Adler sees a real union emerging then, and again in 1905, between the working class and intellectuals. Unfortunately, intellectuals have not remained faithful to this aim of unified freedom. It is only the working class that remains faithful to its historical task.[18]

CONCLUSION

I have read Adler's book as being part of the ideological struggle that Austrian Social Democrats waged against the rival Christian Social party and against the pan-German movement, a struggle in which Austro-Marxists played an important part. Adler claimed that there existed an urgent need for intellectuals to unite with the working class in a common struggle for socialism. He also tried to show how this unity could be built. In my approach to Adler's work I have tried to show the ways in which he sought to achieve this by means of what I call ideological transformation. Adler combined the ideologemes "socialism," "unity," "culture," and "science" in a specific way that changed their respective connotations in order to demonstrate that intellectuals actually had an intrinsic interest in socialism. In order to convince his fellow Social Democrats of this, he had to define intellectuals in a new way, again giving the concept another sociological connotation. Given this, even if he succeeded in his task, there still remained one problem—namely, that of showing the necessary connection between the Austrian Social Democratic party and socialism.

Adler attempted to solve this problem with a theory of human nature. In human nature, he says, there is a tendency toward "unity and harmony" (*Einheit und Harmonie*). This starts in the human mind as an ideal but does not remain there. Instead, this ideal must gain realization in the social world. This "natural" propensity toward unity and harmony is also cultural, and could be called a tendency toward socialism as well. Hence, it should be possible to convince intellectuals that they should become Social Democrats in order to be able to live in unity and harmony with their human nature. If someone says he is a socialist but not a Social Democrat, Adler argues, then he has not understood what he is talking about. It is the Social Democratic party that fights for humanity and its cultural interests. In short, Adler's position is that intellectuals need the Social Democratic party in order to implement their inherent interest, and the Social Democratic party needs the intellectuals so that it can win support from a majority among the population in order to acquire the political influence that will make the realization of socialism possible.

NOTES

1. This paper is related to two current projects on Austro-Marxism, one on Marxism and neo-Kantianism (the study on Austro-Marxism constitutes the second part, preceded by an earlier study of the German development) and another that is part of a comparative project called "Institution and Ideology" being done at the University of Gothenburg on the university systems in Germany, Austria, France, and Sweden.

2. My method is inspired by, on one hand, a project on ideological change carried out at the Institute of History of Ideas and Learning at Gothenburg, and on the other hand by the analysis of fascism made by the group around Projekt Ideologie Theorie in Berlin. The notions of "ideological transformation work" and "ideologem" have been taken from a paper written by H. Bosch, "Ideologische Transformationsarbeit

in Hitlers Rede zum Ersten Mai 1933," Fascismus und Ideologie I, *Argument Sonderband* 60 (1980). See also the more general program of the group "Projekt Ideologie Theorie in Theorien über Ideologie," *Argument Sonderband* 40 (1979).

3. The interest in *fin-de-siècle* Vienna among intellectuals of today has produced some great studies, the following among them: W. M. Johnston, *The Austrian Mind: An Intellectual and Social History 1848–1938* (Berkeley, Los Angeles, London: University of California Press, 1972); A. Fuchs, *Geistige Strömungen in Österreich 1867–1918* (Vienna: Löcker Verlag, 1984); A. Janik and S. Toulmin, *Wittgenstein's Vienna* (New York: Simon & Schuster, 1973); C.-E. Schorske, *Fin-de-siècle Vienna, Politics and Culture* (New York: Alfred A. Knopf, 1980); M. Francis, ed., *The Viennese Enlightment* (London: Croom Helm, 1985).

4. This is a view of Marxism that Max Adler develops in his first larger study, *Kausalität und Teleologie im Streite um die Wissenschaft* (Vienna: Verlag Wiener Volksbuchhandlung, 1904).

5. H. Müller, *Ursprung und Geschichte des Wortes Sozialismus und Seine Verwandten* (Berlin: Verlag J. H. W. Dietz, 1967).

6. Ibid., p. 133.

7. F. Engels and K. Kautsky, *Juristen-Sozialismus Die Neue Zeit* (Stuttgart: Jg. 5, 1887), p. 49 ff.

8. Günter Nenning shows this in his "Biographie," in *Indexband zu Archiv für die Geschichte des Sozialismus und Arbeiterbewegung* (D. Grünberg) (Zurich: Limmat-Verlag, 1973).

9. Leon Trotsky met the Austro-Marxists during his stay in Vienna, and he characterized them in his own lively manner, saying that in "the old imperial, hierarchic, vain and futile Vienna, the academic Marxists would refer to each other with a sort of sensuous delight as 'Herr Doktor.' " L. Trotsky, *My Life* (New York: Pathfinder Press Inc., 1970), p. 209. After meeting the Austro-Marxists at the Café Central, Trotsky concluded that these "people were not revolutionaries. Moreover, they represented the type that was farthest from that of the revolutionary." Ibid., p. 207.

10. My discussion on the connotations of the "intellectuals" is based upon the following: O. W. Müller, "Intelligencija. Untersuchungen zur Geschichte eines politischen Schlagwortes," *Frankfurter Abhandlungen zur Slavistik* 17, 1971; and D. Bering, *Die Intellektuellen. Geschichte eines Schimpfwortes* (Frankfurt am Main: Ullstein, 1982).

11. Müller, "Intelligencija," p. 70.

12. Bering, *Die Intellektuellen,* p. 163 f.

13. Kautsky wrote a series of articles called "Die Intelligenz und die Sozialdemokratie" in *Die Neue Zeit,* Jg. 13, 1894–1895. Max Adler also

took part in this debate. He wrote an article called "Zur Frage der Organisation des Proletariats der Intelligenz," but he didn't publish it under his own name (See A., Max, *Die Neue Zeit*, Jg. 13, 1894–1895).

14. Bering, *Die Intellektuellen*, p. 73.

15. M. Adler, *Marxistische Probleme. Beiträge zur Theorie der materialistischen Geschichtsauffasung und Dialektik* (Berlin: Verlag J. H. W. Dietz [first published in 1913]), p. 13 f.

16. K. Renner, *An der Wende zweier Zeiten* (2nd ed.) (Danubia Verlag, 1946), pp. 278–283; J. Hannak, *Karl Renner und seine Zeit* (Europa Verlag, 1965), pp. 51–60.

17. For a study on the changes of the University of Vienna, see J. Hochgerner, *Studium und Wissenschaftsentwicklung im Habsburgerreich. Studentengeschichte seit Gründung der Universität Wiens bis zum Ersten Weltkrieg* (Verlag der Österreichischen Hochschülerschaft, 1983), esp. chaps. 4 and 5.

18. M. Adler, *1848* (Vienna, 1905), pp. 22–24.

10

The Life Contents and Social Types of Finnish Intellectuals: On the Basis of a Longitudinal Study of Students of the 1960s

Yrjö-Paavo Häyrynen

In materialist interpretations the psychology of various social subjects is understood as the totality of their activities, duties, and contents of life. The study I will be reporting on here constitutes what can be called the *psychology of intellectuals* of a certain historical period.[1] The period studied covers the 1960s to the early 1980s. It concerns the courses of life of present academic workers and intellectuals who in the 1960s finished gymnasium and sought admission to different faculties of Helsinki University. Although focusing on only one generation of intellectuals, this study illuminates the diversity of life contents and careers within the intelligentsia, a group often characterized as one-dimensional, as the new class or the knowledge class. In question is how university selection, gender, social background, and educational experience are related to the formation of different fractions of intellectuals.

Despite the great expansion of university education in Finland from the 1920s onward, the largest group of those acquiring higher education still comes from either the upper middle class or the wealthier agricultural class.[2] The radicalism of the 1960s can be interpreted as a middle-class reaction toward deteriorating social and economic conditions. Only in part can they be said to represent an emancipatory trend of a broader nature. A progressive atmosphere prevailed for a short time in Finnish educational and cultural policy. In the mid-1970s, Finland experienced a counterreaction, which coincided with an economic crisis and the retarding of the growth of resources for the educational system.

In 1950, only 1.5 percent of Finland's population had acquired a university-level education. In 1980 this figure was 6 percent, and the projection for 1995 is 9 percent. It can be assumed that this growth will affect both the internal composition and the external position of the intelligentsia. Only a section of those performing intellectual labor are engaged in traditional core tasks, that is, defining cultural values or carrying out qualified intellectual work. The others perform jobs more narrowly defined by the existing division of labor. In this case, university education may not necessarily guarantee membership in an intellectual class, and it may require additional cultural merits, such as creativity, social influence, or an upper-class background.

According to Michel Foucault, the earlier paradigm of the educated person as the "universal intellectual," an example to other classes, is changing. There has been, Foucault notes,[3] a shift toward the "specific intellectual," whose source of influence is practical expertise. Between these two roles, the universal and the specific, may lie the "new middle class," whose members hold the jobs in the rapidly growing service sector. A rapid expansion of the organization of the public sector occurred in Finland in the 1970s. According to studies on the generational variation of ways of life,[4] this was a period when the new middle class started to form. In our follow-up study, many subjects stressed the communicative and administrative skills they had to learn after university graduation in the practical applications of life.

It can well be asked whether the *period* and the *socially deter-*

mined differentiation of the intelligentsia are reflected in the contents of life of various types of intellectuals. The subjects of our longitudinal study experienced the expansion of the mass university and the rise of student radicalism. They also belong to the large birth cohorts of 1945–48, who in the 1970s competed for jobs in the growing service sector. These may well have been the formative experiences of their generation.

One common denominator of intellectuals is their performance of mental work. For them, the idea of productivity usually refers to those mental aspects rather than to a practical changing of the world. Although creativity is a widely appreciated life goal among the intelligentsia, there are differences in the modes in which various intellectuals are actually involved in creative tasks. On the basis of the findings of our longitudinal study, the appreciation of creativity has grown during the last seventeen years. The scientific and technological revolution has increased the value of theoretical thinking, but at the same time it has made the pattern of change more unpredictable and confused. This may lead to the placing of controversial social pressures on individual creativity. Several psychological studies have attached importance to the contradictory traits of these "creative people": they may be intelligent, sensitive, and tolerant toward ambiguous ideas but at the same time conflicting, hostile, or cynical.[5] This has led to a theory of a complex personality that would underlie the creative potential of such intellectuals (Barron).

Yet the base cause of the complex mind of intellectuals may be their contradictory social position under capitalism. On one hand, in order to prove their merits, they must produce new and acceptable ideas. On the other hand, they must defend their autonomy. The mastery of the "wide" cultural code is regarded as important in the ambiguous tasks of the intellectual worker.[6] But there is also evidence that *work* molds the orientation of people in different social classes, and that people transmit these orientations to their children. Nonconformity and the flexible type of creativity of intellectuals is obviously related to the larger degree of self-direction they have in their work.[7] Sometimes the notion of nonconformity is, however, confused. One should consider the extent to which the academic worker has ideological freedom and the degree to which he or she must conform to the rules of the academic merit system.

It is thus possible to relate the "psychology of intellectuals" to their contradictory positions. Marja Järvelä-Hartikainer applied Erik Wright's conception of class structure in a recent empirical study of the Finnish intelligentsia.[8] She defined four criteria for membership in the intelligentsia: professional authority, position as the organizer of social activities, autonomy at work, and educational qualification. Various subgroups of the intelligentsia were described through the combining of these variables, and those meeting all of these criteria simultaneously were said to belong to the universal core intelligentsia. The idea is interesting, though the relatively small sample did not offer opportunities of analyzing deeply the different fractions of the intelligentsia. The author also admits that these criteria neglect the significance of the subjective definition of intellectuals. According to Antonio Gramsci, a person's *way of thinking*, not his formal qualification, determines whether he is an intellectual. In the present study, we have studied people who can be classified as core intelligentsia on the basis of their *cultural and political influence*. These are contrasted with the other subgroups in our follow-up sample. It can be asked how persons are educated and selected for these fractions of the intelligentsia and how these positions are then reflected in their orientations and life experiences. In this study we are chiefly interested in comparing the psychological characteristics, university and work experiences, and the development of work values of different intellectual fractions. The internal conflicts of the intellectual mind cannot be revealed with the survey method we used.

CAREER SELECTION: ANTICIPATING THE PATTERNS OF INTELLECTUALITY

The first phase of the Student Research Programme sought to reveal the factors of vocational choice of students interested in different educational and occupational alternatives. The theoretical background was provided by the model of self-selection, which hypothesizes that persons will match themselves with existing jobs when choosing their future careers.[9] The first investigation, made in 1965, was of students applying to different disciplines of Helsinki University, with various vocational intentions in mind. The interests and self-ratings of these students were patterned along the lines of vocational orientation, related in a characteristic way to vocational choice, even within a particular field of study. We found *social determinants* affecting these orientations: students from academically educated families strove more often toward intellectual professional tasks or creative self-manifestation, contrasted with the more uncertain orientation of students with lower-middle-class origins.[10]

Among students from the traditional upper middle class—with fathers as lawyers, higher officials, physicians, and so on—intellectual interests were stronger. The proportion of nonconformist and culturally orientated students was also highest in this group.[11] The female students from this class were oriented toward independent professional careers or artistic self-expression; for the males, this orientation meant the choice of a scholarly career or some "feminine" alternative (psychologist, psychiatrist, etc.). The sex-role norms restricting occupational choice appeared stronger among the lower-middle-class students and those from rural areas.

Our results led to the formulation of the model of a *"self-supporting selection circle."*[12] This circle tends to resist changes in the existing differentiation of academic professions and to reinforce the respective trends of selection. It was most clearly observed in the selection of upper-level professions such as medicine and law. The "social-service" intelligentsia, the new middle class, recruits its members more from the lower social strata and also represents a more anomalous and situation-oriented type of vocational choice. The basis of the differentiation of the intelligentsia thus lies in the students' socially determined orientations, developed long before university application.[13] As Bourdieu states, children from the lower social strata distance themselves from education in the early phases of schooling.

DIFFERENTIATION AMONG SUBGROUPS
OF INTELLECTUALS

Our follow-up study of previous subjects was initiated in 1980 in a pilot study carried out by Liisa Häyrynen. For the main study in 1982–83 (cf. table 1) we selected *three samples* from among the persons who had previously participated in our study and could now be located. These included the following:

TABLE 1
Disposition of Academic Careers Study 1965–1982

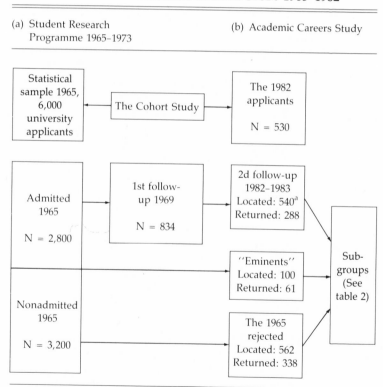

(a) Student Research Programme 1965–1973

(b) Academic Careers Study

[a]Part of the original material is unavailable.

1. A sample from the Student Research Programme (chiefly, present university graduates; due to the composition of the initial sample and the unavailability of material, physicians, theologists, lawyers, and natural scientists were over-represented).
2. A sample of those who were not admitted to university in 1965 (some have received no postsecondary education; the variety of career outcomes is highest in this selection).
3. A sample of those who could be located on the basis of their influential cultural or social position (called "eminents" or influential persons).

The latter were selected *on the basis of several alternative criteria:* an indicated postgraduate degree, published literature, membership in a cultural association, position as head of a governmental department or in public life in general, and so on. The sources used were university catalogs, *Who's Who in Finland, Official Directory,* directories of professional societies, or otherwise recognizable organizations. One hundred were located in this way, and 61 returned the questionnaire.[14] Since there were persons meeting the criteria of "eminence" in the two other samples, a total of 190 of those who answered our questionnaire were grouped into this *"cultural core intelligentsia."* They were divided on the basis of the major field of productivity, as indicated in table 2.

The purpose here is not to contend that these people were eminent on the basis of certain classifiable talents and gifts. Concepts such as eminence, giftedness, and genius are widely discussed in psychology without any definitive clarity.[15] As stated above, the problem is that these categories are formed historically and are related to specific social differentiation. In our study the "eminent" group was selected according to alternative cultural and social criteria, and our interest concerned the ways in which they used their influence and whether their ways of life differed from those of the others. Persons classified into the complementary "noneminent" fraction do not form a unitary group, either; they differ in profession and educational qualification. Therefore, the complementary fraction was divided into two qualification groups: those with university degrees and those with semi-

TABLE 2

COMPOSITION OF THE SUBGROUPS OF THE TOTAL SAMPLE (n=714) AND THE PERCENTAGE OF WOMEN BY SUBGROUP AND SUBTYPE (Academic Careers Study 1965–1982)

| | "Eminent" or Influential Persons[a] | | | | Others: | | | | (b) Semiacademics[c] | |
| | | | | | (a) University Graduates[b] | | | | | TOTAL[d] |
	All	Artistic-cultural	Research and academic	Organizations and politics	All	Scientific-medical	Social-pedagogic and administration	Organizations and administration	All	
Number of subjects	190	43	84	63	402	110	167	125	122	714
Percentage of women	20%	33	20	8	43%	43	55	28	53%	39%

[a]Classified into the subgroup and subtypes on the basis of the major field of productivity.

[b]Classified into the subgroup and subtypes on the basis of profession.

[c]Persons with lower degrees (nurses, technicians, commercial training) or without post-secondary-school education.

[d]Total number of completed questionnaires: in calculations incomplete data excluded. The follow-up study also gathered data on all physicians and theologists who started their studies in 1965, though only these classified as "eminent" (n=27) are included here (in subgroup 1).

academic qualifications. The former subgroup, the largest in our follow-up sample, was further divided into three subtypes (table 2):

1. *Scientific-medical* (physicians, chemists, computer specialists, etc.)
2. *Social-pedagogic* (teachers, priests, those in other humanistic professions)
3. *Organizational-administrative* (lawyers, civil servants, economists)

The disposition of our longitudinal study is summarized in table 1, which also reports the composition of the subgroups and their gender distribution.

Table 2 suggests one differentiating scheme for the contemporary educated intelligentsia. The strategy followed in the selection and location of subjects aimed at achieving a maximum qualitative variation of possible career outcomes and life positions. The follow-up sample does not correspond to the structure of the Finnish intelligentsia as a whole, and its different parts were selected from different basic populations (one limitation is the initial applicant population, which did not represent all types of vocational intentions of Finnish students leaving secondary school). Analysis of the returned questionnaires did not reveal any serious differences between those who did not return it and the 1965 variables. Standardization of the background factors by means of cross-tabulation made the potential bias controllable.

When the different subgroups were compared on the basis of social background, it was seen that eminence, or the influential position, was clearly related to an upper-middle-class social background: 43 percent of the eminent subgroup, 23 percent of the university graduate group, and 19 percent of the semiacademics are representative of this social class. Female cultural-artistic intellectuals and the males in academic positions, in particular, come from this social background. This is related to the initial orientation of upper-middle-class boys and girls. The persons who later achieved eminence in organizational careers do not differ markedly in social background from the subgroup of organizational professions in our sample.

There are also differences in the social backgrounds of different professional fractions: the social-pedagogic intelligentsia appears to stem more from the lower stratum of the middle class or from the industrial working class. *The upper middle class thus directs its children toward eminent positions in general and toward specific professional roles.* This trend was already observable in the selection circle outlined above. Children from academically educated homes seem more persistent in their academic aspirations, even when they are rejected in their first attempt to enter university.

DIVERSITY IN LIFE POSITIONS AND WORK ACTIVITIES

The follow-up study contained questions concerning the subjects' present work, performance, and experience. It can be assumed that if the differentiation that was previously performed has social importance, it would be reflected in these persons' ways of life and work activities. Table 3 provides examples of characteristic differences in work experience. In general, our subjects place high value on challenge and autonomy in their work. This is related to their relatively high educational qualifications in comparison to the working population in general.[16] Still, there are *internal* differences among the various fractions in our sample. The "eminents" value challenge in their work more than do the other subgroups. The degree of self-manifestation, involving the opportunity to use one's talents, is highest among the artistic and scientific subgroups, and the power to influence is highest among the organizational elite. In the "noneminent" subgroups, work content and opportunities for influencing the course of events were evaluated most highly by males in the organizational and legal professions.

Are there any connections between these *subjective experiences* and the nature of the *objective positions* of persons in these subgroups? In order to answer this question, we classified the positions and work contents of our subjects in the context of two theoretical schemes. In the classifications of organizational positions, we used (in a relatively free manner) the conceptions applied by Erik Wright for the analysis of the class positions of different social fractions.[17] This empirical classification is based on

TABLE 3
DIFFERENCES IN CHALLENGE, AUTONOMY, AND AUTHORITY IN WORK AMONG DIFFERENT FRACTIONS OF INTELLECTUALS, IN PERCENTAGES[a] (Academic Careers Study 1965–1982; subgroups are described in table 2)

| | "Eminent" or influential fraction | | | | | | Complementary fraction | | | | | |
| | | | | | | | a) University graduates | | | b) Semi-academics | | |
	All	M	F	Artistic-cultural	Research and academic	Organizations and politics	All	M	F	All	M	F
Challenge of work:												
Extremely challenging	57	57	54	56	60	52	39	42	36	31	36	27
Quite challenging	36	33	46	35	33	40	47	43	52	48	52	45
Not very challenging	5	7	–	5	5	6	9	9	10	14	6	24
Opportunity to use talents (autonomy):												
Very high	55	53	60	58	56	51	38	38	38	33	43	23
Quite high	38	39	35	33	36	44	48	50	46	44	40	48
Rare	4	5	3	2	6	3	12	10	11	17	10	22
Opportunity to influence (authority):												
Many opportunities	40	40	40	35	35	52	21	27	15	27	28	8
Some opportunities	43	44	38	47	43	40	49	51	45	35	35	34
Not many opportunities	14	13	16	12	20	6	25	18	32	40	31	50
N	190	153	37	43	84	63	402	229	173	122	58	64

[a]Self-ratings of the subjects; inaccurate reports not included (sum below 100%).

the features of work the subjects themselves reported in the questionnaire. In addition, we classified the activities the subjects indicated as *major* work content on the basis of the taxonomy of vocational orientation suggested by John Holland (table 4).[18]

A relatively large percentage of "influential" persons either work in independent professions or as managers participating in the decision-making process of their institutions (table 4). In the universities, professors, as the heads of departments, usually represent this type of authority. Many of them are also members of various committees and councils, where they influence public decision making. Among the artistic-cultural intellectuals, about one-third represent the "artisan" role type or "knowledge entrepreneurs," without regular salaried incomes. Nevertheless, the *autonomous*—that is, salaried and relatively qualified—workers are the largest category within the core intelligentsia. These are the people whom Marja Järvelä-Hartikainen called "wage-earner core intelligentsia": those who are highly qualified but who lack organizational authority (1983). Two professional groups, lawyers and physicians, possessed a higher proportion of independent *or* managing positions.

The classification based on Holland's scheme indicates similar differences, but it does so from another angle. An eminent or influential position implies a high proportion of investigative or artistic duties as well as enterprising ones. The percentage of these intellectually more rewarding tasks gradually diminishes if we look at the other subgroups of our sample. Social (welfare, teaching) duties are the most common among the other university graduates, and conventional (clerical) tasks are the most common among the semiacademic group. The amount of investigative and academic retraining activities is particularly low among university graduates of the social-pedagogic professional type.

We must add one more trait to this diversity of inequality in work content: the *gender distribution*. In the eminent group there is no systematic difference between the two genders regarding authority in work and social influence. An eminent position gives a woman practically the same freedom and authority as a man in a similar position. But in each of the subgroups belonging to the complementary sample, women rated their influence—and the semiacademic females their autonomy as well—as systematically

TABLE 4

ORGANIZATORY POSITION AND MAJOR WORK CONTENT AMONG DIFFERENT FRACTIONS OF INTELLECTUALS, IN PERCENTAGES[a] (Academic Careers Study 1965–1982)

	"Eminent" or influential fraction						Complementary fraction					
							(a) University Graduates			(b) Semiacademics		
	All	M	F	Cultural-artistic	Research and academic	Organizations and politics	All	M	F	All	M	F
Organizatory Position:												
1. No accurate report	3	3	—	2	1	5	2	2	3	3	3	2
2. Entrepreneurs or	19	16	27	35	21	3	8	10	8	5	7	3
3. Participating managers	23	25	14	2	16	46	5	8	1	1	2	—
4. Lower managers, section heads, vice principals	20	22	11	14	16	30	19	24	9	16	31	2
5. Autonomous (salaried, professional)	33	29	49	40	43	16	57	54	62	39	41	39
6. Subordinated; semiprof. or irregular	3	4	—	7	4	—	10	1	20	36	16	55
Major Content of Work:[b]												
1. No accurate report	1	1	—	—	1	—	6	1	7	12	5	14
2. Realistic (technical)	2	3	2	1	1	2	6	5	4	18	21	14
3. Artistic (aesthetic)	15	12	27	61	1	3	1	—	1	—	—	—
4. Social (caring)	13	12	19	21	12	10	47	41	54	20	9	30
5. Investigative	40	39	43	7	75	16	13	21	15	2	4	—
6. Enterprising (leadership, decision making)	26	31	3	6	7	64	19	25	8	14	30	—
7. Conventional (clerical)	4	3	5	14	2	6	9	7	10	35	32	40

[a]Based on E. O. Wright; adjusted scale.
[b]Based on J. L. Holland.
Note: The highest number of each subgroup is in italics.

lower than that of their respective male counterparts. This trend is reinforced by the fact that *there generally are fewer women* in the *more rewarding occupations*. Table 2 indicates that women constitute only one-fifth of the eminent subgroup and that only five females (8 percent) belong to the organizational elite, although the general female proportion of our subjects is about 40 percent. Their proportion is also smaller in the specialist and organizational professions in general and greater in social occupations. There is a gender-related distribution of central and peripheral tasks in most professions, and this can be related to Wright's observations about the generally lower-class position of the females in the work force.[19] Only women with exceptional ability get beyond these restrictions on their positions.

THE UNIVERSITY AND THE FORMATION OF THE INTELLECTUAL

One of the chief goals of our study was to analyze the role of university education, both in the development of the individual and in the formation of different fractions of the intelligentsia. In this analysis we followed a "back-dated" procedure in which we examined how the differences in present position were reflected in an earlier course of life. Before presenting this analysis, however, we will illuminate certain retrospective evaluations of our subjects concerning the value of university education and the educational atmosphere of the 1960s. These recollections are categorized in table 5. There, we compare the university graduate sample with *those* members of the eminent subgroup who have university degrees. In their recollections of the educational climate, present eminents stress the relatively more *emancipatory character* of the atmosphere in the 1960s. The "ordinary" university graduates more often recall a restless, polarized, or academically rigid pattern during the same period. Our classification is based on a *qualitative* analysis of the subjects' personal descriptions.

The highest proportion of *all* university graduates stress university qualification as the most important basis for their later careers. Development of thinking and cognition are emphasized more by the cultural core intelligentsia, especially by the artistic intellectuals and the Ph.D.'s of our sample. Among the "ordinary" graduates, those in the organizational professions—often lawyers—also emphasize the development of professional thinking as a significant aspect of university study. This trend indicates that a *university degree forms the basis of many of the present activities, giving both competence and identity to the present professionals.* Direct negative judgment was more common among the intellectuals oriented toward art and culture. These intellectuals mentioned a well-rounded education as a highly valuable aspect of their studies.

Admittedly, it is difficult to discriminate among different sources of impacts on university students. Dormitory living, styles of teaching, the urban way of life, and the period may all be reflected in student development.[20] Newcombe has emphasized in his classical study of Bennington College women both the epochal influence of the period of study and the challenges of that later period, when previously acquired values were transformed into political and intellectual activities. It seems that there is a contradictory relationship between the "emancipatory" 1960s and the "low-profile" 1970s. According to our climate study of 1969, the most homogeneous milieu was found in the professional disciplines (medicine, law, agriculture, and forestry), which were also rated as "goal directed." The radical currents touched the social sciences and the humanities more, where a curriculum crisis was also more acute. Many students in these latter disciplines complained of isolation and anonymity; for them the most formative factor was, apparently, the atmosphere of the period as it was manifested in student radicalism.

The people in our follow-up sample who participated in the Student Research Programme in 1969 provide an opportunity for us to juxtapose the *actual* experiences of persons who are currently in different fractions. Only 50 of those in our present eminent group could be located among the subjects of the student research sample who returned the follow-up questionnaire in 1982. The proportion of scientific intellectuals among them was larger. The answers recorded in 1969 show that the present eminents reported higher academic success then than did the others. An interesting point is that, more often than their peers, they rated theoretical activity and social critique as preferable goals of university teaching, and they judged university education in their particular fields to have failed in the task of developing critical minds. Competitiveness and accuracy were, in their opinion, typical results of university study. They believed, less than did their peers, that student radicalism was only an indicator of the desire of student leaders to appear in public. A proportionally larger number of them regarded it as signaling faults residing in the educational system. One-fifth of the complementary group expressed an open attraction toward student radicalism in 1969, while in the eminent group this rate was about 40 percent. It can be concluded that the stronger reference of the present eminents to the emancipatory nature of the 1960s is founded on their actual student experience. There certainly were scientific intellectuals, particularly M.D.'s or Ph.D.'s in the exact sciences, who stressed the concentration on their studies in the 1960s and who were not favorably disposed toward the cultural and political discourse. Still, the most common feature of the subjects who are currently in influential positions is their generally greater sensitivity to values typical of the students of the 1960s (criticalness; the social relevance of university teaching).

THE INTELLECTUALS' CAREERS
AND CHANGES IN VALUES

A traditional question of longitudinal research concerns change: namely, how students are changed by university education and how work and different job contents mold their initial values.[21] The main problem here concerns what part of any change is attributable to cultural transformation and what part to the specific effects of different life careers. However, since each period has its own particular life courses and developmental schemes, it is not possible to separate the general influences of different ''factors.'' The observations in this last section illuminate the directions in which the value orientations of our different subgroups have developed.

Both in 1965 and 1982–83, our subjects described the features of the ideal job which they would most appreciate (i.e., the "goal-value"). On the basis of these goal-values it is possible to separate out *different types of change* (the typology based on the findings of longitudinal comparisons is presented in table 6).

As can be seen, creative self-manifestation is the most appreciated goal-value of about half of the eminent subgroup (*both* type 2 *and* type 5 indicate appreciation of creativity *in 1982*). This appreciation is strongly represented in the other subgroups as well. Self-manifestation was present in 1965 to a greater degree in the orientation of students who later attained "eminence," and the change type most characteristic of this group between 1965 and 1982 is the *lasting appreciation of creativity* (type 2). It can be observed, however, that the value of *creativity as a life goal has also increased in the complementary fraction*. This is a common trend in the whole longitudinal sample and is also recognizable in the difference between the older and the younger cohorts. It thus may indicate a model of general cultural transmission in the period studied. Another trend related to the career development of our subjects is the increase in the appreciation of a secure future. The orientation toward people was high in 1965, particularly among girls, but it has generally decreased during professional careers. Among the eminent subgroup only 6 percent currently indicate an orientation toward people. This is related to the structure of their activities, in which investigative and artistic-cultural duties are dominant and contact with people is indirect. This decrease in altruistic expectations was also observed among the female university applicants of the 1982 cohort.

Attaining eminence thus contributes to the conservation of an orientation to creativity. Though the appreciation of creativity grows during the life career in all subgroups, it increases most sharply among the females who are currently engaged in creative or influential work. Does the increasing value of creativity indicate a general growth in the need for self-manifestation in all parts of the intelligentsia? It appears that persons in different fractions of the intelligentsia refer to creativity in different types of activities. When asked in which personal activities they felt creative, "influential" persons usually mentioned their work or a field in which they had completed a significant task. The others left the

TABLE 5
Recollections about Higher Education among the University Graduates in Different Fractions of Present Intellectuals; Percentages of Qualitatively Categorized Answers
(Academic Careers Study 1965–1982)

| | "Eminent" or influential fraction | | | Complementary fraction | | | |
| | | | | (a) University Graduates: Candidate's Degree | | | Lower Degrees |
	All	Ph.D.'s	Higher Candidate's Degree	All	Higher	Lower	All[b]
Educational Climate in the 1960s:							
1. No codable description	14	13	14	15	12	23	59
2. Emancipatory; radical as noted positively	33	30	36	18	21	10	11
3. Scholarly; academic; work-centered	17	17	15	15	17	14	4
4. Flexible; social; general positive expression	17	24	13	22	20	25	8
5. Rigidly academic; restless; negative recall	18	17	22	30	30	28	16
%	100	100	100	100	100	100	100
Personal Importance of Completed Studies:							
1. No codable information	12	—	12	13	11	22	36
2. Basis for career and present life	37	37	37	38	39	35	40
3. Learned scientific or professional thinking	26	39	24	14	18	4	2
4. Worldview; general education	11	—	17	13	14	8	5

5. Independence; sociability; general reference	7	8	7	9	8	11	2
6. Useless or other negative evaluation	7	9	4	14	11	20	14
%	100	100	100	100	100	100	100
N	170	47	78	402	296	102	75

a Semiacademic qualifications excluded (n = 29).
b Those with vocational training after secondary school.

TABLE 6

Types of Value Changes between 1965 and 1982 in the Three Fractions of the Intelligentsia: "Eminent," Others with University Degrees, and Others with Semiacademic Qualifications, in Percentages (Academic Careers Study 1965–1982)

Typology of Changes in Goal Values 1965–1982:	"Eminent" or Influential Fraction All	Others	
		University Graduates All	Semiacademics All
1. Security and material rewards; unchanged	18	21	33
2. Self-manifestation, creativity; unchanged	22	8	9
3. Altruism and people; unchanged	3	11	7
4. From one value (1965) toward security (1982)	15	24	14
5. From one value (1965) toward creativity (1982)	26	20	22
6. From one value (1965) toward altruism and people (1982)	3	9	11
7. Data unavailable either in 1965 or 1982	13	7	5
%	100	100	101

Note: The "goal-value" (Kornhauser) was measured both in 1965 and 1982–83 using the same inventory of eleven value orientations, the most important being indicated. The change-matrix 1965–82 (11×11) was reduced to a smaller number of types on the basis of linear analyses computed by T. Tormulainen. On the nature of work-values see Rosenberg (1957).

concretization of creativeness open or, more usually, listed activities belonging to the private life sphere: hobbies, family, and friendship. This may signify that these people seek creative self-manifestation in life areas other than those of work or public position.

CONCLUDING REMARKS

Our findings confirm the notion that different types and paradigms of the intelligentsia exist. One line of demarcation runs between eminence and noneminence. Eminence is related to a high degree of self-direction, but it also has a *social dimension*: the people belonging to the eminent subgroup to a significant degree worked in independent or managerial positions, and they had more investigative, artistic, or leadership duties. The profile of their duties can be related to a better connection into "information streams," and can be reflected in activities and values. University education appears to be a significant basis for later life career. For most persons it guarantees a qualification that connects them to the mainstreams of cultural exchange and prevents a decrease in intellectual ability. In the past, university education granted access to an intellectual class. Today, it no longer appears sufficient; attaining the preferred career position requires additional cultural merits. Alongside the formal procedure of university admission, a selection linked to the course of life has developed in which one criterion is the capacity to endure reverses and to persist in the attainment of the chosen vocational goal and another is the capacity to be oriented toward creativity. These capacities are related to a cultural code and are manifested as flexibility, courage, or a clear professional image. Very often these properties are related to the students' social background. *University teaching does not generally initiate a creative orientation in students who do not initially exhibit it.* To transform university education into creative action requires high selectivity from the student, and for most students present teaching does not produce such an orientation.

There are epoch-related factors that help form intellectual personalities. For some persons the radical years of the 1960s represented this kind of strong formative experience. Still, for the majority of our subjects, the university was mainly the place to acquire their present competence. Our present universities do not look like hotbeds of intellectualism.

The eminent subgroup and the other subgroups that comprise the intelligentsia can be divided into *subtypes* on the basis of their central life orientations. Tentatively, we might differentiate among the following types of orientation:

1. cultural-artistic (the missionary or teleological role)
2. artisan-entrepreneur (persons with creative life-strategies)
3. specific intellectual (the leading experts; the possessors of "knowledge capital")
4. managerial consultant
5. work-centered professional
6. local activist (community leaders and the "provincial eminents")
7. uncertain intellectual (those with identity problems)
8. family or privacy-centered (those resembling the conception of the new middle class)

Though the first four types are most common among the eminents, all subtypes may be present in the same profession.

Our concept of eminence is, in the final analysis, rather individualistic. It may be that new germs of eminence are situated in *collective* types of intellectual work, in the awareness of common professional interests. The growing interest in creativity may increase the demand among the academic middle class for meaningful work.

Whether cultural reproduction occurs through which the intellectual class secures its positions (see Bourdieu) cannot be answered in this kind of empirical survey. Undoubtedly, the cultural position of the elite is reproduced through the motivational "habitus" of its offspring, and the various fractions of the professional intelligentsia have diverging social bases, with the service sector representing the "degrading" field. Still, the system of professions and the psychology of its different fractions is in a state of transition, allowing no existing structures to be repeated as such. Melvin Kohn's thesis—according to which work molds all facets of personality—contrasts with the idea of cultural reproduction of the social position. Our findings show that although anticipatory social selection occurs for different fractions of the intelligentsia, work-career also influences a person's value orientation. Creative work increases self-confidence, especially among the women, and the subject's image of his or her own scholarly ability seems related to the amount of research and investigative activities undertaken in the later course of life. One of the chief advantages of the materialist—Marxist and macro-orientated—psychology is that it sees the social orientation of persons and its development as a *relational* concept: tied to life positions and the activities these make possible. More research along the lines of the "typical sites of intellectuals" (Cornelis Disco in this volume) and about "professions as the factions of the intelligentsia" would be quite valuable. The observations made in this paper and the picture outlined of orientational types which has been outlined may help illuminate the new life modes of intellectuals.

NOTES

1. On the macropsychological question cf. Häyrynen 1984.
2. See the comparative study by Adamski and Häyrynen 1978.
3. Foucault 1981.
4. J. P. Roos 1981.
5. See Barron and Harrington 1981.
6. On the *cultural capital* transmitted between generations cf. Bourdieu 1973; Bourdieu and Passeron 1977; in this volume, C. Levy and B. Martin and I. Szelényi.
7. See Kohn 1969, Kohn and Schooler 1978.
8. See Järvelä 1983.
9. See Rosenberg 1957, Holland 1973.
10. See Häyrynen 1970.
11. See Häyrynen 1983.
12. Häyrynen and Perho 1976.
13. See Adamski and Häyrynen 1978.
14. Liisa Häyrynen and Raimo Jaakkola also participated in the gathering of data concerning the eminent subgroup.
15. See Albert 1983.
16. See the findings concerning the autonomy of work in different class fractions, Blom et al. 1983.
17. See Wright et al. 1982.

18. See Holland 1973.
19. Wright et al. 1982.
20. See Astin 1978.
21. See Melvin Kohn's argument.

REFERENCES

Adamski, W. W., and Y.-P. Häyrynen. 1978. "Educational Systems." In *Social Structure and Change. Finland and Poland. Comparative perspective*, edited by E. Allardt and W. Wesolowski. Warszawa: Polish Scientific Publishers: pp. 217–244.

Albert, R. S. 1983. *Genius and Eminence: The Social Psychology of Eminence and Exceptional Achievement*. Oxford: Pergamon Press.

Astin, A. W. 1978. *Four Critical Years: Effects of College on Beliefs, Attitudes and Knowledge*. San Francisco: Jossey-Bass.

Barron, F., and D. M. Harington. 1981. "Creativity, Intelligence and Personality." *Annual Review of Psychology* 32:439–476.

Blom, R. et al. 1983. "Tutkimuksia luokkateoriasta—vertaileva luokkarakenne—ja luokkatietoisuustutkimus. *Tampereen yliopiston sosiologian ja sosiaalipsykologian laitoksen työraportteja*. [Studies into class theory; comparative research programme on class structure and class consciousness.] B 2/1983. University of Tempere: Department of Sociology and Social Psychology.

Bourdieu, P. 1973. "Cultural Reproduction and Social Reproduction." *Knowledge, Education and Cultural Change*, edited by R. Brown, pp. 71–112. London: Tavistock Publications.

Bourdieu, P., and J.-C. Passeron. 1977. *Reproduction in Education, Society and Culture* (English ed.). London: Sage.

Foucault, M. 1981. "Truth and Power." Edited by Ch. C. Lemert, pp. 293–307. In *French Sociology: Rupture and Renewal Since 1968*. New York: Columbia University Press.

Häyrynen, Y.-P. 1970. "The Flow of New Students to Different Fields of Study: Educational Choice, Career Motivation and Discrimination Effects of University Admission." *Annales Academiae Scientiarum Fennicae*, ser. B, TOM 168.

———. 1983. "Performance, Self-Concept, and Creativity: A Discourse Based on Longitudinal Studies of Finnish Students." *Higher Education in Europe*, 2/VIII: 35–44.

———.1984. "Research Object of Psychology in the 1990s: How Changes in Man Are Reflected in the Psychology We Are Studying." In *Psychology in the 1990s*, edited by K. M. J. Lagerspetz and P. Niemi, pp. 483–

506. Amsterdam: Elsevier Science Publishers B. V.

Häyrynen, V.-P., and H. Perho. 1976. Student Flows and Educational Streams in University. *University of Joensuu*, ser. A:20.

Holland, J. L. 1973. *Making Vocational Choice: A Theory of Careers*. New Jersey: Prentice-Hall.

Järvelä-Hartikainen, M. 1983. Palkkatyö ja Sivistyneistö [Wage labor and the intellectuals]. In *Uria ja ulottuvuuksia: Festschrift for Prof. Y.-P. Häyrynen*, edited by J. P. Savola, pp. 28–49. Joensuun Korkeakoulu 19.

Kohn, M. L. 1969. *Class and conformity: A study of values*. Homewood, Ill.: The Dorsey Press.

Kohn, M. L., and C. Schooler. 1979. "The Reciprocal Effects of Substantive Complexity of Work and Intellectual Flexibility: A Longitudinal Assessment." *American Journal of Sociological Review* 84:24–52.

Roos, J. P. 1981. "On Typologies of the Way of Life." Edited by J. P. and B. Roos In *Ways of Life: Subjective and Objective, Publications of the Research Programme on the Change of Way of Life*, no. 11: University of Helsinki.

Rosenberg, M. J. 1957. *Occupations and Values*. Glencoe, Ill.: The Free Press.

Wright, E. O. et al. 1982. "The American Class Structure." *American Sociological Review* 47:709–726.

Epilogue: Intellectuals and Power or The Power of Intellectuals?

Anders Björnsson

In 1959, C. P. Snow published his now well-known essay "Two Cultures." "I believe," he wrote," that cultural life in the West is fast becoming split into two opposing groups." On one side he placed the humanists and on the other the natural scientists, with physicists as perhaps the most representative group. "Between these two poles, a chasm of mutual ignorance about the other side is spreading—often (especially among the younger members) animosity and dislike, but mostly a lack of understanding." Intellectually and emotionally, these groups show "extremely little common ground" between them (from the Swedish version of "The Two Cultures and the Scientific Revolution," 1961).

Who reads Snow today? A quarter of a century later, the discussion has taken other paths. Today it concerns a real or imagined interchange among various groups of intellectuals rather than between "two cultures." The impulses toward new ideas, if one dare use such a strong expression (for doing so risks giving to Snow's thesis a paradigmatic meaning that he never intended), have been many. These can certainly be dated further back than the time of the publication of Snow's essay twenty-five years ago. Here, names such as Bakunin, Machajski, Burnham, and Djilas come immediately to mind. A turning point in this discussion came with Alvin Gouldner's *The Future of Intellectuals and the Rise of the New Class* (New York, 1979). Gouldner pointed to an underlying common culture—*the culture of critical discourse*—which could serve as a basis for the rise of intellectuals to power in a new type of society.

It was Gouldner's spirit rather than Snow's which presided over the discussion at the Nordic Workshop, "Intellectuals, Universities and the State," held at Fiskebäckskil, Sweden, January 12–15, 1984.

In looking at the assembled group of scholars, someone with an untrained eye would have been inclined to agree with Gouldner's judgment. For here sat men (there was only one woman present, which is perhaps symbolic) from various disciplines who, though they proved to be greatly at odds, displayed no animosity and, at the same time, found terminology and a language common enough to all present. Was this merely illusion?

With only a few exceptions, however, the participants were closer to the humanities pole of Snow's dichotomy. The dichotomy itself would perhaps have to be amended today to include a third group of equal priority: social scientists.

Still, I wondered, was there commonality in all this diversity?

I also wondered about my own role at such a conference. Since I am a journalist, my job is to observe and report, to be both insider and outsider. As a journalist I belong to no clearly defined intellectual milieu, yet I participate—willingly or not—in an intellectual discourse. My professional identity is split, as is that of the entire profession, between an occupational identity and a highly individualized perspective. Today's journalist is trying to get a grip on his own profession. But he cannot say, as perhaps the scientist can, that a new sense of professional identity is emerging. This ambiguity is inherent in the occupation itself: the task of presenting impressions, loosely connected pictures, which are still meant to be believable and trustworthy.

With such self-reflection always in mind, this conference report is offered as a journalistic product. These are impressions—trustworthy, I hope—of an outsider with an insider's interest in the subject matter.

I can begin where one must sooner or later end up, with the problem of defining intellectuals. The first is phenomenological, beginning from the self-understanding and perception of an individual, from his or her particular ways of thinking and acting. The second begins from an objective, observable position in the social structure. It is possible, but hardly likely, that these two can coincide; more likely, they complement each other.

In Yrjö-Paavo Häyrynen's study of post-1968 academic careers in Finland, one can find the making of both types of definition. Häyrynen expresses himself in this way:

> It . . . seems that professional or educational qualifications are not sufficient criteria for classifying various subgroups of intellectuals: their life products, even their subjective orientations and goals in life, appear to be significant in this respect. The fact is, the influence of intellectuals on social development is rather dependent upon their ideological and mental positions.

This subjective element, taking account of an intellectual's interaction with other social groups, is the basis for Häyrynen's separating out a special group of "eminent intellectuals" from the rest. This group includes all those who sought academic training fifteen years ago. Häyrynen uncovered a polarization following from a divergence within those professions requiring academic training, where the experience of "creativity" at work was a major factor in determining and sorting out an elite.

Häyrynen suggests that this polarization runs right through the entire academically trained labor market. A professor in rehabilitation research, for example, is probably not a member of this elite (the "eminent"). Another participant, Katrín Fridjónsdóttir, also pointed to creativity as a dividing factor. For her, the difference between the academically trained "professional" and the "scientist" could be expressed as the difference between those who worked with ready-made theories and those who produced theories themselves—in other words, the difference between the intellectual as producer or as consumer of theoretical knowledge.

But if, as in this case, knowledge is to function as a basis of power (and power is the key point in the attempt to circumscribe the idea of an intellectual elite), it is not sufficient merely to distinguish between those with or without theoretical or scientific competence, as Gernot Böhme and several others pointed out. Knowledge must to some extent be "objective knowledge," a criterion that Ron Eyerman's commentary on modern new-class theory sharpened to include those who accumulated as well as disposed of "cultural capital." (I will talk more about this later.)

In a presentation that gave an account of the struggle between Socrates and the Sophists, Böhme drew a distinction between philosophical schools in terms of differing social strategies. The aim of a particular tradition of thought was to acquire a monopoly over a field of knowledge, to draw a "demarcation line" that excluded competing schools from an area. For the Socratics, Plato and his followers, the struggle concerned power within the ancient state. According to them, only the philosopher possessed the required knowledge proper to statesmanship. Since only he was skilled enough to rule, he must be afforded that role over all others. Other contenders were to be cast out from the community of scholars and relegates to second-class citizenship. Cast below even artisans and farmers, they were given pejorative names: poet, rhetorician, sophist. Were they all intellectuals?

The step from ancient Greece to contemporary Swedish literary criticism is perhaps a long one. Yet there is a rather interesting comparison to be made, especially when taking into account Donald Broady's investigation of the issues raised on the cultural pages of Stockholm newspapers between 1980 and 1982.

Broady applied P. Bourdieu's conception of an intellectual "field of struggle" to what was perhaps a paradigmatic shift in Swedish literary criticism. In the early 1980s a group of young critics schooled in poststructuralist theory outmaneuvered and replaced an older generation that had made its mark in the late sixties and early seventies. The members of this older generation had celebrated such values as realism and documentary literature. They had stressed political content at the same time as they had been uninterested in—or ignorant of—literary tradition as such. Success in such a struggle between schools and generations requires the investment of "cultural capital" in just that area where an opponent is weakest. In this case, it proved to be aesthetic judgment. Winners on the field must adopt—to use Broady's phrase—a strategy that undermines an opponent:

> That is, their strategy was to restore and reestablish the legitimacy of all the boundaries enclosing the fields of art, literature, and criticism, which means reverting those fields to their former, "normal," more autonomous state. Thereby, the new entrant can bring forth a *baisse* (reduction) in the value of those specific investments which had helped the previous generation attain their positions on literary magazines, daily newspapers, publishing houses, etc.

In contrast to Böhme, Broady stressed that combatants must be in agreement about some basic issues in order for the struggle to take place at all. Their ideologies may diverge, but neither side can afford to attack the intellectual field itself (in this case, the value of literary criticism). Here, to cite Bourdieu, lies the bottom line of common interest. Acceptance of the intellectual field is itself a precondition for their contention and struggle to attain dominance. On this common ground, struggle takes place as a group struggle, not as a clash of unrelated individuals.

If the intellectual shows up in so many different guises, so many different activities and historical settings, how is it at all meaningful to attempt to locate a particular position in a social structure to capture this diversity? How is it possible, one may ask, to grasp the intellectual as a macrosociological phenomenon?

The message from the conference on this point was indecisive and split, just as it was on the level upon which to analyze the issues involved. In itself this is not entirely negative. With various and divergent methods and levels of analysis, it may be possible to study a phenomenon from many angles, giving an increasingly sharper picture. In the mind of this layman, methodological pluralism is just what is required in the study of so amorphous a phenomenon as the intellectual. How should the heterogeneity of the intellectual be evaluated, however? Many at the conference (Adam Westoby, for one) pointed to a leveling out of earlier differences in various types of intellectual labor, while others (Häyrynen, for example) stressed functional differentiation and the diversity.

Several presentations warned of the dangers of "economism" in the analysis of intellectuals. Svante Nordin argued for the relative autonomy of the ideological vis-à-vis the economic in his analysis of Swedish intellectuals in the nineteenth century. From another angle, Ivan Szelényi pointed out that it is necessary to take account of economic relations in order to investigate the conditions under which intellectuals are produced and reproduced. This does not mean, however, that it is necessary or even desirable to begin analysis with economic relations for the definition and classification of intellectuals. Rather, intellectuals have historically shown themselves to be relatively flexible in relation to economic conditions.

A good illustration of this thesis could be found in Nordin's presentation. He showed that the bureaucratic power that ruled Sweden in the early nineteenth century was anchored in an academic ideology, which claimed that legitimate rule was grounded neither in aristocratic birth nor in money (the liberal view). Rather, it claimed that legitimate rule lies with those who have insight into the proper aim or goal of the state. This was an ideology especially constructed for civil servants, a new class of public officials. This institutionalized ideology built upon an idealist vision of the "reasonable state," a Hegelian and Platonic spirit that was teleological from beginning to end. In an aside to his paper, Nordin compared this ideology to contemporary Eastern Europe, where a bureaucratic class legitimates its rule through another form of teleological reason called Marxism-Leninism.

Around the turn of the century, there occurred in Sweden several fundamental transformations that undercut the "scientific" roots of this civil-servant ideology. A new philosophy of science called positivism gained a foothold in the Swedish academic world, largely through the influence of the philosopher Axel Hägerström. Positivism challenged the entire idea of teleological knowledge, particularly the idea that something like the "goal" of the state could exist at all. For Hägerström, only the knowledge of means, not ends, was possible. Goals or ends are something that politicians, not civil servants, should deal with. The latter should content themselves with perfecting the techniques of proper means. With this, Nordin argued, the civil servant was transformed from teleocrat to technocrat, from generalist to particularist in statesmanship. Edmund Dahlström pointed out in response that some of these old teleological ideas were still around in the 1930s and 1940s among Swedish intellectuals. One could find social scientists connected with social planning who saw themselves as "philosophers," with the responsibility for rational social and economic development.

Returning to Szelényi's suggestion, if the connection of intellectuals to the economy is currently weak, it may be because they have developed a stronger relationship to the state, as they had earlier vis-à-vis the church. Obviously, there exists a clear connection here. The modern intellectual is educated in a state-funded university, is likely to work in a state agency, and is likely to be paid through a grant from the state or even to receive his or her research grants from the state.

The question, of course, is how much this influences his or her role and behavior as an intellectual. Szelényi, for his part, argued strongly that if intellectuals are to become a class, this can only occur through the state—that is, through the state as a lever for self-formation, for the realization of power ambitions.

For a Marxist like Bengt Furåker (I will come back to Marx-inspired interpretations of intellectuals), the Western state remains a capitalist state, that is, a sphere dominated by economic interests. This itself must be interpreted as a hindrance to any power ambitions of intellectuals. Yet, in his view the state performs a double function. On one hand, the growing public sector has reduced the power of private capital. On the other hand, a new system that separates the power of ownership from that of control of capital has pushed a new stratum of professionals into leading positions. There exists, then, according to Furåker, a latent tendency in contemporary social structure:

> The complex combination and transformation of social forces, involving a decline of the petty bourgeoisie and the industrial proletariat and the growth of the middle layers and intelligentsia, may *undermine* the position of the capitalist class. Together with the working class and other wage earners, the intelligentsia may *use the state* as an instrument for cutting the power of capital owners. (Emphasis added.)

This, of course, is at present only speculation. Even so, Furåker saw a marked tendency for an intelligentsia to find new avenues of political expression—in trade unions and political parties (organizations that already reveal an overrepresentation of intellectuals in leadership positions), in the bureaucracy and the mass media. The last is certainly not the least important. Through the mass media, the sphere of opinion making, ''they (intellectuals) have a key role in shaping the whole cultural context in which political and ideological issues arise.''

The power to decide the day's agenda, to determine what ought to happen, may be teleology on the comeback trail.

However, the ''state'' is not a unified, one-dimensional complex, not to mention the diversity of ways in which intellectuals relate to this complex called the state. In the discussion concerning the crisis of the welfare state—currently a major issue in Sweden, as it is elsewhere—groups of intellectuals have revealed themselves to be sharply critical of the structure and function of the modern state. This critique has focused on the state intervention in and the consequent rationalization of more and more areas of social life. As could be seen in Bo Lindensjö's presentation, however, this criticism, along with the proposed solutions that follow it, is greatly divided along ideological lines. At the same time, these critical intellectuals are themselves most likely involved in some part of the public sector (here one should probably add that the left-wing critique of the state as such, very popular at the end of the sixties, has practically ended).

What struck me most about Lindensjö's contribution was the calling into question of the very concept of the ''state.'' This occurred most explicitly in connection with a discussion of the Norwegian power structure study. This policy study discusses breaking up the centralized Norwegian state and replacing it with decentralized sectors, with each state organ more closely tied to formally independent institutions (corporations, interest groups, etc.) than to other state offices. The sense of community is thought to be greater within a sector than within the state as a whole. This is a exciting theory.

Assume for the moment that a flood of intellectual expertise could be channeled into such a sector—for instance, that of health care. We might then find intellectual careers looking something like this: college/university degree, administrative post in an agency dealing with drug abuse, social-problems reporter for a big-city newspaper, trade-union expert on social problems, and public relations chief for a privately owned drug company—while all the time remaining within one sector, within the same field, to cite Bourdieu. The roles may vary, but the personnel are exchangeable. The example I have chosen is, of course, "ideal-typical." This offers a distinct advantage, since it is microscopic and can be projected against a less clear background.

But is this really what is called to mind when one talks of a "culture of critical discourse"? What would Gouldner have to say here?

Gouldner maintains that humanistic and technical intelligent-sias have emerged in contemporary society and are in the process of uniting forces to establish themselves as the dominant class in both the capitalist West and the socialist East. This class, he maintains, is fast replacing the proletariat as the "universal" class (in the Marxist sense) and will soon subordinate the traditional bourgeoisie. This intelligentsia has become a "cultural bourgeoisie" that exercises power and influence through the control and dispensation of "cultural capital." Such capital is not material in the way we usually think of it; rather, it is symbolic. Cultural capital takes material form, however, in cultural products (information, usable forms of knowledge), which returns to its owners an ever-increasing portion of society's surplus product.

Cultural capital must be distinguished from human capital. The latter refers to professional skills and the like, which can be measured through standard productivity equations. Opposite this is cultural capital, which directly concerns social relations, relations of power and domination in society. In this, cultural capital refers to a special type of (theoretical) knowledge that permits or equips its owners to control and dominate other people, to represent society's goals and meaning in logical, rational terminology (rather than in terms of economic growth or human happiness, to take two competing examples). Thus, the power aspirations of intellectuals remain hidden in and legitimated through scientific language.

It is certainly possible to question the link between this conception of capital and that of Marx. As the discussion showed, however, there is a fruitful—but also risky—analogy to be drawn here, the key to which is that a new social relationship and a new power (class) struggle is emerging.

Criticism of Gouldner's thesis formed along different lines. In a provocative presentation, Thomas Söderqvist suggested that one could find this new dominant/subordinate relationship in many different settings: from a "therapeutic situation" where a client is made subordinate to the knowledge of the expert, to a general situation where individual competence is being slowly undermined by "planning agencies" controlled by intellectuals (CIA, KGB) who monitor their activities. Even if one wanted to do so, applying the category of "class" to these various modes of domination/subordination would be difficult indeed. Westoby pointed out the additional difficulty in applying the notion of "capital" as its source. Classical political economics, which includes Marxism, tied capital to the factory system and to the technical revolution. In precapitalist society there existed no such "capital" relationship. Therefore, cultural capital cannot be seen as a precondition for a new intellectual class. Dahlström argued further that while one can acknowledge the obvious similarities in the division of labor in capitalist and socialist societies, the relationships of power and domination in these societies are very dissimilar.

Clearly, however, Marxist categories are useful in this context, if only as points of reference. In his enthusiastic—if not uncritical—defense of Gouldner, Cornelis Disco argued that Marxist class theory was the most "suitable" place to begin. Cultural capital *is* a useful concept for the analysis of social relations in contemporary society, according to him. Current capitalist society is subject to the infiltration of a growing—but not yet fully grown—new class. This class of "theory bearers" (Disco's term) has introduced a new set of rules, and principles are couched in the language of the culture of critical discourse:

> Not only the legitimations but even the ground for an increasing number of critical decisions refer to the survival of systems rather than private property, to human self-realization rather than the capacity to labor, or to rational conservation rather than profitable exploitation.

This does not mean, however, that older forms of domination and exploitation are entirely disappearing:

> What seems beyond doubt, however, is that social formation, the kinship-bound bourgeoisie, is now definitely being eroded as a coherent dominant class.

This is a development that has been occurring with increasing speed since World War II. It includes, among other things, state intervention in traditional processes of (money) capital accumulation and reproduction, the takeover by a technocratic elite of decision making within private corporations, and the replacement of hereditary rights by principles of merit. All of this was interpreted in an entirely different manner by the Marxist Disco than by the Marxist Furåker.

From Disco's presentation one was left with the impression of a charge of intellectuals against the castle walls of the enemy bourgeoisie. The cultural sphere is the ground of this attack. From here, especially from strategic positions within the media but also from positions within education and science, thrusts are made into the corridors of established power. These forays are not open and direct but covert, made from the inside. Such intellectuals are "bearers of cultural traditions, actively engaged in transforming those traditions into effective cultural capitals, and occupants of specific sites in the functional and hierarchical division of labor *all at once.*"

Totally in opposition to Disco, Ivan Szelényi (with coauthor Bill Martin) subjected Gouldner's ideas to heavy criticism. The non-Marxist Szelényi's main point was that Gouldner could not account for how this new class of intellectuals would undermine the traditional bourgeoisie, in just that sphere where their power is really concentrated, the sphere of material production.

As Gouldner defines it, cultural capital cannot be transformed into material ownership. There exists nothing in the theory, according to Szelényi, which allows cultural dominance to become economic dominance. As opposed to material capital, cultural capital cannot be easily separated from its physical bearer; it is nonconvertible. It cannot be accumulated, except through demographic expansion. Even if one could point to the emergence of a cultural bourgeoisie, he contended, it still would be necessary to show a nonowning class that stood in a direct subordinate relation to this culturally based power. Where Szelényi asked, is this new underclass?

Gouldner's weakness lies in that "his cultural capital is strikingly similar to human capital." Therefore, he cannot see "the procapitalism of those with lots of human capital and with little or no cultural capital." Gouldner simply overlooks the anticapitalism of intellectuals, because he does not understand that the majority of them are owners of human capital. They are, therefore, excluded by definition from that special situation that the culture of critical discourse is supposed to afford them. The main problem with Gouldner's theory, then, according to Szelényi, is that he does not show how cultural capital can be used to dominate others. Rather, he ties the notion too closely to a form of income grounded in differences in productivity and technical competence.

Thus, in this formulation intellectuals are no class, since class relationships are by definition those of domination/subordination. The only possible way for intellectuals to dominate society, according to Szelényi, is in conjunction with a social formation totally under state control. In such a situation the cultural sphere has already been conflated with the economic. Here, cultural capital is entirely convertible—for example, through a party bureaucracy and a party school, where an old bourgeoisie has been replaced by a bureaucratic class, which then dominates the entire field. This, however, is not the situation in the West (at least not yet).

Class or not, after this discussion it should be fruitful to look more closely at the various historical forms and shapes of intellectuals. Or course, models are necessary, but empirical studies are necessary as well. This need for empirical evidence was fulfilled by several of the presentations.

Söderqvist labored with the thought that relationships of cultural domination can be found in the interactions among individuals. For investigating this relationship he recommended a "microsocial, cognitive-emotive" approach. This approach would help reveal how one party voluntarily accepted the domination of others. Lennart Svensson offered two intellectual professions—architects and psychologists—as groups worthy of further research. Clearly empirically oriented, Tomas Gerholm presented his plans to study intellectual life in the Polish city on Krakow. Westoby's sharp presentation of intellectual labor covered many empirical angles. He asked, for example, how a theory of a new class can account for the apparent degradation and proletarianization of many facets of intellectual labor.

After Westoby's insightful portrait of intellectual labor in which he brought forward such "soft data" as attitudes, personality types, and the like, a journalist like me could have added many details of support.

We are now speaking about the criteria, the definition, and the concepts through which to delimit and locate the intellectual. There exists a weakness here which is not theoretical but practical, should one wish to test these new instruments in concrete circumstances. Here one finds that an intellectual plays not one but many roles. He or she acts in many spheres and in various fields and may also create new ones.

Kjell Jonsson showed this in his study of turn-of-the-century Swedish middle-class radicalism. A circle of enlightened aristocrats with various political points of view anticipated and constructed "questions" to which later generations were to find institutionalized solutions. Jonsson took his examples from the area of social policy in the broadest sense—health care, education, demography. In terms of their own self-understanding, these middle-class radicals saw these "issues" being handled by an educated elite, that is, themselves. Formulated in this way, professionalized and made into an object of knowledge and control, solutions to social "problems" could lie only in their expert hands.

To say that intellectuals play many roles can sound like an indefensible truism. The key issue is whether or not these roles are all played in the same game, if the content of the role is the same in all the fields.

The heavily ideological character of intellectual debate speaks clearly against such a view. But what if this ideological posturing—to again connect to Broady—is itself part of the game, the very basis of the intellectuals' field, as such? And why shouldn't it be possible to find a least common denominator (of some type) between, say, an atomic physicist who constructs weapons in a supermodern laboratory and plays tennis during leisure time, and a literary critic who works in a poorly furnished room and demonstrates against middle-distance rockets when work is through? This seems at least as likely as finding commonality in any greatly diversified occupational group, diversity that may unify at a union meeting or during a labor-market conflict. Or is this only rhetoric?

I will discuss one final theme: the "workers' " movement and intellectuals. Often debated in the last hundred years, this issue has most often been treated as an important yet separate phenomenon. Historically, however, the modern workers' movement (in the sense of organized political parties) has known many intellectuals in important leadership positions.

In his presentation of Austro-Marxism, Lennart Olausson pointed out that a leading ideologue, Max Adler, argued that the working class required the knowledge provided by intellectuals and that the latter found their natural allies in social democracy. The intellectual was nothing more than a "cultural worker" with, like the rest of the working class, an objective interest in socialism. What socialism lacked, according to Adler, was a Marxist science, the highest form of knowledge of nature and society. Because intellectuals were the carriers of science, there existed a natural connection between them and socialism. The key to this natural link lies in culture, which was said to emanate from human nature and to be ideologically neutral. Culture bound together all those in a society who saw in socialism the solution to their problems.

This harmonic conception, orchestrated by the Social Democratic party leadership, had its roots in turn-of-the-century Viennese student circles.

Carl Levy has studied the conceptualization and forms of relationships between intellectuals and working-class movements. In the period from 1870 to 1914, great numbers of intellectuals (members of the "educated middle class") were attracted to working-class political parties. In many European countries, and especially in Italy and France, these intellectuals attained leading positions. Ideological debate provided them with a springboard from which to capture these strategic positions. Such ideological debate functioned as a glue, binding together groups of functionaries otherwise indifferent to one another, who acted together at the same time that they fought one another.

This "intellectualization" of working-class parties also created a new type of party functionary: the self-educated worker. Levy placed these former manual workers in a special category of "former workers, would-be journalists, and skillful machine men who might have working-class roots but (who) were born late enough to enter the first wave of new white-collar workers." This type of functionary was an autodidact, an educated man, who attracted great respect from those around him. He and his like knew "how to control their rank and file, especially during periods of radicalization." The point is that this social mobility was intimately linked with intellectual or cognitive mobility. Superior knowledge thus acted as the filter that sorted out those who would rise up. A turning point was reached, "that existential break when one becomes one's own boss," and the former manual worker found a new world opened up, new possibilities, new goals in life, both for himself and for others.

What is it we have seen here? A man on his way to power, the emergence of a new ruling class? What kind of road is it he travels on his way to power, and what kind of power will he take? Just where have we ended up after this conference discussion, in a conference that sought to capture the intellectual at the birth of a new epoch?

It is with such open-endedness that I will close this report, for the conference itself offered this very character of openness as its most pervasive form.

Anders Björnsson
July 1984

Contributors

Cornelis Disco
Department of Philosophy
and Social Sciences
University of Technology
Delft, The Netherlands

Edmund Dahlström
Department of Sociology
University of Gothenburg,
Sweden

Ron Eyerman
Department of Sociology
University of Lund, Sweden

Katrín Fridjónsdóttir
Department of Sociology
University of Lund, Sweden

Bengt Furåker
Department of Sociology
University of Umeå, Sweden

Yrjö-Paavo Häyrynen
Department of Psychology
University of Joensuu,
Finland

Carl Levy
Faculty of Social Sciences
University of Kent at
Canterbury, England

Bill Martin
Department of Sociology
University of Wisconsin
Madison, United States

Lennart Olausson
Department of History of
Ideas and Learning
University of Gothenburg,
Sweden

Thomas Söderqvist
Department of Biology
Roskilde University Center,
Denmark

Lennart G. Svensson
Department of Sociology
University of Gothenburg,
Sweden

Ivan Szelényi
Department of Sociology
University of Wisconsin
Madison, United States

Adam Westoby
School of Education
The Open University
Milton Keynes, England

Subject Index

Name Index

Designer: U.C. Press Staff
Compositor: Freedmen's Organization
Text: 10/12 Palatino
Display: Palatino